The Openhearted Audience

The Openhearted Audience
Ten Authors Talk about Writing for Children

Edited and with an Introduction by
Virginia Haviland
Children's Literature Center

LIBRARY OF CONGRESS   WASHINGTON   1980

Library of Congress Cataloging in Publication Data

Main entry under title:

The openhearted audience.

Bibliography: p.
COMMENTS: Travers, P. L. Only connect.—Sendak, M.
and Haviland, V. Questions to an artist who is also an
author.—Aiken, J. Between family and fantasy [etc.]
  1. Children's literature—History and criticism—addresses, essays, lectures. 2. Books and reading for
children—Addresses, essays, lectures. I. Haviland,
Virginia, 1911–
PN1009.A1063   809'.89282   79-15085
ISBN 0-8444-0288-5

For sale by the Superintendent of Documents, U.S. Government Printing Office
Washington, D.C. 20402

Contents

Introduction

In its program of lectures, the Library of Congress has introduced a succession of distinguished contributors to children's literature. The first of the annual lectures on children's books was presented in 1963, the year the Children's Book Section, as it was then called, was established at the Library. With the reorganization of the Library of Congress in 1978, this center for reference, advisory, and bibliographical services was renamed. Today as the Children's Literature Center it works with the new Center for the Book in continuing to plan lectures and symposia, inviting speakers from this country and abroad.

The ten lecturers whose papers are gathered here have much to say about the genesis of their own writing for children, revealing influences and impulses they feel account for particular qualities that define their books. They speak convincingly also about creative writing and children's literature in general.

What is imagination and where do the ideas expressed in fiction come from? Why do some people feel compelled to write and to what end do they compose their stories? Dreams are a key, says Eleanor Cameron. She calls dreams a significant part of her life, as are the experiences held in the unconscious, where through "slow transformation over the years" they are turned into "treasure." Similarly, Virginia Hamilton points to the significance symbols hold for her, describing in particular the symbol of *the Street,* especially meaningful to her in connoting "the need for sharing life with others." Her intention in writing is to break down symbols and "free the reality." "Standing on the brink of a work about to begin," Jill Paton Walsh finds her "mind on fire"—and indeed she must enter such an area of excitement to be able to begin a narrative fiction.

All these authors share a conviction about the worth and complexity of children's literature. They deplore negative attitudes toward creative writing for children, looking beyond their own individual approaches to the whole existing body of literature for children. Ivan Southall, like many a children's writer, is concerned about the low regard some people have for authors writing for children. Ursula Le Guin discusses a "puritanical distrust" of fantasy she recognizes in some people, who see a pathological regression and strange amorality in fairy tales, not realizing the function and worth the tales have in children's lives.

The respect for fairy tales, myths, and legends held by these authors, on the other hand, is great. P. L. Travers, especially, stresses their importance, describing her own childhood as having been "drenched in a Celtic twilight." Both an author and an illustrator, Maurice Sendak states that there is probably "no such thing as creativity without fantasy." And Joan Aiken expresses her belief that one of the functions of books is to feed a child's own imagination: "reading provides the child with matter for creating his own fantasy."

How do these creators of distinguished examples of children's literature view their craft? Writing, for Virginia Hamilton, is an attempt at "literary radicalism." Jill Paton Walsh, believing that a writer must have "intellectual passions," has developed the metaphor of a trajectory to describe the creative planning of a story. Eleanor Cameron brings together many authors' comments about the mysterious process of writing, where a story seems to well up from the unconscious or to grow of its own, surprising even its creator. Like Eleanor Cameron both critic and author, John Rowe Townsend considers the interplay between the two creative arts, wondering whether or not it is desirable for authors to be critics too. And Erik Haugaard, discussing the art of translating, speculates that "if Hans Christian Andersen had not had an idealized picture of the artist and the importance of art, would he not have ended his life as a shoemaker?" Thus dreams and ideals are important in many different ways to many different storytellers.

Whatever direction they may have taken, all these writers agree in their respect for the child audience. "The largest literate, openhearted audience in the history of the world," Ivan Southall calls children today. He recalls an "emotional brilliance" that left him as a child "all-of-a-tremble." An important as well as sensitive audience, stresses Jill Paton Walsh, children are "the Lords of Time," to whom it will fall to carry forth all ideas that we value today.

The ten articles printed here have had earlier publication in the *Quarterly Journal of the Library of Congress* or as separate pamphlets. As the brief biographical notes for each author indicate, the lecturers are each known for a substantial history of publishing, and their works include a number of widely recognized prizewinning books. Bibliographies supplied indicate the range of their writing.

The majority of the lectures were given in observance of National Children's Book Week. This occasion has had a place in the programs of libraries, schools, and bookstores since 1919, when the American Booksellers Association organized a committee to promote it.

VIRGINIA HAVILAND

The Openhearted Audience

Pamela L. Travers was born in Queensland, Australia, in 1906 and was privately educated. She became a journalist, actress, and dancer. After moving to England, she became a regular contributor to the *Irish Statesman* in the 1920s and 1930s, and during World War II she served the British Ministry of Information in the United States. For her own entertainment while recovering from an illness, she began to write the Mary Poppins stories. She was writer-in-residence at Radcliffe College, Cambridge, Massachusetts, 1965-66; at Smith College, 1966; and at Scripps College, Claremont, California, 1970. She received the Order of the British Empire in 1977.

Books for children:
Mary Poppins (1934), *Mary Poppins Comes Back* (1935), *Happy Ever After* (1940), *I Go by Sea, I Go by Land* (1941), *Mary Poppins Opens the Door* (1943), *Mary Poppins in the Park* (1952), *The Fox at the Manger* (1962), *Mary Poppins from A to Z* (1963), *Friend Monkey* (1971), *About Sleeping Beauty* (1975), and *Mary Poppins in the Kitchen: A Cookery Book with a Story* (1975).

For adults:
Moscow Excursion (1935) and *Aunt Sass* (1941).

Based on a talk given at the Library of Congress on October 31, 1966, this article was first published in the *Quarterly Journal of the Library of Congress* for October 1967.

2

Only Connect

by P. L. Travers

It was suggested to me when the Library of Congress did me the honor of asking me to address you that I should talk about how *Mary Poppins* came to be written. Now, I know that there are many people who can talk, and at great length, on subjects of which they are totally ignorant. But I'm not one of them. I can't speak of what I don't know and this is not from an excess of modesty but from lack of relevant data. Any work of fiction, any work of imagination, has, inevitably, something of the quality of poetry or of those strange flashes of realization that happen for no apparent reason or rhyme—it can't be described. Words are like the notes on a piano, instruments of communication, not the poem—or the music—itself. Once a piece of work is finished, it has said all there is to be said. My instinct is always to whittle down, not to enlarge upon, and hasn't your own poet, Randall Jarrell, said—I forget the exact phrase for the moment—that a writer must remain silent about the way in which he writes? Even what he writes. Nothing, however, prevents a writer from speaking about the earth—the compost, as it were—from which his work arises. He can't help knowing something about that because it is, of course, his very self.

And this brings me to my title. I don't have to tell you where it comes from. When I was at Radcliffe last year students from that college and Harvard used to crowd into my small apartment once a week and the talk was so good—they were all so alive, so open to ideas, and so ready to fight me for them. I liked that. And I remember that on one occasion I said—and it still seems to me true—that thinking was linking. At that, one marvelous girl blazed out at me, "Yes! Only connect!" and began searching for pencil and paper. But I begged her not, for the life of her, to write it down in a notebook. E. M. Forster has made the connection already, and now it was really her own. Once you write things down you've lost them. They are simply dead words on dead paper.

But "Only connect" was the exact phrase I had been leading up to and it has been precious to me ever since I read *Howards End,* of which it is the

3

epigraph. Perhaps, indeed, it's the theme of all Forster's writing, the attempt to link a passionate scepticism with the desire for meaning, to find the human key to the inhuman world about us; to connect the individual with the community, the known with the unknown; to relate the past to the present and both to the future. Oh, it's a marvelous phrase and I seized upon it for this lecture because—well, what else *is* there to seize upon? This question of linking is, anyway, very close to me and since that is what I am talking about tonight inevitably I have to go back to the past.

The illustrations in this chapter are by Mary Shepard and are from Mary Poppins, Mary Poppins Comes Back, Mary Poppins from A to Z, Mary Poppins in the Park *and* Mary Poppins Opens the Door, *copyright 1934, 1935, 1943, 1952, 1962, 1963, 1971 by P. L. Travers;* © *1962 by John Lyndon Ltd. and are reproduced by permission of Harcourt Brace Jovanovich, Inc.*

You remember Blake's "Little Black Boy?" "My mother bore me in the Southern wild." In that sense I was a little black boy, too, for I was born in the subtropics of Australia. Not that I spent all my life there, only my young years, and most of it far from cities. I lived a life that was at once new and old. The country was new and the land itself very old—the oldest in the world, geologists say, and in spite of all the brash pioneering atmosphere that still existed, even a child could sense the antiquity of it. We had also strong family traditions; we couldn't escape them, caught as we were between the horns of an Irish father and a mother of Scottish and Irish descent. It was simple, not rich, not centered at all around possessions or the search for status symbols. It seems to me that there were few *things* of any kind—furniture, of course, clothes and food, all the modest necessities. But of toys, and personal treasures, very few. If we wanted them we had to invent them, not by parental edict but from necessity. And there were very few books: Dickens and Scott, of course, Shakespeare, Tennyson, and some of the Irish poets. I ate my way through these like a bookworm not because of any highbrow leanings but simply because they were books. But for the children who, as far as I can remember, were seldom specially catered for, it was the grownup world that was important. There was a modest hodgepodge of good and bad: Beatrix Potter, simple—even babyish—comics, an odd book that nobody else seems ever to have heard of called *The Wallypug of Why*, Ethel Turner's stories, Alice, Kingsley's *Heroes*. Hawthorne I never met till I was grown up and it seems to me, as I read him now, though perhaps I wouldn't have thought so then, that he rather talks down to children, "tinifying," if I may coin a word, and inventing dear little curly haired daughters to make people like Midas more acceptable. Kingsley doesn't do those things. He gives you the myths straight.

Then, too, we had something that no child could find today, not anywhere in the world. We had penny books. You could buy a fairy tale for a penny—that's how their lore went into me. And just as good, perhaps even better at that age, you could buy a *Buffalo Bill*. I don't know whether anybody in this audience remembers such books? Indeed, not long ago—for it seemed so unlikely—I began to wonder whether I hadn't made them up. It was a great relief to me when Rosamond Lehmann, the novelist, assured me that I hadn't. "Of *course* we had penny books," she said, and we dreamed over them together. Oh, why didn't I keep them? What grownup, with no eye for the future, tossed the raggedy little morsels—as I myself have done since with many a child's tattered paper treasure—into a nearby dustbin? Last year, when I was in Toronto visiting the Osborne collection of children's books that goes back to the seventeenth century, I eagerly searched the glass cases. "If only," I said, quite by chance, "I could see a penny book." A conspiratorial, Guy Fawkes sort of look passed between the librarians, and one hurried away and quickly came back with something held secretively behind her. She put it on the case before me and there was a *Buffalo Bill*—almost, it seemed, the very one, in the faded blacks and blues and reds that I had so long remembered. On the back of the cover was the advertisement for the two-and-sixpenny alarm clock that I had saved up for long ago but never quite achieved. And there, also—much more important—was the air rifle for nineteen-and-elevenpence that would kill an elephant at five yards. Alas, I never got that, either. What would I have done with it, if I had, you may ask. I never had a moment's doubt about what I was saving for. It was to slay the enemies of Ireland! The sorrows of the "most distressful country" got into me very early—how could it help doing so with my

father's nostalgia for it continually feeding the imagination? My body ran about in the Southern sunlight but my inner world had subtler colors, the grays and snows of England where Little Joe swept all the crossings and the numberless greens of Ireland which seemed to be inhabited solely by poets plucking harps, heroes lordlily cutting off each other's heads, and veiled ladies sitting on the ground keening.

I think, perhaps, if there was any special virtue in my upbringing, it lay in the fact that my parents, both of them, were very allusive talkers. Neither of them ever read anything that didn't very quickly come out in conversation and from there pass into the family idiom. If my father discovered a poem he liked, even a piece of doggerel, it would presently be, as it were, on the breakfast table. Many a phrase, as ordinary to me then as the daily porridge, began its life, as I later learned, as a quotation from a poem or snatch from a ballad. As an instance, my father, who was a great lover of horses—and tricky, dangerous horses at that—would call out, whenever he returned from riding or driving, "Bonnie George Campbell is home!" And my mother from somewhere in the house would always answer "Thank God!" But *who* has come home, I used to wonder, for my father was neither George nor Campbell. It was not until much later, when I began to read the Scottish ballads, that I understood. You remember it?

> Booted and saddled
> And bridled rode he,
> To hame cam' his guid horse
> But never cam' he.

For all Bonnie Georges that come safely home the Lord should, indeed, be praised.

"Oh, what can ail thee, knight-at-arms?" my mother would sometimes say to a weeping child. Who was this knight, I often wondered. And yet, when you come to think of it, all children are knights-at-arms at times, alone and palely loitering. It is then they need to be comforted. But sometimes my father would prevent that. "No, no," he would say "let her weep. You know we need the rain." Thinking of this, with hindsight, I see how really antique that was, that we cannot really escape the myths, even if we wish to. You can call it, perhaps, sympathetic magic. And it is a fact that still, in countries suffering from drought, a cup of water is poured on the ground in the hope of bringing rain. In Sumeria, the oldest civilization the world knows, the rain god was invoked by the pouring of a cup of wine. I remembered this recently when a journalist, who had been talking to people in Ireland about the assassination of President Kennedy, told me that one old man had said gravely, "We cried the rain down for him that night." What an epitaph! The rain cried down!

Then, too, there were maxims galore and proverbs and aphorisms. I was so often told—being a passionately lazy child—to "Make an effort, Mrs. Dombey," that I began to think that Dombey was one of my own names. How could I know it was out of Dickens?

Then, there were other, closer, connections with myth. In those lucky days there was always help to be had in the house. Such people are wonderful meat for children. The life they live, from the child's point of view—because to him it is strange and unknown—seems to be filled with all the glamor that his own dailiness lacks. One of them—Bella, or was it Bertha?—had a parrot-headed umbrella. This fascinated me. On days out, it swung beside Bella's furbelows—she was far more elegant, I then thought, than my mother—and was carefully put away in tissue paper on her return, while she told us the always fantastic story of what she had done and seen. Well, she never *quite* told—she did more, she hinted. "Ah," she would say, looking like Cassandra, "if you could know what's happened to me cousin's brother-in-law!" But all too often, when prayed to continue, she would assure us, looking doomed and splendid, that the story was really beyond all telling and not for the ears of children. Oh, those inadequate ears of children! We were left to wonder, always mythologically—had he perhaps been chained to the mast because of someone's siren voice? Was his liver being slowly eaten by a baldheaded local eagle? Whatever they were, the things she didn't tell, they were always larger than life. Once, however, she spoke plain. "I saw Paddy Liston in the gutter," she said, "and him as drunk as an English duke!" Well, what a sight for the inward eye! It filled out imagination to such an extent that now I can never think of our poor, probably sober, dukes without seeing them en masse under tables, robed and crowned and in the last stages of alcoholic dissolution. We didn't, as you see, need television! In a world where there are few possessions, where nobody answers questions, where nobody explains—I say this with joy not sorrow—children must build life for themselves. One child is forced this way, one another. I went into imagination and poetry—perhaps I should more modestly say versifying—and never with grownup approbation. Come to that, I never sought it.

"Hardly W. B. Yeats," said father once, when my mother showed him a scrap of mine. And remembering it now I feel bound to agree with him, though at the age of seven it would have been hard even for *Yeats* to be W.B. Yeats. My father, as you see, perhaps because he was so far away from her, was in love with Cathleen ni Houlihan. Nothing that Ireland did was wrong, nothing that other countries did was completely right. Even his maxims came from Ireland. "Never put a baby in a drawer," was one of them. But who would ever do such a thing? Even if he saw a doll in a drawer, he would pluck it out, saying "Remember Parnell!" We had never even *heard* of Parnell and I had to wait to make the connection till I read a life of him a few years ago. Soon after he was born his mother, called away on some pretext, put him down quickly and came back to discover that her baby had disappeared. She looked everywhere, servants searched the house, gardeners rummaged in the shrubberies—no sign of Charles Stewart Parnell. I hope I'm not inventing it, but I think the police, too, were sent for. And while they were once more searching the nursery a mewling little sound came from the bureau. And there was Charles Stewart, six weeks old and at his last gasp because his mother, absentmindedly dumping him into an open drawer had, also absentmindedly, shut it! I am sure my father knew this story. Where else could the maxim have come from?

So you see, I was drenched in the Celtic twilight before I ever came to it. Indeed I only came to it when it was over and had practically turned into night. I had dreamed of it all my life and although my father was long dead, I had to test what my childhood had taught me. So the first thing I did on arriving in England was to send a piece of writing to A.E. (George Russell), who was then editor of *The Irish Statesman*. With all the hauteur of youth I deliberately sent no covering letter, just a stamped addressed envelope for return. And sure enough the stamped envelope came back, as I had fully expected it to do, but inside—instead of my manuscript—was a check for three guineas and a letter from A.E. It said "If you have any more, please let me see them and if you are ever in Ireland let us meet." So, you see, even if I hadn't been already going to Ireland I would have been off on the next train.

That was how I came under the wing of A.E. and got to know Yeats and the gifted people in their circle, all of whom cheerfully licked me into shape like a set of mother cats with a kitten. As you can imagine, this was a blessing and far beyond my deserving. But I was not the only kitten, no young person was ever sent empty away, the riches were poured out upon all. It was strong meat, this first introduction to my father's country, among the poets and the makers of history. Perhaps it was just as well that my first contact with my Irish relatives should take me down several pegs. I needed it. They, I discovered, were not at all in love with Cathleen ni Houlihan. Living cheek by jowl with her, they saw her without any trappings. Irish to the marrow, full of local lore and story, lovers of horses and the countryside, they weren't at all sure that life depended on poetry and they took the Celtic Renaissance with more than a grain of salt. "I don't like you gallivanting around with men who see fairies," said one. "And the thought of you, a young girl, in Fleet Street, that terrible place— its beyond thinking about!" From his description of it, I saw myself suffering nameless indignities at the hands of newspaper tycoons or being dragged up dark alleys by drunken reporters, and looked forward to it all with the greatest enthusiasm—though of course I didn't say so. "And you'll meet such frightful people," he said. "There's one who lived down the road a way—old now, of course, but a terrible great boastful fellow. If you meet him, be courteous, but do not pursue the acquaintance. His name is Shaw, George Bernard Shaw."

Gradually I learned to dissemble my enthusiasm for all that the elderly relatives of my father's generation found so reprehensible. One of them even remarked approvingly, "You're not nearly so mad as you used to be." Yet, he was the one who, on his deathbed, hearing his wife asking the doctor if he was likely to last till the next morning, remarked sardonically, "I don't need to. I've seen plenty of mornings. All I want to know is, will I live to hear the result of the boat race?" Among last words this spartan, if eccentric, phrase deserves, I think, a place.

Not so mad as I used to be? Little did he know! It was coming back from visiting him that one of what he would have called my maddest moments occurred. I knew that on the way back to Dublin the train would pass Lough Gill. And I remembered that in Lough Gill lay Yeat's Lake Isle of Innisfree. So I leapt from the carriage and charged a boatman on the lapping shore to take me there.

"Ach, there's no such place," he said.

"Oh, but there is, I assure you. W. B. Yeats wrote about it."

"And who would he be?"

I told him.

"Ah, I know them, those poets, always stravaging through their minds, inventing outlandish things. *We* call it Rat Island!" Rat Island! Well!

So we set out, under grey hovering clouds, with me in the bows and a young priest, who suddenly arose out of the earth, it seemed, joining us in the stern. At last, after a rough passage, there was Innisfree. No hive for the honeybee and no log cabin but of course I hadn't expected them. They were only in the bee-loud glade of Yeats's stravaging mind. But the whole island was covered with rowan trees, wearing their red berries like jewels and the thought suddenly came to me—a most disastrous one, as it turned out—"I'll take back some branches to the poet." In no time, for the island is diminutive, I had broken off pretty nearly every branch from the rowans and was staggering with them toward the boat. By now a strong wind had sprung up and the rain was falling and the lake was wild. Those Irish loughs beat up into a great sea very quickly. As we embarked, the waves seemed as high as the Statue of Liberty and I wished I'd had more swimming practice. Then I noticed, between one trough and the next, that the priest, pale as paper, was telling his beads with one hand and with the other plucking off my rowan berries and dropping them into the water. "Ah, Father," said the boatman, pulling stertorously on the oars, "it's not the weight of a berry or two that will save us now." He gave me a reflective glance and I got the idea, remembering that in times of shipwreck women are notoriously unlucky, that he was planning to throw me overboard, if the worse came to the worst. I wished *I* had a string of beads! However, perhaps because of the priest's prayers, we came at last safely to shore. I hurried through the rain with my burden and took the next train for Dublin. The other passengers edged away from my streaming garments as though I were some sort of ancient mariner. I should never have started this, I knew, but there is an unfortunate streak of obstinancy in me that would not let me stop. From Dublin station, through curtains of cloud—taxis did not exist for me in those days—I carried the great branches to Yeats's house in Merrion Square and stood there, with my hair like rats' tails, my tattered branches equally ratlike, looking like Birnam come to Dunsinane and wishing I was dead. I prayed, as I rang the bell, that Yeats would not open the door himself, but my prayer went unheard.

For an articulate man to be struck dumb is, you can imagine, rare. But struck dumb he was at the sight of me. In shame, I heard him cry a name into the dark beyond of the house and saw him hurriedly escape upstairs. Then the name came forward in human shape and took me gently, as though I were ill or lost or witless, down to the basement kitchen. There I was warmed and dried and given cocoa; the dreadful branches were taken away. I felt like someone who had died and was now contentedly on the other side, certain that nothing more could happen. In this dreamlike state, I was gathering myself to go—out the back way if possible—never to be seen again. But a maid came bustling kindly in and said—as though to someone still alive!—"The master will see you now." I was horrified. This was the last straw. "What for?" I wanted to know. "Ah, then, you'll see. He has his ways."

And so, up the stairs—or the seven-story mountain—I went and there he was in his room with the blue curtains.

"My canary has laid an egg!" he said and joyously led me to the cages by the window. From there we went round the room together, I getting better every minute and he telling me which of his books he liked and how, when he got an idea for a poem—There was long momentous pause, here. He was always the bard, always filling the role of poet, not play-acting but knowing well the role's requirements and giving them their due. He never came into a room, he *entered* it; walking around his study was a ceremonial peregrination, wonderful to witness. "When I get an idea for a poem," he went on, oracularly, "I take down one of my own books and read it and then I go on from there." Moses explaining his tablets couldn't have moved me more. And so, serenely, we came to the end of the pilgrimage and I was just about to bid him good-bye when I noticed on his desk a vase of water and in it one sprig of fruiting rowan. I glanced at him distrustfully. "Was he teaching me a lesson?" I wondered, for at that age one cannot accept to be taught. But he wasn't; I knew it by the look on his face. He would do nothing so banal. He was not trying to enlighten me and so I was enlightened and found a connection in the process. It needed only a sprig, said the lesson. And I learned, also, something about writing. The secret is to say less than you need. You don't want a forest, a leaf will do.

Next day, when I was lunching with A.E., he said to me, "Yeats was very touched that you brought him a sprig of rowan from Innisfree." So I had to tell him the whole story. You couldn't be untruthful with A.E. "I hope," he said slyly, "when you go to Dunfanaghay"—his own favorite part of Ireland—"you won't cut down all the willows for me. What about the tree spirits? Remember the dryads!" Dryads! I'd grown up on a diet of mythology and on Innisfree I'd forgotten it all. It was A.E. who had to remind me, A.E. whose thought was crystal-clear and hard—and still had room for dryads. These men—he, Yeats, James Stephens, and the rest—had aristocratic minds. For them, the world was not fragmented. An idea did not suddenly grow, like Topsy, all alone and separate. For them, all things had antecedents, and long family trees. They saw nothing shameful or silly in myths and fairy stories, nor did they shovel them out of sight in some cupboard marked Only for Children. They were always willing to concede that there were more things in heaven and earth than philosophy dreamed of. They allowed for the unknown. And, as you can imagine, I took great heart from this.

It was A.E. who showed me how to look at and learn from one's own writing. "Popkins," he said once—he always called her just plain Popkins, whether deliberately mistaking the name or not, I never knew, his humor was always subtle—"Popkins, had she lived in another age, in the old times to which she certainly belongs, would undoubtedly have had long golden tresses, a wreath of flowers in one hand, and perhaps a spear in the other. Her eyes would have been like the sea, her nose comely, and on her feet winged sandals. But, this being Kali Yuga, as the Hindus call it—in our terms, the Iron Age—she comes in the habiliments most suited to it.

Well, golden tresses and all that pretty paraphernalia didn't interest me; she could only be as she *was*. But that A.E. could really know so much about it astonished me, that he should guess at her antecedents and genealogy when I hadn't thought of them myself—it put me on my mettle. I began to *read* the book. But it was only after many years that I realized what he meant, that she had come out of the same world as the fairy tales.

My childish love for the tales had continued to increase in me—Tolkien says somewhere that if you are natively attached to the fairy tales (lots of people are not and there's no blame in that), that habit grows on you as you grow older. And it has certainly grown on me. "Only connect" comes strongly into this. Not long ago, I read in the *New York Times* about how the eels from America and Europe make their way to the Sargasso Sea to mate and lay their eggs, the journey for American eels taking one year, for Europeans two. Afterward, they make their long way back to their respective homes and apparently feel it was worth it. Well, for me the tales are a sort of Saragasso Sea and I am a kind of eel. And all these years of pondering on the fairy tale, first of all for love of it—because to learn about anything, it seems to me you have to love it first—and later because I became enthralled by it, all this pondering has led me to believe that the true fairy tales (I'm not talking now about invented ones) come straight out of myth; they are, as it were, miniscule reaffirmations of myth, or perhaps the myth made accessible· to the local folkly mind. In the nineteenth century, as you know, Andrew Lang and all his fellow pundits treated them as the meanderings of the primitive intelligence—and therefore, apparently suitable for children! Then the anthropologists had a go at them and later they descended, if I may so put it, to the psychoanalysts. But none of these seem to have been able to exhaust their meaning; there is still plenty left. They're like the magic pitcher in the Greek myth of Baucis and Philemon—you remember it retold in Hawthorne?—no matter how much milk you poured out, it was still full to the brim. This, of course, is where Jack's magic purse comes from; whenever you take out the last coin there is always another there.

Of course, you may ask—indeed, people are always asking—who invented the myths? And do you think they are true? Well, true? What is true? As far as I am concerned it doesn't matter tuppence if the incidents in the myths never happened. That does not make them any less true, for, indeed, in one way or another, they're happening all the time. You only have to open a newspaper to find them crowding into it. Life itself continually reenacts them. Not long ago, staying with friends in Virginia, I watched from the terrace as two little girls of six and four performed the rite of burial over a dead bird. I guessed that they did not want to touch it but they gathered all their grandfather's flowers and covered the body with them. Over these they laid branches and set a fence of sticks around them. Then they stood up and began to dance, not wildly, not gaily, not childishly, but formally, with measured steps. After that they knelt down—one on either side of the grave—were they praying? I couldn't see—and then they leaned across the sticks and gravely embraced each other. They had never been to church or a funeral, never before seen anything dead, knew nothing about the rite they were enacting out of ancestral memory, and the whole performance was true. I don't insist that you make anything out of it, but it meant something to me—the assurance that the myths and rites run around in our blood; that when old drums beat we stamp our feet, if only metaphorically. Time and the past are getting at us. The Australian aborigines have a word for this. For any happening further back than a grandmother their memories cannot go, any event further forward than a grandson, they cannot pretend to envisage. Beyond these times, when knowing is relatively possible, they can only reach by speaking of what lies there as the Dreaming. "It is gone into Dreaming," they say of the past. "It will come in the Dreaming," they say of the future.

There is a wonderful Japanese phrase, used as a Zen koan, which says, "Not created but summoned." It seems to me that this is all that can be said of the myths, "They are in the Dreaming. They are not created but summoned." But it is the fairy tale, not the myth, that is really my province. One might say that fairy tales are the myths fallen into time and locality. For instance, if this glass of water is myth, and I drink it, the last drop—or the lees of the wine—is the fairy tale. The drop is the same stuff, all the essentials are there. It is small, but perfect. Not minimized, not to be made digestible for children. I think it is more and more realized that the fairy tales are not entertainments for children at all. In their primal state, that is. They've been bowdlerized and had the essentials removed in order not to frighten—but to my mind it is better not to tell them at all than to take out all the vital organs and leave only the skin. And what *isn't* frightening, after all? What *doesn't* carry a stern lesson? Even the nursery rhymes present us with very difficult truths. And they, too, like the fairy tales, have long family trees, though it would not be easy, I admit, to prove it legally. Take Humpty Dumpty. All the king's horses and all the king's men couldn't put him together again. That some things are broken irrevocably, never to be whole again, is a hard truth and this is a good way of teaching it. Away back in Egypt, the myth was telling the same thing. You remember how, when the body of Osiris was cut up and scattered, his sister-wife Isis searched the world for the fourteen pieces, trying to remember him and always unable to recover the fourteenth. I'm not trying here to suggest that whoever wrote "Humpty Dumpty" had Isis and Osiris in mind. Of course not. I merely make the connection between them. And what about the cow that jumped over the moon? In Egypt the sky was always thought of as a cow, her body arching over the earth and her four legs standing firmly upon it. Again, it is I who make the link, not the writer of the rhyme. "How many miles to Babylon?" What is that telling us, I wonder, with its three score and ten, the life of man? There is a gloss upon this rhyme that makes it perhaps a little clearer.

> How many miles to Babylon?
> If it's three score and ten
> Bury me under the cold gravestone
> For my time is come, but make no moan,
> I shall be back by candle-light—
>   Many times again!

You may think this is hocus-pocus and mumbo jumbo—and well it may be, except to me—but if you look in the Oxford dictionary, you will find that hocus-pocus itself derives from *hoc est corpus*—and we are, after all, talking here about the body, if I may so put it, of an idea. Mumbo jumbo has, alas, no known derivation. It is a figure supposed to have been invented by African chiefs in order to keep their wives properly disciplined and to give them a sense of awe. As for fee fi fo fum, you must go back to ancient Greece for that. It was the great incantation of the Erinyes, the triple furies born from the drops of blood of Cronus; and the old world rang with it as they pursued their prey. What a long and circuitous way it took before it found a home in our Western nurseries!

You may, of course, feel that this is drawing a long bow. But, as I see it, what is a long bow for but to be drawn? And our phrase "the long bow" itself comes from the great bow of Philoctetes, one of the Argonauts, who inherited it from Hercules. A man had to be a hero inwardly and outwardly to be able to draw that bow.

Or it may be that you will categorize all this as "old wives' tales." But I am one who believes in old wives' tales and that it is the proper function of old wives to tell tales. Old wives have the best stories in the world, and long memories. Why should we treat them with contempt? The tales have to be told in order that we may understand that in the long run, whatever it may be, every man must become the hero of his own story; his own fairy tale, if you like, a real fairy tale. Hans Andersen, for me, in spite of the fact that he often used old material, is an inventor of fairy tales; so is Oscar Wilde. They both have an element of nostalgia in them, a devitalizing element that the true tale never has. Perhaps those that most clearly derive from myth, those that clearly show their antecedents, are the Greek stories, the Norse tales, and Grimms'. These are old trees, rooted in the folk, full of meaning and ritual; they retell the myths in terms that can be understood by unlettered people. For originally they were for the listener rather than the reader; they came long before books. Every one of these tales, it seems to me, is asking something of us, telling us something about life. Of course I am now on my hobbyhorse and anyone who wishes may get up and shoot at me or at any rate ask a question. I am not here to stand and assert but to share my questioning with you.

Doesn't it seem to you, too, that there is more in the tales than meets the eye? Think of all those stories of the three brothers, who go off in search of various treasures. As a child, naturally, I thought of them as separate entities—the eldest so handsome, always delayed at the crossroads or prevented from going farther because of some temptation. He's handsome and brave, and relying on this, he assures himself that when the time comes, he'll find the treasure. Then the second, sure of his cleverness, a cleverness that proves to be groundless, also fails in the quest. Lastly, the third brother sets out, realizing his ignorance, knowing himself a simpleton. And so he is. Simple and humble, willing to accept help from anyone who will give it. You'll remember the story of "Puddocky," a prime example of this. I always loved that youngest son. Nowadays, however, I think of the brothers, not as single adventurers, but as three stages of one man. In the beginning he sets out bravely, young and handsome, and quickly gets to the end of that; but "I'm still clever," he thinks to himself; yet soon he finds even that's not true. He ends by knowing he knows nothing. And once he knows nothing he begins to know something and from there it is really only a step to happy ever after.

The fairy tales also tell us a great deal about women—or, perhaps about woman and her role in life, the triple role of maiden, mother, and crone. Each of us, of course, begins as a maiden and whether she becomes a physical mother or not makes no difference, the role of mother is the next step, the flowering of the bud. Last of all comes the grandmother—again, not the physical grandmother, but the stage where the flower withers into seed pod. To become a crone, it seems to me, is the last great hope of woman, supremely worth achieving. An old woman who remembers, who has gathered up all the threads of life and sits by the fire with her hands in her lap—not doing anything any more—what a marvelous thing! This is what it is to become wise. There you sit in your rocking chair as in the fairy tales—I hope I shall, anyway—aware of all you have learned and garnered and having it available in case the young ones want it. You will not force it on them, but simply tell it. That's what the crones—all those good and bad fairies— are doing in the tales.

Of course, it is not always easy to see the relation between the fairy tale and the myth. They do not *all* insist on telling you of their great-grandparents. But many of them have lineaments that loudly proclaim their breeding. Cinderella, for instance,whose story is so ancient that she is found in one guise or another in practically every mythology known to man. She has been grossly ill-treated, however, by writers of pantomime and by illustrators who retell the tales in terms of their own illustrations. Chop off a nose or leg, what does it matter? All tellers of the Cinderella story, ever since Perrault himself retold it, make the mistake of assuming that it is because she wishes that she goes to the ball. If that were so, wouldn't we all be married to princes? No, the wishing has much more behind it; it must be so if the happy ending is to be achieved. Grimms' comes near to the true theme. There, it is not because she wishes but because she has performed the necessary rites at her mother's grave, and because, above all, she has accepted her fate, that she meets the little benevolent bird who gives her the golden gown and all the magnificent rest. And then, the story has so many sisters. There is a book—the author's names is Cox—which has over three hundred versions of the Cinderella story. But I like to make my own connections. Would you not say she was the girl in "King Cophetua and the Beggar Maid?" Isn't she, as near as makes no matter, Patient Griselda? And who but Cinderella is Lear's Cordelia, with those two monstrous sisters? Going back to myth, you will find her in the garb of Sita, the prototype of all feminine virtue in the epic of the Ramayana, in India, which is as old as history.

And what about that recurrent theme where a character in the story agrees—for a price—to give the villain the first thing that runs to greet him on his return home? It's a wonderful story. You find it in "The King of the Golden Mountain" and "The Singing, Soaring Lark" and it goes back to Methuselah—or at any rate the Old Testament, in the story of Jephthah's daughter. None of the true stories was born yesterday; they all come from far and have a long way yet to go. One that was dear to me as a child—I still think it most beautiful, even though others protest that it is brutal and bloody—was "The Juniper Tree." There is a wicked stepmother, of course, who, when the little stepson bends down to get an apple from a chest, drops the lid and cuts his head off. Even now I never bend over a chest without making quite sure that the top won't fall on me. And so the story goes from bad to worse. Sitting the body at the table, with the head balanced on top of it, she orders the little sister to call her brother to supper. Naturally, he does not answer, so the little sister gives him a shake and down falls the severed head. And now worse hurries on to worst. The stepmother cooks the child in a stew and gives this meal to the father when he comes home from work. "Ah," he exclaims, "how truly delicious. I feel as though it were all mine." As, indeed, of course, it is. Eventually the little watching bird puts all to rights, the little sister is freed of her supposed guilt, the little boy comes alive again, the stepmother—and serve her right!—is finished off with a millstone. It sounds, I admit, like a mess of horrors. But it never bothered me at all. Knowing the power of the little bird I never doubted that the boy would be safe. If, indeed, the father ate him, it was inevitable, even natural, that the boy would somehow, and in good time, return to his proper shape. After all, hadn't Cronus, the father of the gods, eaten up his children? Son after son was born to Rhea and each time Cronus said "He'll supplant me!" and promptly swallowed him down. But with her last child Rhea grew cunning, swaddled a stone and gave it her husband who, feeling—though erroneously—that it was all his, let it go the way of the others. Thus Zeus was saved to become king of the gods. And, once on his throne he, himself, performed the same act—or an aspect of it—when he took his unborn son

Dionysus into his own thigh—his mother having been burnt to death—
and at the full period of nine months brought him forth, unharmed and
perfect.

And then there are the countless stories that warn against trying to see
too much; of the demon lover who persuades the maiden to marry him on
the understanding that she must never, once the night falls, attempt to
look at him. And always the maiden—who could help it?—always the
maiden fails. Either she is persuaded by her family, as—again!—in the
"Singing Soaring Lark" and "Melusine," or she is overcome by curiosity,
as in "Cupid and Psyche." And as a result he disappears or has to go
through grave vicissitudes before he comes to himself once more. This
theme comes directly out of myth, it goes back to the farthest limits of time
when Semele, not knowing that her bridegroom was divine, yet
suspecting it, begs him to grant her one boon, that she may see him in all
his splendor. Reluctantly Zeus unveils himself and she, unable to endure
the lightning, is herself turned to ash. The story is a warning, repeated
down the centuries, through myth, folk and fairy tale, that it is dangerous
to look upon the face of the god. Seek him rather with the inward eye.

"Rumpelstiltskin" was another of my favorites, for its meaning lay very
close to me. Everyone knows the story of how the miller's daughter, in
order to become a queen, promises the little old man her first child if he
will spin her straw into gold. Of course he does it. It is no problem. To
him they are one and the same. But when the child is born she cannot bear
to part with it and he agrees to let her off if she can discover his name. So
for three days she tries this and she tries that, always unsuccessfully, and
he warns her that when tomorrow comes he will take the child away. In
despair, she sends riders far and wide, east of the sun and west of the moon.
Only one comes back with a clue. "In the land where the wolf and the hare
say goodnight to each other, I came upon an old man, jumping up and
down and singing "My name is Rumpelstiltskin." And so, the next day,
making a great pretence of it, she asks the old man "Is it
Rumpelstiltskin?" And with that he shrieks a great "Yes!" and stamps his
foot into the earth and tears himself in two. His name is known, therefore
he is finished. This role has been played out.

This idea of the secrecy of the name, the taboo against making it
known, goes back to man's very early days, to the time, perhaps, when he
had no name. During the war I spent two summers with the Navaho
Indians and when they gave me an Indian name they warned me that it
would be bad luck for me and the tribe if I ever disclosed it to anyone. And
I never have. For one thing, I do not want to receive or give bad luck, and
for another I have a strong atavistic feeling—one, I think, that is strongly
shared by unlettered people all over the world—that to disclose one's
name or take another's before the time for it is ripe—well, it's dangerous. I
tremble inwardly and withdraw when my Christian name is seized before
I have given it, and I have the same hesitancy about using that of another

person. An Indian—or a gypsy—would understand this very well. It is a very ancient taboo and I relate it—though I don't suggest that anyone else relate it—to the earliest times when men built altars "To the Unknown God." If I were ever to build an altar, I would put that inscription above it.

In making these connections, I do not want to assert or impose. But, in fact, all things are separate and fragmentary until man himself connects them, sometimes wrongly and sometimes rightly. As far as I am concerned, it is all a matter of hint and suggestion, something seen at the corner of the eye and linked with another thing, equally fleeting. You remember Walt Whitman's poem "On the Beach at Night." "I give you the first suggestion, the problem, the indirection." Isn't that wonderful? Turn your back on it and you'll find it! It's like Shakespeare's "By indirection find direction out." And with these quotations I connect Swift's dictum "Vision is the art of seeing things invisible." Doesn't this relate to the unknown name?

But now let me make one last link. I was rereading recently how Aeneas came to Campania—which is now Naples—seeking some means of getting into contact with the ghost of his father, Anchises. First, for piety, he prays at the temple of Apollo, begging the god to inspire the Cumean Sybil, whose cave is at hand, to help him on his way to the underworld. Nearby is the great forest where lies the terrible Lake of Avernus over which no bird flies, and at the edge of that is the rift between the great rocks that guard the way to the realm of Pluto. You know the story. She tells him to break from one tree in the forest a small golden branch. With that in his hand he will be able to descend into the depths. So, holding the branch before him as an amulet, he begins the dreadful journey. Of course, the whole of Frazer's *Golden Bough* is about this branch and many of the fairy stories repeat it; "The Shoes That Were Danced to Pieces," for instance, where the twelve princesses are followed each night to the underworld by a soldier who breaks off a little golden branch to bring back as a sign that he has, indeed, been there. Not for nothing, I thought, as I read again of Aeneas, were those four sites so close together— the temple of Apollo, the cave of the Sybil, the Lake of Avernus, the Land of the Dead. It is inevitable that they should touch and interpenetrate each other, not only in myth, but in life. Life, in a sense, *is* myth, one might say; the one is a part of the other. In both of them, the good and the bad, the dangerous and the safe, live very close together. And I remembered, as I thought about this, how Aeneas had begged the Sybil to speak her oracle in words and not, as was her usual practice, to write it on leaves that would blow away. That struck a chord in me, for I knew a story where this had actually happened. In this story, the wind blows leaves into the hands of two children. And on each leaf a message is written. One says "Come" and the other "Tonight." Now, the story I'm talking about is "Halloween." It is in *Mary Poppins in the Park*. And there is the Sybil obeying Aeneas by writing the oracle down on leaves! And I thought I had invented it!

There's a poem by Rupert Brooke, one verse of which says:

There's wisdom in women, of more than they have known,
And thoughts go blowing through them, are wiser than their own.

Truly, I had far wiser thoughts than my own when I wrote that story. You may remember—though why should you?—that it is about a party in the park where all the shadows are free. They go out to enjoy themselves and leave their owners at home. The only one whose shadow refuses to go without her is—guess!—Mary Poppins.

I find another connection here in the fact that tonight happens to be Halloween. In ancient times this used to be the festival of the dead. I think it was one of the popes, Boniface IV, perhaps, in the seventh century, who decided to do away with the pagan saturnalia and turn it from what it so significantly was, into a commemoration of the saints and martyrs. But in spite of him the myth never lost its mystery; men needed the festival rites for the dead; they needed to find a way out of grieving that would ease their fear that the spirits of the dead might come back to earth and haunt them. They put on masks and disguised their faces, wrapping themselves, to cheat the ghosts, in the garments of black that became for us, their late descendants, simply mourning clothes. The wake that the Irish hold for the dead is part of this ancient saturnalia. It gives an opportunity and a justification for the living to turn their faces again to life: it also provides a propitious moment, a ritual moment, one could say, a kind of crack through which some element of the unknown can be brought into the known.

Is anyone thinking of saints and martyrs on this Halloween, I wonder? And who knows, when they leave this hall, that their shadows will be with them? For me the fairy tales are abroad tonight. Good fairies and demons, Beauty and the Beast—they are all knocking at the doors, rattling their money boxes and holding out grubby hands for candy. It's a pagan festival still, be sure, swinging between trick and treat, angel and devil, yes and no. It is a night of ghosts and shadows, a night that links the past and the present, a night perhaps when that crack between known and unknown could open, and we could believe the old Greek poet Aratus when he declared: "Full of Zeus are the cities, full of Zeus are the harbors, full of Zeus are all the ways of men."

If it was true then it is true always, time cannot change the timeless. It could be—could it not?—*this* city, full of lighted, grinning pumpkin faces; *that* harbor out on Chesapeake Bay; *we* men—if we could only connect. What do you think?

Maurice B. Sendak was born in Brooklyn in 1928. He studied at the Art Students' League in New York, 1949-51. His early work included drawing for All American Comics in the 1940s and then designing and constructing window displays for Timely Service and F.A.O. Schwartz in New York. His unusual talents soon came to the attention of Ursula Nordstrom, the children's book editor at Harper's, for whom he illustrated Marcel Aymé's story *The Wonderful Farm*. He has had numerous one-man shows in New York, Philadelphia, Hartford, Zurich, and Oxford. He received the American Library Association Caldecott Medal in 1964 and the Hans Christian Andersen International Medal in 1970. In 1977 he was given an honorary doctorate from Boston University. He lives in Ridgefield, Connecticut.

Written and illustrated by Sendak:
Kenny's Window (1956), *Very Far Away* (1957), *The Sign on Rosie's Door* (1960), *Where the Wild Things Are* (1963), *Higglety Pigglety Pop! Or, There Must Be More to Life* (1967), and *In the Night Kitchen* (1970). Also, in verse, *The Nutshell Library* (4 vols., 1962) and *Seven Little Monsters* (1977), and *Really Rosie* (1975), a play for stage and for television.

Illustrated by Sendak, among many:
Atomics for the Millions (1947), *A Hole Is to Dig, a First Book of First Definitions* (1952), *The Wheel on the School* (1954), *Charlotte and the White Horse* (1955), *The House of Sixty Fathers* (1956), *Little Bear* (1957, and sequels), *Seven Tales*, by Hans Christian Andersen (1959), *The Moon Jumpers* (1959), *Mr. Rabbit and the Lovely Present* (1962), *The Griffin and the Minor Canon* (1963), *The Bat-Poet* (1964), *The Animal Family* (1965), *Hector Protector, and As I Went Over the Water, Two Nursery Rhymes with Pictures* (1965), *Lullabies and Night Songs* (1965), *Zlateh the Goat, and Other Stories* (1966), *The Golden Key* (1967), *The Light Princess* (1969), *King Grisly-Beard* (1973), and *The Juniper Tree, and Other Tales from Grimm* (1973).

In a National Children's Book Week program on November 16, 1970, Maurice Sendak presented some of his ideas about children's literature in an informal question-and-answer session. This article was published in the October 1971 *Quarterly Journal of the Library of Congress*.

Questions to an Artist Who Is Also an Author

Maurice Sendak with Virginia Haviland

Miss Haviland: *As a starter, let's ask: What did a book mean to you as a child? And what kinds of books did you have?*

Mr. Sendak: I think I'll start with the kinds of books, because back in the thirties I didn't have any "official" children's books (I refer to the classics). The only thing I can remember is cheap paperbacks, comic books. That's principally where I started. My sister bought me my first book, *The Prince and the Pauper.* A ritual began with that book which I recall very clearly. The first thing was to set it up on the table and stare at it for a long time. Not because I was impressed with Mark Twain; it was just such a beautiful object. Then came the smelling of it. I think the smelling of books began with *The Prince and the Pauper,* because it was printed on particularly fine paper, unlike the Disney books I had gotten previous to that, which were printed on very poor paper and smelled poor. *The Prince and the Pauper* smelled good and it also had a shiny cover, a laminated cover. I flipped over that. And it was very solid. I mean, it was bound very tightly. I remember trying to bite into it, which I don't imagine is what my sister intended when she bought the book for me. But the last thing I did with the book was to read it. It was all right. But I think it started then, a passion for books and bookmaking. I wanted to be an illustrator very early in my life; to be involved in books in some way—to make books. And the making of books, and the touching of books—there's so much more to a book than just the reading; there is a sensuousness. I've seen children touch books, fondle books, smell books, and it's all the reason in the world why books should be beautifully produced.

Miss Haviland: *Our questions to you, which are questions I think you have often answered for university and other groups, come as questions to you as an author and questions to you as an artist. Let's begin with the*

25

group of questions that have to do with you as an author. What part do you think fantasy should play in a child's life?

Mr. Sendak: Well, fantasy is so all-pervasive in a child's life: I believe there's no part of our lives, our adult as well as child life, when we're not fantasizing, but we prefer to relegate fantasy to children, as though it were some tomfoolery only fit for the immature minds of the young. Children do live in fantasy *and* reality; they move back and forth very easily in a way that we no longer remember how to do. And in writing for children you just must assume they have this incredible flexibility, this cool sense of the logic of illogic, and that they can move with you very easily from one sphere to another without any problems. Fantasy is the core of all writing for children, as I think it is for the writing of any book, for any creative act, perhaps for the act of living. Certainly it is crucial to my work. There are many kinds of fantasy and levels of fantasy and subtleties of fantasy—but that would be another question. There is probably no such thing as creativity without fantasy. My books don't come about by "ideas" or by thinking of a particular subject and exclaiming "Gee, that's a terrific idea, I'll put it down!" They never quite come to me that way; they well up. In the way a dream comes to us at night, feelings come to me, and then I must rush to put them down. But these fantasies have to be given physical form, so you build a house around them, and the house is what you call a story, and the painting of the house is the bookmaking. But essentially it's a dream, or it's a fantasy.

Miss Haviland: *Are you, yourself, remembering daydreams? And a belief in fantasy that came out of your own childhood?*

From Where the Wild Things Are *by Maurice Sendak. Copyright © 1963 by Maurice Sendak. Courtesy of Harper & Row, Publishers, Inc.*

Mr. Sendak: I can't recall my childhood any more than most of us can. There are sequences and scenes I remember much as we all do. But I do seem to have the knack of recalling the emotional quality of childhood, so that in *Wild Things*—I can remember the feeling, when I was a child (I don't remember who the people were, but there were people who had come to our house, relatives perhaps) and I remember they looked extremely ugly to me. I remember this quite clearly, and that when people came and, with endearments, they leaned over and said "Oh, I could eat you up!" I was very nervous because I really believed they probably could if they had a mind to. They had great big teeth, immense nostrils, and very sweaty foreheads. I often remember that vision and how it frightened me. There was one particular relative (I have some relatives in the audience, so I won't mention who it was) who did this to me, and it was really quite terrifying. Well, he is forever immortalized in *Wild Things*. *Wild Things* really is the anxiety and pleasure and immense problem of being a small child. And what do children do with themselves? They fantasize, they control fantasies or they don't control fantasies. It's not the recollection of my own particular childhood that I put down in books, but the feeling— like that particular feeling of fear of adults, who are totally unaware that what they say to children is sometimes taken quite literally. And that when they pinch your cheek out of affection, it hurts; and that, when they suggest they could "hug you to death," you back away—any number of such things.

Miss Haviland: *It would be interesting to find out whether you can account for the fact that college students seem to enjoy* Where the Wild Things Are *and* Higglety Pigglety Pop! *as much as children do. The question is: whom do you see as your audience?*

Mr. Sendak: Well, I suppose primarily children, but not really. Because I don't write for children specifically. I certainly am not conscious of sitting down and writing a book for children. I think it would be fatal if one did. So I write *books*, and I hope that they are books anybody can read. I mean, there was a time in history when books like *Alice in Wonderland* and the fairy tales of George Macdonald were read by everybody. They were not segregated for children. So I'd like to think I have a large audience, and if college students like my books, that's fine. I think young people tend to be freer about reading children's books. They don't think it's an odd thing to do particularly, if it's a good piece of fantasy, or even if it's just a good piece of fun. They aren't as hung up as perhaps we were about reading "children's" books. I know a lot of students think that I was "turned on" when I wrote some of my books. That is not just a guess, because I've had lots of inquiries about what I smoked during certain chapters of certain books. And that may be partly the interest that they have in such things. Writing fantasies is really being quite sufficiently high (without anything more than an Empirin).

Miss Haviland: *Some other college students have asked how you, as a
writer in this post-Freudian era, can resolve the problem of not
consciously manipulating the unconscious.*

Mr. Sendak: [After a pause] Well, that's a problem. The Victorians were
very fortunate. *Alice in Wonderland* is full of images and symbols, which
are extremely beautiful and sometimes frightening. We know that Carroll
had no Freud, and the book came pouring out of his unconscious, as
happened with George Macdonald in *The Princess and the Goblin.* These
authors touched on some very primal images in quite a fascinating way. It
is more difficult for us to do because we do know so much, we've read so
much. I hope I don't consciously manipulate my material. I do not
analyze my work; if something strikes me and I get excited, then I want it
to be a book. If it begins to die as I work, then of course it's not a book. But
I think I do get away occasionally with walking that fine unconscious
line. The things I've written in which there are conscious unconscious
things, are very—you can't put your finger on it, certainly children can
put their fingers on it, they are *the* most critical audience in the world,

they smell a rat instantly. You cannot fool them, you really cannot fool them. They're tough to work for. And if they sense—and they know adults do these books—if they sense for one minute that I was faking this, I would know it. Now, *Wild Things* walked a very fine line in this particular sense. It was accepted by children largely, and that's the only proof I have that I've done it.

Miss Haviland: *Another college student has asked about the recurring symbol of something eating something, ingesting something, and then giving it out again. For instance in* Pierre *the lion eats Pierre and then gives him out; and in* As I Went Over the Water *a sea monster ingests a boat, then gives it out; in* Higglety Pigglety Pop! *Jenny eats a mop and then gives it out; and in* The Night Kitchen *Mickey is engulfed in dough and then springs out. Would you comment on this?*

Mr. Sendak: I don't know if it's safe to, but I began by telling you how much I liked to bite into my first books, and that is perhaps a clue to this subject. And, so far as I'm aware, I'm not an overeating person, but perhaps it is a hang-up from childhood. A pleasant one, I think. The

Max. From Where the Wild
Things Are *by Maurice Sen-
dak. Copyright © 1963 by
Maurice Sendak. Courtesy of
Harper & Row, Publishers,
Inc.*

business of eating is such an immensely important part of life for a child.
Grimm's *Fairy Tales* is full of things being eaten and then disgorged. It's
an image that constantly appeals to me; I love it. In *As I Went Over the
Water*, the scene where the monster eats the boat and then regurgitates it is
hilarious! I have the mind of a child, I think that's very funny. I will sit
home and laugh myself sick over what I've done. Whether it appeals or
makes sense to anyone else, I honestly don't know. It just seems right and
occasioinally children laugh too, so we laugh together.

Miss Haviland: *Some readers have been intrigued by the relationships
between your characters Kenny, Martin, Max, and Mickey. Would you say
in what way these children may be the same child, or in what ways they are
not?*

Mr. Sendak: They are the same child, of course. Three of them have the
initial "M." I don't think that's an accident, although I thought of that
only while I was working on the last book. The first boy was Kenny, and
he was named after a specific person. But a thread of meaning connects all
the children. I can do a very rough analysis, I suppose. Kenny is a
frustrated and introverted child. And Martin is fussy and sulking and not
very brave. Max is tremendously brave but in a rage. And Mickey is

Martin. From Very Far Away *by Maurice Sendak. Copyright © 1957 by Maurice Sendak. Courtesy of Harper & Row, Publishers, Inc.*

extremely brave and very happy. I can follow that—I don't know if you can—but in the characters there is a kind of progress from holding back to coming forth which I'd like to think is me, not so much as a child or pretending that I'm a child but as a creative artist who also gets freer and freer with each book and opens up more and more.

Mickey. From In the Night Kitchen *by Maurice Sendak. Copyright © 1970 by Maurice Sendak. Courtesy Harper & Row, Publishers, Inc.*

Miss Haviland: *Many persons right now are asking what inspired you to produce this new book,* In the Night Kitchen.

Mr. Sendak: Well, that is a difficult question. It comes out of a lot of things, and they are very hard to describe, because they are not so clear to me. There are a few clues. When I was a child there was an advertisement which I remember very clearly. It was for the Sunshine Bakers. And the advertisement read "We Bake While You Sleep!" It seemed to me the most sadistic thing in the world, because all I wanted to do was stay up and watch. And it seemed so absurdly cruel and arbitrary for them to do it while I slept. And also for them to think I would think that was terrific stuff on their part, you know, and would eat their product on top of it. It bothered me a good deal, and I remember I used to save the coupons showing the three fat little Sunshine bakers going off to this magic place, wherever it was, at night to have their fun, while I had to go to bed. This book was a sort of vendetta book to get back at them and to say that I am now old enough to stay up at night and know what is happening in the Night Kitchen! The other clue is a rather odd fantasy of mine when I was a child. I lived in Brooklyn and to travel to Manhattan was a big deal, even though it was so close. I couldn't go by myself, and I counted a good deal on my elder sister. She took us—my brother and myself—to Radio City Music Hall, or the Roxy, or some such place. Now, the point of going to New York was that you *ate* in New York. Now we get back to eating again. Somehow to me New York represented eating. And eating in a very fashionable, elegant, superlatively mysterious place like Longchamps. You got dressed up, and you went uptown, and it was night when you got there, and there were lots of windows blinking, and you went straight to a place to eat. It was one of the most exciting things of my childhood, to do this. Cross the bridge, and see the city approaching, and get there, and have your dinner, and then go to a movie, and come home. So, again, *In the Night Kitchen* is a kind of homage to New York City, the city I loved so much and still love. It had a special quality for me as a child. It also is homage to the things that really affected me esthetically. I did not get to museums, I did not see art books. I was really quite rough in the sense of what was going on artistically. *Fantasia* was perhaps the most esthetic experience of my childhood, and that's a very dubious experience. But mainly there were the comic books and there was Walt Disney, and, more than anything else, there were the movies and radio, especially the movies. The early films, such as the Gold Digger movies and *King Kong* and other monster films, were the stuff that my books are composed of now. I am surprised, and this is really unconscious—I was looking at *Where the Wild Things Are* not too long ago with a friend, who had found something which amused her a great deal. She is a film collector, and she opened to one page of the book, where one of the wild things is leaning out of the cave. And then she held alongside it a still from *King Kong;* and it was, literally, a copy. But I had not seen the still, of course; I could not

From In the Night Kitchen *by Maurice Sendak. Copyright © 1970 by Maurice Sendak. Courtesy of Harper & Row, Publishers, Inc.*

have remembered the sequence. Obviously, it had impressed itself on my brain, and there it was: I mean, exactly the proportions of cave to cliff, and proportions of monster coming out of cave. It was really quite extraordinary, the effect the films did have on me.

It was only much later, when I was a practicing illustrator and writer, that I got to know the classic children's books and read them. I did not know them as a child; I did not know pictures or paintings or writing when I was growing up. Brooklyn was a more or less civilized place, let me assure you, but this particular thing didn't get to me until quite late. And I think it's reflected in my work. I am what is commonly referred to as a late bloomer. I am happy for that.

Miss Haviland: *That brings us to the question of whom you believe to be some of the great writers for children? You have made some allusions already, but would you enlarge on that?*

Illustrations by Maurice Sendak from A Hole Is to Dig, *by Ruth Krauss. Illustrations copyright 1952 by Maurice Sendak. Courtesy of Harper & Row, Publishers, Inc.*

Mr. Sendak: George Macdonald I think of as probably the greatest of the Victorian writers for children. It's the combination of planes, levels, that he worked on. George Macdonald can tell a conventional fairy tale; it has all the form that a fairy tale must have. At the same time, he manages to inundate the story with a kind of dream–magic, or unconscious power. *The Princess and the Goblin:* Irene's travels through the cave with the goblins are so strange, they can only come out of the deepest dream stuff. The fact that he can weave both of these things together is exactly what I love so much in his work, and what I try to emulate. And he is a model; he is someone I try to copy in many ways. There are other writers, like Charles Dickens, who has precisely this quality of the urgency of

childhood. The peculiar charm of being in a room in a Dickens novel, where the furniture is alive, the fire is alive, where saucepans are alive, where chairs move, where every inanimate object has a personality. This is that particularly vivid quality that children have, of endowing everything with life. And Dickens sees and hears as children do. He has a marvelous ear for what's going on socially and politically, and on one level he's telling you a straightforward story. But underneath there is the intensity of the little boy staring out of everything and looking, and examining, and watching, and feeling intensely, and suffering immensely, which is what I think makes Dickens a superb writer. The same is true of George Macdonald. Another favorite writer is Henry James. I first became enthusiastic over Henry James when I read some of the earlier novels about young children. His incredible power of putting himself in the position of young children, viewing the adult world; and his uncanny sense of how difficult and painful it is to be a child. And even

harder to be an adolescent. Now, these are people who write from their child sources, their dream sources. They don't forget them. William Blake is my favorite—and, of course, *The Songs of Innocence* and *The Songs of Experience* tell you all about this: what it is to be a child—not childish, but a child inside your adult self—and how much better a person you are for being such. So that my favorite writers are never writers who have written books specifically for children. I don't believe in that kind of writing. I don't believe in people who consciously write for children. The great ones have always just written books. And there are many more, but I can't think of them now.

Miss Haviland: *Now let's take a group of questions set to you as an artist. In a photo bulletin issued by our State Department, a comment is made that critics credit—and I'm quoting now—"a hidden little boy, Maurice, between four and eight, with the dreamlike quality of the pictures created by Sendak the man." And further in this piece, the journalist quoted you as saying that your new book,* In the Night Kitchen, *is your idea of what books looked like to you as a four-year-old. Would you elaborate on this quotation?*

Mr. Sendak: Well, I think I did that already. I mean, the city as I felt it as a child. It also was an attempt to capture the look of the books that meant so much to me in the thirties and the early forties—they were not glamorous, "artistic" books; they were very cheap, full-color books that, up to a short time ago, I thought were contemptible. But for some odd reason, my old love for them has returned. My taste in English graphics and German fairy tales came much later, and it really is, I think, on my part at least an honest attempt to get back to those things that did mean an awful lot to me as a child. They weren't fancy, they were good, and *In the Night Kitchen* was an attempt to make a beautiful book that at the same time still suggested those early inexpensive books that were read by most children I knew.

Miss Haviland: *One librarian recalls hearing you speak in the 1950s, a time between the publishing of your illustrations for* A Hole Is To Dig *and of those for* Little Bear, *when you said that your roots go back to Caldecott. And this past April, when you accepted the Hans Christian Andersen International Medal, you named another string of artists whom you credit with stimulating you. I remember you mentioned William Blake, whom you've already spoken of here, George Cruikshank and Boutet de Monvel, Wilhelm Busch, Heinrich Hoffmann.*

Mr. Sendak: That's right.

Miss Haviland: *Could you talk about the specific elements that you think you find there that are particularly relevant to the children's book illustrator?*

Reproduced with the permission of Farrar, Straus & Giroux, Inc. from The Light Princess
by George MacDonald. Pictures by Maurice Sendak. Pictures Copyright © 1969 by Maurice Sendak.

Mr. Sendak: I hated school and my own particular way was to learn by myself. Many of the artists who influenced me were illustrators I accidentally came upon. I knew the Grimm's *Fairy Tales* illustrated by George Cruikshank, and I just went after everything I could put my hands on that was illustrated by Cruikshank and copied his style. Quite as simply as that. I wanted to crosshatch the way he did. Then I found Wilhelm Busch and I was off again. But happily Wilhelm Busch also crosshatched, so the Cruikshank crosshatching wasn't entirely wasted. And so an artist grows. I leaned very heavily on these people. I developed taste from these illustrators. Boutet de Monvel, the French illustrator, who is still not terribly well known (which is a great surprise to me), illustrated in the twenties, or earlier perhaps—and had the most glorious sense of design and refinement of style. His pictures are so beautifully felt and they are supremely elegant as only French illustration can be. They are very clear, very transparent, extremely fine. At the same time, they can be very tragic. There are things in his drawings, which perhaps now would even seem too strong for children—although at one point, they did not. There is a perfect example of his method in one of his illustrations for the *Fables* of La Fontaine—"The Wolf and the Lamb." They are a series of drawings, very much like a comic strip. It's like a ballet. The little lamb moves toward the stream and begins to drink, and the ferocious wolf appears and says: "What are you doing here? This is my water!" Of course, he's rationalizing the whole thing, he's going to eat the lamb up anyway, but he's putting on this big act about it being his water. Now, the lamb knows that there's no chance for escape, and while the wolf is bristling—and in each drawing his chest gets puffier and his fangs get fangier, and his eyes are blazing, and he looks horrendous—now, in proportion to him, growing larger on the page, the lamb dwindles. It has immediately accepted its fate, it can't outrun the wolf, it doesn't even listen to the words of the wolf, this is all beside the point: it is going to die, and it prepares itself for death. And while the wolf goes through this inane harrangue, the lamb folds itself in preparation for its death. It leans down, it puts its head to one side, it curls up very gently, and its final gesture is to lay its head down on the ground. And at that moment the wolf pounces and destroys the lamb. It is one of the most beautiful sequences I've ever seen and one of the most honest in a children's book. There's no pretense of the lamb escaping, or of there being a happy ending—this is the way it is, it does happen this way sometimes, that's what de Monvel is saying. And this is what I believe children appreciate. People rage against the Grimm's fairy tales, forgetting that originally the brothers Grimm had— I'm going off the track a little bit—assembled the tales not for children but for historical and philological reasons. They were afraid their past was being lost in all the upheavals of that period, and the tales were put out as a scholarly edition of peasant tales not to be forgotten as part of the heritage of their homeland. Well, lo and behold, children began to read them. And the second edition was called *The Household Tales* because children were devouring the books—not literally—I'm going to be so conscious of that from here on. The whole point I'm making, although I have forgotten the point frankly, is that those illustrators and writers that attracted me were the ones who did not seem at all to be hung up by the fact that their audiences were small people. They were telling the truth, just the way it was. This could be done if it were esthetically beautiful, if it were well written—simply, if it were a work of art, then it was fine. Now *Der Struwwelpeter* was one of the books that I loved very much—graphically, it *is* one of the most beautiful books in the world. One might complain about the cutting off of fingers, and the choking to death, and being burned alive, and might well have a case there—but, esthetically, for an artist growing up it was a good book to look at and a lot of my early books were affected strongly by the German illustrators. When I came to picture books, it was Randolph Caldecott who really did put me where I wanted to be. Caldecott is an illustrator, he is a songwriter, he is a choreographer, he is a stage manager, he is a decorator, he is a theater person; he's superb, simply. And he can take four lines of verse and have very little meaning in themselves and stretch them into a book that has tremendous meaning—not overloaded, no sentimentality in it. Everybody meets with a bad ending in *Froggie Went A-Courting*. Froggie gets eaten at the end by a duck, which is very sad, and the story usually ends on that note. But in Caldecott's version, he introduces, oddly enough, a human family. They observe the tragedy much as a Greek chorus might—one can almost hear their comments. In the last picture, we see Froggie's hat going downstream, all that remains of him. And standing on the bank are mother, father, and child—and it's startling for a moment until you realize what he's done: the little girl is clutching the mother's long Victorian skirt. And it's as though she's just been told the story, she's very upset, obviously. There are no words: I'm just inventing what I think this means—Froggie is dead, it alarms her, and for support she's hanging on to her mother's skirt. Her mother has a very quiet, resigned expression on her face. She's very gently pointing with her parasol toward the stream as the hat moves away, and the father is looking very sad. They're both expressing to the child, "Yes, it is very sad, but this does happen—that is the way the story ended, it can't be helped. But you have us. Hold on, everything is all right." And this is impressive in a simple rhyming book for children; it's extremely beautiful. It's full of fun, it's full of beautiful drawings, and it's full of truth. And I think Caldecott did it best, much better than anyone else who ever lived.

Miss Haviland: *One critic, at the last Biennale of Illustration at Bratislava, said: "There is no fundamental difference between illustrations for children and those for adults." Would you comment on that?*

Mr. Sendak: I don't agree at all, of course. I intensely do not believe in illustrations for adults. For preschool children who cannot read, pictures are extremely valuable. But even children who do read move in a very different world. As for adults, I personally find it offensive to read, I will *not* read, a novel that is illustrated. I always use this example, and many people here who know me have heard me carry on about this particular one, the case of *Anna Karenina:* the audacity of any illustrator who would draw Anna after Tolstoy has described her in the best way possible! Now, everyone who's read the book knows exactly what she looks like, or what he wants her to look like. Tolstoy is superb. And then to get an artist so asinine as to think he's going to draw Anna! Or Melville: it's incredible. People illustrate *Moby-Dick.* It's an insane thing to do, in my estimation. There is every difference in the world between illustrations for adults and illustrations for children. I don't know why there *are* illustrations for adults. They make no sense to me at all.

Miss Haviland: *Out of that same Biennale of Illustration, where you represented the United States as our juror, there was considerable disagreement, I recall disagreement in theory, on the importance of kinds of art as illustrations. You were there, could you bring this into the picture?*

Mr. Sendak: Well, I'm not sure I know exactly what you mean, but as I recall there was a European point of view as to what illustrations accomplish in a children's book, as opposed to what we believe is the function of illustration. I didn't know such a difference of opinion existed until we were in Czechoslovakia. And it was quite extraordinary. Partly, perhaps, because there is a dearth of original writing, they tend more often to reillustrate their classic and fairy tales, and the illustrations take on a dominance and importance which I, as an illustrator, do not approve of. The books often become showcases for artists. I mean, you turn pages and there are extremely beautiful illustrations, but so far as I can see they could be taken out of one book and put into another. Whereas here, we are very much involved in making the illustrations work in a very specific way inside a book. Now, a picture is there, not because there should be a picture there; there is a purpose for a picture—we are embellishing, or we are enlarging, or we are involving ourselves in some very deep way with the writer of the book, so that the book (when it is finally illustrated) means more than it did when it was just written. Which is not to say we are making the words more important; we are perhaps opening up the words in a way that children at first did not see was possible. In the United States we work to bring pictures and words together to achieve a wholeness in the book, which I was very surprised to find is not at all important in many European countries. It's not a matter of right or wrong, it's just that it is so different! There it was so much a matter of graphics, of beauty of picture; here graphic acrobatics are less important.

Miss Haviland: *One critic has asked why you changed from the "fine engraved style" of* Higglety Pigglety Pop! *back to what this person calls the "fat style" of your earlier work.*

Mr. Sendak: Umm, "fat style." Well, I think the only way to answer that is to discuss the business of style. Style, to me, is purely a means to an end, and the more styles you have, the better. One should be able to junk a style very quickly. I think one of the worst things that can happen in some of the training schools for young men and women who are going to be illustrators is the tremendous focusing on "style," on preparation for coming out into the world and meeting the great, horned monsters, book editors. And how to take them on. And style seems to be one of the things. It's a great mistake. To get trapped in a style is to lose all flexibility. And I have worked very hard not to get trapped in that way. Now, I think my work looks like me, generally speaking; over a series of books, you can tell I've done them (much as I may regret many of them). I worked up a very elaborate pen and ink style in *Higglety*, which is very finely crosshatched. But I can abandon that for a magic marker, as I did in *Night Kitchen*, and just go back to very simple, outlined, broad drawings with flat, or flatter, colors. Each book obviously demands an individual stylistic approach. If you have one style, then you're going to do the same book over and over, which is, of course, pretty dull. Lots of styles permit you to walk in and out of all kinds of books. It is a great bore worrying about style. So, my point is to have a fine style, a fat style, a fairly slim style, and an extremely stout style.

Miss Haviland: *This question comes to you as both an artist and an author. Do you think of your books first in words or in pictures?*

Mr. Sendak: In words. In fact, I don't think of the pictures at all. It's a very strange, schizophrenic sort of thing; I've thought of that very often. Sometimes after I've written something I find that there are things in my story that I don't draw well. And if it were any other person's book, I'd consider not doing it. But I've written it and I'm stuck with it, which is proof to me that I have not (at least consciously) been seduced by the tale's graphic potential. I don't think in terms of pictures at all; I find it's much more interesting and difficult to write, and illustration now becomes secondary in my life. So far as I'm aware, I think strictly in terms of words. And then when it's finished, it is almost a surprise as to "How'm I going to draw *that?* or "Why did I do that?" I'm stuck with an airplane, or I'm stuck with a building. If I'm stuck with an automobile, I'm ready to blow my brains out.

Miss Haviland: *Some artists feel that creating a work is a very separate experience and vastly more satisfying than what happens when the work goes out into the world. How do you evaluate the private experience as compared with the public experience?*

Illustration by Maurice Sendak from Seven Tales *by H. C. Andersen, translated from the Danish by Eva Le Gallienne. Illustration © 1959 by Maurice Sendak. Courtesy of Harper & Row, Publishers, Inc.*

Mr. Sendak: Well, there really is no comparison. The private experience is extraordinary, because it's all yours, nobody knows about it, nobody's going to find out about it, and you have it all to yourself for as long as it takes you to finish the book. *In the Night Kitchen* took two years of concentrated work. *The Wild Things* took about the same length of time, maybe a little less. During that time you are completely absorbed in this dream, this fantasy, whatever it is. The pleasure you get is extraordinary. You live in a very strange world, really quite divorced from this dull, real world. When I'm working on a book, I see very few people, do very few things but think about my book, dream about my book, love it, hate it, pull hairs out of my head; and the only time I speak to people is when I want to complain about it. And then it's over, and then it's finished, and the great shock comes when it is printed! And that's much like giving birth, and always a difficult birth. A book being printed is a major topic in itself; it is a very difficult thing to see through. What was once very dreamlike and transparent and what you thought was a magic moment has now become a real thing in a printing press, and it's going through a big machine, and it looks lousy, and it has to be done all over again. And so gradually your particular transparent little dream is becoming more real, and more terrible every moment. And then finally it is a book. And you become extremely depressed, because you realize that what was so superb and different is really just another book! How strange. It looks like all the other things you've done. And then it goes out into the world, and your child, who was so private and who was living with you for two years, now is everybody's child. Some people knock him on the head, some kick him in the rump, and others like him very much. It's a totally different experience. It takes me a long time to shift gears. I am now in the process. It's only a few weeks since the book came out, and I don't know quite yet how to adjust to the fact that people are looking at it, and criticizing it.

Miss Haviland: *Looking at the publishing world, we can see a very big question: Do you think that children's book publishing is significantly different today than it was when you began in the early fifties? And, if you do, in what respect do you see this?*

Mr. Sendak: Well, yes, of course, it is very different than when I began in the early fifties. For one thing, the world seemed quieter then, and there was more opportunity to do experimental kinds of books. More important, there was time for young people to grow quietly. If you're an artist, you really need the time to grow quietly and not feel competitive or pushed. It was that way in the early fifties. One could develop gradually. Now, of course, it is much more competitive, and we do many more books but, alas, not many more great books. Something is lost. There is a rush, we are flooded with books, books come pouring out of the publishing meat grinder. And, the quality has dropped severely. We may be able to print a book better, but intrinsically the book, perhaps, is not better than it was. We have a backlist of books, superb books, by Margaret Wise Brown, by Ruth Krauss, by lots of people. I'd much rather we just took a year off, a moratorium: no more books. For a year, maybe two—just stop publishing. And get those old books back, let the children see them! Books don't go out of fashion with children; they only go out of fashion with adults. So that kids are deprived of the works of art which are no longer around simply because new ones keep coming out. Every Christmas we are inundated with new books, and it's the inundation which I really find quite depressing.

Miss Haviland: *Would you generalize in any way on what has been happening in other countries as you have traveled abroad and looked at picture books?*

Mr. Sendak: Since I've generalized all this time, I could go a little further. There was a great moment in the middle fifties when, suddenly, the foreign books came to America. Books from Switzerland, the Hans Fischer books and the Carigiet books. We'd never seen them; it was a revolution in American bookmaking. We suddenly began to look very European. It was the best thing that could have happened to us, we *looked* terrific! But, of course, Europeans were then doing the most superb books. England invented the children's book as we know it. And now in the sixties and seventies, certainly America is leading the world in the manufacture of children's books. It's disappointing, I find, going to Europe (with the exception of England and Switzerland) and finding so few contemporary children's books. I don't know if you found this to be true, but I did. In France there is *Babar* and the great old ones, but there are very few new ones. There *are* new ones, of course, but none that we get to see and none that seemingly even French people or Italians get to see—it seems they have dropped back considerably. I could be wrong. In my travels I've discussed this matter with illustrators and editors—and this is certainly the impression I've gotten.

Miss Haviland: *Is there any point that you would like to make, aside from the questions that have been brought up to you before and which you've answered again tonight?*

Mr. Sendak: I love my work very much, it means everything to me. I would like to see a time when children's books were not segregated from adult books, a time when people didn't think of children's books as a minor art form, a little Peterpanville, a cutesy-darling place where you could Have Fun, Laugh Your Head Off. I know so many adult writers whom I would happily chop into pieces, who say, "Well, I think I'll take a moment and sit down and knock off a kiddy book! It looks like so much fun, it's obviously easy—." And, of course, they write a lousy book. You hope they will and they do! It would be so much better if everyone felt that children's books are for everybody, that we simply write books, that we are a community of writers and artists, that we are all seriously involved in the business of writing. And if everyone felt that writing for children is a serious business, perhaps even more serious than a lot of other forms of writing, and if, when such books are reviewed and discussed, they were discussed on this serious level, and that we would be taken seriously as artists. I would like to do away with the division into age categories of children over here and adults over there, which is confusing to me and I think probably confusing to children. It's very confusing to many people who don't even know how to buy a children's book. I think if I have any particular hope it is this: that we all should simply be artists and just write books and stop pretending that there is such a thing as being able to sit down and write a book for a child: it is quite impossible. One simply writes books.

From Where the Wild Things Are *by Maurice Sendak. Copyright © 1963 by Maurice Sendak. Courtesy of Harper & Row, Publishers, Inc.*

Joan D. Aiken was born in Rye, England, in 1924, the daughter of Conrad Aiken. She was educated at Wychwood School, Oxford, 1936–40. She married Ronald George Brown in 1945 (he died in 1955) and has one son and a daughter. She worked for the British Broadcasting Corporation; as librarian for the United Nations Information Centre, London; as an editor for *Argosy* magazine; and as a copywriter for an advertising concern. For her books for children she received the Manchester *Guardian* Award in 1969 and the Mystery Writers of America Edgar Allan Poe Award in 1972.

Books for children:
More Than You Bargained For, and Other Stories (1960), *The Kingdom and the Cave* (1960), *The Wolves of Willoughby Chase* (1963), *Black Hearts in Battersea* (1964), *Nightbirds on Nantucket* (1966), *A Necklace of Raindrops, and Other Stories* (1968), *Armitage, Armitage, Fly Away Home* (1968), *The Whispering Mountain*, (1969), *Smoke from Cromwell's Time, and Other Stories* (1970), *The Green Flash, and Other Tales of Horror, Suspense, and Fantasy* (1971), *Night Fall* (1971), *The Cuckoo Tree* (1971), *The Kingdom under the Sea and .Other Stories* (1972), *Arabel's Raven* (1974), *Midnight Is a Place* (1974), *Not What You Expected: A Collection of Short Stories* (1974), and a book of verse, *The Skin Spinners* (1976), *Go Saddle the Sea* (1977), *The Far Forests: Tales of Romance, Fantasy, and Suspense* (1977), and *The Faithless Lollybird* (1978).

Plays for young people:
Winterthing; A Play for Children (1972), *The Mooncusser's Daughter* (1974), and *Street: A Play* (1978).

Novels for adults:
The Silence of Herondale (1964), *The Fortune Hunters* (1965), *Beware of the Bouquet* (1966), *Dark Interval* (1967), *The Crystal Crow* (1968), *The Embroidered Sunset* (1970), *Died on a Rainy Sunday* (1972), *A Cluster of Separate Sparks* (1972), *Voices in an Empty House* (1975), *Castle Barebane* (1976), *Last Movement* (1977), *The Five-Minute Marriage* (1978), and *The Smile of the Stranger* (1978).

This article is based on a lecture given at the Library of Congress on November 15, 1971, for National Children's Book Week, and was originally published in October 1972 in the *Quarterly Journal of the Library of Congress*.

46

Between Family and Fantasy
An Author's Perspectives on Children's Books

by Joan Aiken

America always had a tremendously powerful imaginative significance for me when I was a child. This was to a very great degree due to the large number of American children's books that there were in our household. My parents had moved from America to England about three years before I was born, and my elder brother and sister must have brought as many of their favorite books with them as they were allowed to, which was a good lot. This was in the early twenties. So, besides hearing their homesick and nostalgic reminiscences of Cape Cod and South Yarmouth and Boston Common, I germinated all sorts of ideas about America, nourished on *The Wide Wide World*, and *Little Women*, and *The Story of a Bad Boy* (by Thomas Bailey Aldrich), *Two Little Savages*, *Uncle Remus*, and the *Katy* books, and, of course, Tom Sawyer and Huck Finn. Consequently I had a very romantic idealized notion of America, which I didn't actually set foot in till after I was thirty.

America was a place where people sat rocking on the porch (this was a linguistic perplexity, because it would be quite impossible to sit rocking on an English porch; a porch in England is a small external roof above the front door to prevent the rain blowing over the threshold). It was a place where children went coasting in winter and picked huckleberries into tin pails in summer, attended fish-fries, ate molasses cookies, hot biscuits, cornmeal mush, and chowder, drank root beer (which sounded delicious), listened to loons and mockingbirds, chewed sassafras sticks, wore muffs and high shoes, were bitten by rattlesnakes and attacked in trees by lynxes, and slept in trundle beds.

Some of these details were borne out by the reminiscences of my elder brother and sister, others were not; but they were all highly sustaining to the imagination. As time went on, my elders lost their American accents and turns of phrase—I can remember much family discussion as to

47

whether one said pavement or sidewalk, automobile or car, biscuit or cracker—but we still had the books, and by degrees acquired more: *Queechy, Freckles,* and *A Girl of the Limberlost, Melbourne House,* and the Daisy books, *Daddy-Long-Legs, Betsey, Elsie Dinsmore, St. Elmo, Rebecca of Sunnybrook Farm, Pollyanna* and *Anne of Green Gables.* I know that Anne, geographically, belongs to Canada, but in every essential way she fitted into the American scene.

Now there was one interesting factor which, looking back, I can see all those old books had in common, besides being American. Some of them were laid in the city, some in the country; some were set in the North, some in the South; some dealt with personal relationships or moral struggles and others were simple tales of adventure or domestic sagas; some were great literature, others were fairly humdrum bits of work; some were about boys, others about girls; but the unifying feature connecting them all was that, almost without exception, they were stories about parentless children—about orphans. The central characters in these books had lost at least one parent. Often it was the father: maybe he was away at the war,

Illustration from Night Fall *by Joan Aiken, designed by Aileen Friedman. Copyright © 1969 by Joan Aiken. Published by Holt, Rinehart and Winston. Reproduced courtesy of CBS, Inc.*

as in the case of the March family; sometimes he died midway through the book, as in *Melbourne House* or *The Story of a Bad Boy;* sometimes the parents were simply elsewhere, as in *Two Little Savages;* but a very large proportion of those children were bona fide orphans, doomed either to be brought up by tough-minded aunts, like Tom Sawyer or Ellen in *The Wide Wide World,* or to be reared by even more thick-skinned and uncomprehending strangers who had adopted them from the local orphanage.

Now, doesn't this seem significant? I suppose most of these books were written around the turn of the century; some, like *Little Women,* of course, a good deal earlier. One can propound various reasons for such a scarcity of parents—the recent memory of the Civil War, for instance. Or the American pioneer spirit—the idea that parents were something you early left behind as you hewed your way from log cabin to White House. It was not that adults, as such, were unimportant in these books; there was almost always some guide, philosopher, and friend—Uncle Jerry Cobb, Caleb Clark, The Bird Woman, Dr. Sanford, Mr. Ladd, John Humphreys—who appeared midway through the tale to protect and advise the child who was the central character and to reconcile him or her to the harsh and arbitrary behavior of the adoptive parents. Over and over again in these books one comes across the episode where the child, driven to despair by some piece of adult injustice, has decided to run away complete with huckleberry pail and battered umbrella, but meets the friendly counselor somewhere along the way and is persuaded to go back and give the uncongenial environment just one more try.

We can probably take it that *Melbourne House, The Wide Wide World,* and *A Girl of the Limberlost* were written in ignorance of the Oedipus complex and all its connotations. Freud was born in 1856 and published *The Interpretation of Dreams* in 1900 but it wasn't, I'd guess, for another thirty years after that, at least, that any trickles from the tidal wave of his innovatory ideas began to reach the inland lagoons of children's literature. So one can probably assume that all this hacking away of the parental undergrowth was just a simple, healthy, unconscious instinct, a rebellion against the rigid family structures of the nineteenth century and its didactic family books such as *Sandford and Merton* and *The Fairchild Family.* Now, whether these books about orphans were written from an unacknowledged wish to massacre the writers' own parents or a yearning to shunt off their children to the nearest orphanage, the resulting benefit to the reader is indisputable.

When my fourth book for children was in process of being published, its English editor objected that the title I'd given it—*Bonnie Green*—was unexciting, and asked me to think of something better. At that time I was working as an advertising copywriter for J. Walter Thompson, and I asked the very intelligent friend with whom I shared an office what she thought of my alternative, *The Orphans of Willoughby.* "It's not bad," she said. "At some point, every child longs to be an orphan."

Illustration by Robin Jacques from Black Hearts in Battersea, *by Joan Aiken. Copyright ©*
1964 by Joan Aiken. Reprinted by permission of Doubleday & Company, Inc.

As soon as she said it I saw that she was right. All these late nineteenth-century books about poor orphans wrestling with unjust guardians and adverse circumstances exactly meet the needs of children, who, from time to time, want endorsement for their feeling that parents are utterly tyrannical and unreasonable. In these books, children's ambivalent feelings toward their parents are neatly polarized: horrible Aunt Fortune, who dyes Ellen's stockings brown and withholds her mail, is mother seen in her most baleful aspect; kind Alice Humphreys, who reads French with Ellen and takes her for walks (but also dies halfway through the book) is mother viewed on her benevolent and sympathetic side.

It's easier for a young child to polarize; not to have to think of the same person in two different ways, not to have to realize that good people have their defects and even the bad can have some likable qualities. And, another important point which ties up with what I want to talk about presently, it is one of children's most basic pretend-games to imagine a situation in which their parents have vanished; it's a kind of primary imaginative exercise.

Of course, in the end, psychology caught up with even children's literature. About the time I was six or seven, spanking began to be frowned on, parents were reluctantly becoming more permissive, it was the fashion to say, "Mother is not *angry*, just terribly, terribly hurt," and so it became acknowledged that, in children's fiction also, even if parents were not always a hundred percent sympathetic, fun-loving, jolly good sorts, at least they ought to be represented that way. The era of warmhearted, down-to-earth, outgoing, sensible family novels was on its way in. Nasty tyrannical parental figures were on their way out. For about thirty years—starting, I suppose, with the Arthur Ransome books?—fictional families remained at an alltime high of sunny reasonableness. Whether the child readers enjoyed this as much as they were assumed to, I doubt. Anyway it was partly in reaction against all this sweetness that I evolved my own pseudo-nineteenth century, harking back to the good old days of wicked adults and put-upon children.

But forward evolution was going on at the same time. By the time I had grown up, fictional families were beginning once more to face real problems: from illness to poverty, from poverty to crime, the trend went on. The teenage situation novel was arriving. Parents got divorced, girls became pregnant, boys took drugs; it was all very true to life.

So, in a way, we are now back where we were at the end of the nineteenth century: the family is very much to the fore again. Or, rather, it is in the doghouse. In the literature of psychology and in adult fiction, one is constantly reminded of Thurber's aphorism about women: Woman's place is in the wrong. Only now it is the family. R. D. Laing and A. Esterson, in *Sanity, Madness, and the Family,* have demonstrated how a family environment can produce schizophrenics. David G. Cooper advanced this theme even further in *The Death of the Family*, advocating the removal of the family and the family-structured society. Earlier, Wilhelm Reich said the same thing. Bernice Rubens, in her prize-winning novel *The Elected Member*, depicted the frightful way in which the family unloads all its neuroses and hangups onto one victim. The family itself has become the scapegoat. And partly, I am sure, in reaction to all this concentration on family—profamily, antifamily, family served up however you like it, medium, rare, or with french fries— fantasy is flourishing as never before (though for this too there was literary parallel, in a lesser degree, at the end of the nineteenth century).

I must say I don't find this swing to fantasy at all surprising. After all, among all the earnest pursuit of reality, this torrent of books about dropouts and teenage mothers, I often wonder how much attention is paid to the literary preferences of the dropouts themselves, if anyone asks teenage mothers whether they want to read books about other teenage mothers. Or whether, as the state of the market might indicate, they don't prefer a bit of a letup from their own circumstances and wish to read about Hobbits.

There does certainly seem to be a profound cleavage between pure fantasy on one side and pure realism on the other. Please understand that I don't wish to take sides, one way or the other. My books, I consider, come in the middle. They are about orphans, following the American tradition.

Last summer I attended the third conference on children's literature in education, at Exeter, England. After one of the main speeches, the whole conference became involved in a brisk debate as to whether realism or *un*realism was best in children's fiction; it didn't seem to occur to any of the people who leapt up and argued vigorously on one side or the other that children like different books at different times. That some children like one kind of book and others like another. That the same child can read seven different books on seven consecutive days. Nobody but a fanatic sticks to the same diet, day in, day out, every day of his life. And children, bless them, are anything but fanatics. They are empirical; they change; even if they don't feel like trying something new just now, they may well try it next month.

But, people say, even if you offer some alternative diet to books about the family, whether in its good or bad aspect, why should the alternative be fantasy? What has fantasy got to offer? Shouldn't children be learning useful facts as they read, can't they have historical novels or stories set in far-off lands, or at least proper Greek myths or Indian legends, so that while they read they are also stocking up on their cultural heritage?

People quite often say all this to me. "You write fantasy," they say, sometimes fairly accusingly. "Do you think it is right to stuff children's heads with all this moonshine?" Or words to that effect. In fact, as I've suggested, I wouldn't entirely agree that what I write *is* fantasy; I'll come back to that presently. But I quite often find myself putting the case for fantasy in this kind of argument, so I'll put it now.

Straightaway, one comes up against the problem of definition. I daresay everybody has their own rough definition of fantasy, but though these overlap to some degree, one soon discovers in conversation that they are by no means identical. Arthur C. Clarke, grand master of science fiction, said in a radio interview recently: "You may not be able to define fantasy, but you know it when you see it." I am not sure that even that is true.

I found about four different meanings of the simple word itself. First, the general conception of something odd, exaggerated, eccentric, varying from the normal. Then, Shakespeare's use: dandified, fond of finery. In musical or poetic terms a fantasy is a work that follows no formal pattern. In fiction, one tends to think of it as a paperback—maybe with a monster on the cover and beams of prismatic light flowing about, science fiction with an added element of the supernatural.

In psychology the definition of fantasy is more exact, and to underline this difference in status, the word is often spelled with a ph instead of an f. Here it is held to mean imagination, daydreaming, as opposed to adaptive thought; that is, thought processes not hinging onto, or intended to produce results in, reality. But, as well as this, fantasy is the imaginative activity underlying *all* conscious thought—the underground mental processes which support and enliven and nourish the more overt and connective processes.

Having laid out these rough and ready definitions, I will now give an equally rough and ready and very subjective account of my own relations with fantasy, overlapping from the psychological category to the fictional, with some excursions into theory about fantasy's general function in the lives of children.

When does fantasy begin? Very early indeed. According to leading authorities on child psychology, the newborn baby receives messages from the outside world; right away, it starts to accompany these stimuli with its own mental images of what is happening to it, and from an amazingly early age it can make rational deductions. It has been proved, for instance, that a five-week-old baby can learn to switch on a light by moving its head, in a quite complicated way, maybe two turns to the right and one to the left. So then, extrapolating from what has already happened to it, the baby is able to create images, not of what is happening now, but of what will presently happen again. The baby's next step is to imagine what could or might happen, on more accumulations of evidence. His mother might vanish entirely and never reappear. Or she might stay with him always and never again go off to answer the door. Babies have this preoccupation with appearances and disappearances which, of course, is later reflected in fairy tales. Countless stories deal with cloaks or caps of invisibility; it's the old nursery blanket that one's mother used to hide behind, dressed up a bit.

Then the baby's imagination takes another leap, and from things that could happen but are not likely, he proceeds to imagine events that could not happen, that are right outside the bounds of possibility. In his despair and outrage at the mother who does not come when he cries, he conceives—so psychology tells us—the notion of eating her up entirely, of eating up the whole exterior world. I find this conception credible because it, too, is plainly reflected in some fairy tales. In "Hansel and Gretel," for instance, the children are deserted by their parents, so they eat the gingerbread cottage and finally bake the witch (mother again, the deserting mother in her most evil aspect) in her own oven. Some people consider "Hansel and Gretel" too frightening for small children. Certainly it is a very basic and horrid tale, but I don't think there is the slightest sense in keeping such stories from children, in view of the fact that they are quite capable of forming these conceptions for themselves; it's an example of the horse and the stable door.

It's interesting, to diverge for a moment, that this notion of eating up the world—of an edible world all composed of foodstuffs—doesn't crop up more in myth and folklore. I can think of various nursery rhymes and songs—"If all the trees were bread-and-cheese," "The big rock-candy mountain"—there are some poems by the nineteenth century American Eugene Field in his book *Songs of Childhood*. Jean de Bosschere wrote a book called *The City Curious* in which even the characters were edible, Erich Kastner used the idea in *The 35th of May*, Roald Dahl did in *Charlie and the Chocolate Factory*, Sendak has in his *Night Kitchen*. But on the whole, the edible-world fantasy seems a product of the individual imagination, rather than genuine myth. And it seems to have cropped up more at the turn of the century than at any earlier time. I haven't done much research on this; anyone who wants to correct me is welcome. But I wonder if imaginations around then weren't starved in some curious way, that they had to nourish themselves on images of marzipan flowerbeds and chocolate trees. Maybe this notion of an edible world is too frightening and shameful, one we would prefer to forget.

Anyway, back to the developing baby. Experimental work done at Harvard, at Johns Hopkins, at Edinburgh University, Scotland, and at the Tavistock Institute, London, has shown that babies have two distinct ways of reacting to objects and to people, and that these two modes of development are in competition—either one bit of your brain develops, or the other. Which is a pretty serious thought. Also that babies can get bored, if the experience they receive (finding they can switch on a light by turning their head, perhaps) is not relevant to their stage of development. This seems to me even more thought provoking. One of the most important things possible for a child to learn is that he can entertain himself by his own mental processes. I simply hate to think of babies being bored by being presented with the wrong sort of experience, even in the interests of science.

At age one or so, which apparently is about the most crucial stage of our mental development, equipped with these conceptual powers—the power to imagine things as they are, as they will be, as they might be, as they might not be, and as they could not possibly be—the baby climbs out of his cot, explores the world, and acquires a lot more external ingredients for internal fantasy. His dreams and imaginings, instead of being concerned simply with food and physical processes and love and hate for the people who do things to him and for him, become full of dogs, and cars, and trees, and toys, and furniture, and supermarkets. And all this material he manipulates with complete omnipotence; partly, of course, this is to compensate for the fact that in reality he doesn't have much power over his surroundings.

The raven Mortimer and the bread bin. From The Bread Bin; As Told in Jackanory by Bernard Cribbins, *by Joan Aiken. Illustrated by Quentin Blake. Published by the British Broadcasting Corporation. Illustrations © Quentin Blake 1974. Reproduced courtesy of the publisher.*

Young children's fantasies come in all graduations and variations of depth: total belief, semibelief, pure pretense. When I was six or seven I used to have a game about putting the eggcups away—if the cupboard door wasn't closed within a couple of minutes of my putting the first one in, all the eggcups would turn hostile, would turn into wicked little threatening creatures—so it was a kind of giggling frantic rush to get them all in and the door shut as fast as possible. That was really a game, really pretense. But then, later, going to bed in our house at Rye that was slightly haunted, at age twelve or thirteen, I had to cross an unlighted double room to get to my bedroom, passing a big, book-lined alcove. Again, it was a desperate rush to get to my safe bedroom, but this time I wasn't giggling; I never was certain that *something* wouldn't come out of that dark alcove.

Children are capable of tremendous double-think; they can know that something is true, and that it is not true, with equal certainty. I suppose in a way fantasy is like a kind of homeopathic magic; if you know you can switch on terror and switch it off again, give yourself just the right amount for a delicious tingle, it is like an immunizing dose against other, larger fears.

Of course all children's fantasies aren't frightening. Most are wishful. My stick is a horse, this brick is a birthday cake, let's say we're all going to the circus. Sometimes the wish is the first step toward action. Children's wishes, of course, can assume such powerful substance and reality that the letdown, if the wish doesn't come true, may be shattering. Remember Hoodoo McFiggin's Christmas, in Stephen Leacock's *Literary Lapses:* he prayed every night for a pair of skates, a puppy, an air gun, a bicycle, a watch, and a drum—what he got was a box of collars, a pair of pants, a toothbrush, and a Bible. I could never bear to read that as a child though I knew it was supposed to be funny; it just seemed tragic to me.

Children's fantasies, being so strong, so near the edge of reality, can easily get out of hand. I had to judge a competition recently which required a description of an imaginary friend: some of these children's imaginary friends, obviously described from genuine experience, were exasperatingly superior, punctual, and faultless; others had become real tyrants, selfish, demanding, time-wasting, and liable to give false information; one could see that it might not be a step from such overbearing familiars to real demonic possession.

Arabel pulling Mortimer on a roller skate. From The Bread Bin *by Joan Aiken. Illustrated by Quentin Blake. Published by the British Broadcasting Corporation. Illustrations © Quentin Blake 1974.*

In the course of childhood, naturally, children acquire a kind of library, or catacomb, or compost-heap, of outgrown, discarded fantasies, which, even though discarded, are not lost, merely stowed away somewhere lower down in the less accessible regions of mental experience: images of heaven or hell, of the North Pole, of what school is going to be like, of the hospital where Mrs. Jones has gone, of South Carolina or Switzerland or the Sargasso Sea. Just as one can, long after, call up the imaginary picture of a place or person which one had entertained before actually going to the place or meeting the person, just as one can recall and review this discarded preconception, so one can also recall the discarded images of childhood. I can still remember my visions of what America was like from age four on. I can remember my early ideas of heaven and Kubla Khan's pleasure dome with equal distinctness; I am sure you can all do the same. Not to mention the attic of the March family and David Copperfield's aunt's parlor.

Some fictional places had such a strong reality for me as a child that they became incorporated in my dreams. So did fictional characters. When I read *The Three Musketeers*, at the age of eight or nine, the figure of Cardinal Richelieu so impressed me—he was represented as an extremely powerful, sinister, almost omnipotent character, if you recall— that he figured as the villain in my dreams over quite an extended period. He was sinister, in those dreams, rather than terrifying, presumably because, in the book, though so powerful and wily, he was in fact worsted by the musketeers. Richelieu was the central character in the first wholly fictional dream I can remember having. In that dream he was called The Lord Abbot, and he interfered in a war between three kings, behaving in a very ruthless and destructive manner. This was the first dream I had in which I was merely a spectator, taking no part in the action. It was also the first dream that I wrote down, and I still have it.

Like most children from the age of five on, I was continually telling myself stories and acting stories and writing stories down. Maybe some children don't get to the writing-down part, but the stories are there just the same; they have a very powerful existence. And a story can have as many images as any chunk of reality. With my own, as with the real and fantasy memories of people and places, I can distinguish between my memory of a story as I first conceived it and the final form—usually very impoverished and abbreviated—in which I managed to get it written. In fact, what I put down—particularly between the ages of five and nine, before I learned to join letters together and write reasonably fast—what I put down was just a kind of synopsis or shorthand or hieroglyphic, a symbol of what my intention had been. That's all my work ever is, really. I'm invariably disheartened, at the end of a book, by the amount that has had to be left out, at the skimpiness of the concrete outcome, compared with the largeness and richness of the original conception.

This is one reason why I think vocabulary is terribly important for children. Those experimenters at Harvard also did research on the amount of time that mothers spend actually conversing with their small children, and they discovered that ten minutes a day is the average; even the best mothers don't do much longer. A preschool experiment on children from deprived areas, in the West Riding of Yorkshire, England, showed that aggression always goes along with lack of language. And a pilot study on emotionally disturbed children in Hampshire, England, found that the whole group studied were more backward in their reading than they ought to have been, judging from their I.Q.'s, that they had small vocabularies, and that 40 percent of them were bored all the time.

My next-door neighbor in Petworth, England, happens to be a sociology graduate from Berkeley, California, who did a year's work with very backward children; she told me that when she first met her class they didn't know how to use scissors, except just to stab each other. I felt a lot of sympathy with them; to have a tool without the knowledge of how to use it is just about the most frustrating experience in life.

Conversely, I can remember at, I suppose, about the age of three or four, the tremendous feeling of astonishment and elation I had in discovering some of the uses and shades of meaning and adaptability of words. For instance, I can remember listening to my mother talking to my elder brother and sister and realizing that the word "few" could be used in opposing ways: if you said "quite a few" that meant a lot, whereas "only a few" meant not very many. A research team in Nottingham, England, discovered that families with a very small arsenal of adjectives got on with each other significantly worse than those with higher descriptive faculties; if you can relieve your tension with some Krushchevian turn of phrase it apparently helps to avert bloodshed; and they found that families who hadn't very many nouns in regular use tended to be even more bad tempered.

This is all pretty rudimentary; what I am getting around to saying is that the faculties of imagination can be trained and fed like any other. Children are poets, or should be, if they are equipped with the means; I don't mean that they should necessarily be set to write little verses about the rain and the cat and going to the dentist—though that's okay too—but that they should be shown the possibilities and pleasures of words, of analogies between things and processes, that language and behavior are symbols of feeling. And that they should be given the right equipment so that they can make use of their mental resources. There's a Welsh saying: Three things enrich the poet—myth, poetic power, and a store of ancient verse. Exactly the same things enrich the child, call them what you like. Last month I was driving an eight-year-old boy in my car and we happened to pass an old farm cart on which was piled a great tangle of rusty wire. "It's like a lyre," he said. "I expect it was dropped there by a hurricane, and someone's hunting for it on the other side of the world." Three leaps of thought in quick succession; he couldn't have done that without the equipment.

Sister Bridget washing soot off Mortimer. From The Bread Bin *by Joan Aiken. Illustrated by Quentin Blake. Published by the British Broadcasting Corporation. Illustrations © Quentin Blake 1974.*

By the age of four—I think Johns Hopkins found this one out—we have already acquired 50 percent of our final intelligence; by the age of eight we have 80 percent of it; if we haven't made good use of our minds by then we have wasted a lot of time. In fact some will be irretrievably lost.

I'm sure that wherever there is real trouble in the world, the basic cause of it is lack of imagination, simply failure to project, treating other people as if they were things. In a way, that's even more disastrous than greed. Science and imagination are getting farther and farther apart; it seems to be the duty of people who worry about this to try to start a reverse trend going. I feel that, if the imaginations of young children are nourished and given full scope right from the start, then, at least, if they later become scientists, they will have more chance of remembering from time to time that they are humans too (and also they'll very likely be better scientists).

Children who have access to the language of the imagination, who are able to conduct a dialogue between the inner, imaginative self and the outer world—I'm sure such children are more adjustable, more resourceful, likelier to see all the possibilities of a situation. I read somewhere that bilingual children tend to have a higher intelligence than those who speak only one language. I'm not sure that's proved; I've heard the converse stated, too, but I prefer to believe it because it endorses my point.

At the Exeter conference on children's literature which I referred to earlier, I spent four days in the commission on mythology, discussing, with about thirty other people, the uses of myth in education—whether myth was a good or a bad thing, what kinds of myths should be told to children, if at all, whether children should hear their own indigenous myths first, rather than those from other parts of the world, whether frightening myths ought to be left out, what myth does for us anyway, and, most basic of all, what myth is.

To the best of my recollection, not one of those questions really got answered, though we were all talking our heads off all the time. Certainly we couldn't come to any consensus of opinion as to what myth is. A collective dream? Universal logic? Sacred mysteries? But it was agreed that myth overlaps fantasy, and in some way is needed by everyone—not simply as moral exhortation or parable, any more than the purpose of religion is simply to make people behave better, but because myth is the basic material of a rich inner life, and because a rich inner life does seem to be essential for human equilibrium.

A myth is like one of those tremendous old maps, with dragons and monsters and blowing winds, a map in which, by choice and elimination, by trial and error, one can perhaps discover one's own whereabouts, one's own identity, and get some notion of the boundaries between reality and imagination. And also perceive that these boundaries—between what we call sanity and what we call madness—are more flexible than we have been in the habit of believing.

I sometimes imagine a human being—I'm afraid I have a terribly concrete mind, I simply love analogies—as a kind of mixed freight and passenger train, traveling along at night. The driver is there in front: the conscious, the ego. Behind him are all those trucks and cars, containing goodness knows what, all going heaven knows where. The driver can make his way back along the train if he wants to and have a look through various doors to see what is there, who is there, if he can see *anything* in the dark; some drivers choose to, others prefer just to keep driving. But, of course, the driver is not in control of the train or its motive power; all he can do is pull a few levers and hope there's nothing on the track ahead.

Reading, like direct experience, provides a child's mind with freight, with ingredients for creating his own fantasies, as I've indicated with my dreams about Cardinal Richelieu. And, perhaps most important of all, reading provides a child with a world absolutely of his own, unshared by anybody, unless he chooses to share. Almost any reading is nutritious in some way. Almost any reading will provide something. But I do have reservations about one area of literature which I shall now discuss.

Illustration by Susan Obrant from The Cuckoo Tree *by Joan Aiken. Copyright © 1971 by Joan Aiken. Reprinted by permission of Doubleday & Company, Inc.*

When I was a child I read all the time. As well as all those splendid books about orphans, which I loved so much, I read myths and fairy tales and historical fiction and ghost stories and nineteenth-century novels and poetry. Some things I liked better than others, some I didn't like much at all, but I would rather read anything than nothing; and it didn't occur to me not to read something just because I didn't like it; in a curious way, because the books were there, I felt it was my duty to read them, not just once, but over and over.

And of all the books we had, looking back now and classifying, I can't say that any particular kind of reading was my favorite. Fantasy came at both ends of the spectrum. One fantasy story was just about my best-loved bit of reading for years: that was Walter de la Mare's *The Three Mulla-Mulgars.* And I still think it's a beautiful, poetic, imaginative book. And the book, or books, that I liked least of all were also fantasy, those by Lewis Carroll—*Alice in Wonderland, Through the Looking-Glass, Sylvie and Bruno,* and *Phantasmagoria.* I can't remember when I met them first; I must have had them read to me at a pre-reading age. I certainly have a mental image of the room with the looking-glass, where Alice talks to the chess pieces, as the sitting room in the house where I was born.

I had a really deep dislike of those Lewis Carroll books, which I'll try to analyze. It wasn't so much because of the sharpness and unkindness of the characters, the way they were constantly snubbing one another, though that was very disagreeable; but what made me profoundly uneasy about the books was the texture of chaos, the dream-feeling that at any moment some random occurrence might upset the action; that, as in a nightmare, innumerable obstacles were going to prevent Alice from ever achieving her objective; that, as in a nightmare, she might even forget what her objective had been. The Alice books for me had the depressing effect of listening to a recital of somebody's long, boring dream (as a matter of fact, now I very much enjoy listening to people's dreams, because of the insights that they give, but then, of course, I had no such notion and they seemed like chartless wildernesses).

Recently I came across Carroll's introduction to *Sylvie and Bruno* again and I'm going to quote a bit of it, first because it's a very interesting illustration of the creative process and secondly because it seems to me an absolute blueprint of how *not* to construct a children's book. Carroll says:

> As the years went on, I jotted down, at odd moments, all sorts of odd ideas, and fragments of dialogue, that occurred to me—who knows how?—with a transitory suddenness that left me no choice but either to record them then and there, or to abandon them to oblivion. Sometimes one could trace to their source these random flashes of thought—as being suggested by the book one was reading, or struck out from the "flint" of one's own mind by the "steel" of a friend's chance remark—but they had also a way of their own, of occurring, *a propos* of nothing—specimens of that hopelessly illogical phenomenon, "an effect without a cause." Such, for example, was the last line of "The Hunting of the Snark," which came into my head...quite suddenly, during a solitary walk: and such, again, have been passages which have occurred in dreams, and which I cannot trace to any antecedent cause whatever.

Please note that I am not for a moment criticizing Carroll's habit of making use of his various flashes of inspiration—every writer does the same; every writer has unprompted sparks of thought, sudden eruptions of dialogue, meaningful passages in dreams; every writer makes use of them to enrich his work; I do myself all the time. But, instead of controlling his fantasies, I feel that Carroll let them roll away from him at random; it was this sense of undirected force, of an engine, as it were, out of gear, which distressed me as a child, so that I found his books far more upsetting, than, for instance, Bram Stoker's *Dracula*, in which the elements, though evil, were subject to a high degree of organization. Certainly there were vampires, but their habits were known and charted— one carried garlic, one made the sign of the cross, one buried them at the crossroads, and they were done for. Whereas in the Carroll books it was not even at all clear who was good and who was bad; which was another very upsetting factor.

Carroll goes on in his preface:

And thus it came to pass that I found myself at last in possession of a huge unwieldly mass of literature—if the reader will kindly excuse the spelling—which only needed stringing together, upon the thread of a consecutive story, to constitute the book I hope to write. Only! The task, at first, seemed absolutely hopeless, and gave me a far clearer idea, than I ever had before, of the meaning of the word "chaos"; and I think it must have been ten years, or more, before I had succeeded in classifying these odds-and-ends sufficiently to see what sort of a story they indicated; for the story had to grow out of the incidents, not the incident out of the story.

Exercising any degree of control over the kind of books written for or read by children is a highly doubtful policy. It has been suggested that fantasy could be dangerous because it might create for children images more frightening than anything they could construct for themselves. Actually I think this is even more likely to happen in a context of reality. But, in any case, what terrifies one child may seem merely comic to another, or may be completely ignored; one can't legislate for fear. But if one is to exercise any kind of censorship whatever over children's reading matter, it seems to me that this kind of uncontrolled, almost sick, fantasy is a better candidate for the axe than, for instance, comics, the usual target for parental or educational disapproval. Comics may be vulgar, silly, violent, but they are not mad; it is the incipient madness of Carroll that I feel is risky. I think that, in writing for children, the real sin against the Holy Ghost is to depress them; anything else is more forgivable. They may ignore—or assimilate—hate, anger, fear, stupidity, vulgarity, but despair is just too damaging. One feels that Carroll's plunge into unreason was an attempted escape from despair, and I'm sure that was what distressed me as a child.

And furthermore, his whole preface affronts me. You should not make a children's book out of "odds-and-ends." It seems to be the Victorian idea that leftovers from the adults-lunch are suitable to be sent up to the nursery for the children's meal. You certainly should not spend years in a desultory attempt at classification, pushing random elements about, to see if they can be forced into some kind of story. A children's book should be written with a high degree of care and intent, remembering how few books children have time to read in the course of childhood and that the impact of each one is probably equivalent to a dozen, or twenty, encountered at a later age.

These were very personal reactions to Carroll; other people may be quite differently affected by those books. But often, discussing fantasy with friends and colleagues and children, I've encountered fairly similar reactions and the feeling that fantasy without any touch of reality whatever can be much more demoralizing than stories which, though they may have an intrinsically more frightening content, are laid in reality. I'm distinguishing between simple fear and the distress caused by chaos; obviously this uneasiness at fantasy arises from fear of the chaos inside oneself; if one were truly well adjusted, one could be perfectly calm about Alice's inability to get into the garden, about the inconsequential suddenness with which characters in *Sylvie and Bruno* appear and disappear, but how many of us are truly well adjusted? And children, it may be said, are not adjusted at all; they are still trying to find a world to fit them.

Children, I think, are not opposed to an orderly existence; in fact, left to organize themselves, they invent far more severe regulations than any adult would ever dare impose on them, and I think they like a degree of orderliness in their reading matter, too. Remember how structured the traditional fairy tales are. Even nursery rhymes, though they often start off with a wild leap outside logic, nearly always end up by working their way back into sense again.

At this point, of course, having waded into Carroll's writing technique so unmercifully, I lay myself open to perfectly reasonable inquiries as to how I write my own books. And to that I can at least answer truthfully that I write them with very great care. I think about them for a year or two beforehand, until I have them fairly firm in my mind; I make notes about characters, I do research on details, I discard things that don't seem to belong, and I wait, if there seems to be a gap, until the necessary thing to fill it emerges in my mind.

I know that my full-length children's books are said to fall into the fantasy category. I'd agree that my short stories do. But I would claim that my novels are not fantasy proper. There is no supernatural element—no dragons, no wizards, no time travel, no magic rings, no invisibility, no spells, no runes, no monsters, no magic at all. Humans do not speak animal language. There are exaggerations, to be sure: my dukes have gold doorknobs and mix their mustard with champagne, people travel by elephant or air balloon to reach their destination more speedily, a character can fall asleep for nine months, there are occasionally wolves in Hyde Park, London, but nothing actually impossible occurs, no natural laws are broken.

And I do like to collect as many genuine details as I can, to interlard with the exaggerations. I like my family heirloom to be not just any valuable miniature but a genuine lost Breughel; I like the language my farmers speak in *The Cuckoo Tree*, for instance, to be proper Sussex dialect (I think children enjoy lively, unusual language), and my locations to be real ones, my streets to be real streets, so that, up to a point, the places I write about can be found on the map. I like to do this for several reasons, apart from the simple pleasure of getting things right. First, a rather improbable story line is more credible if it is fenced about with genuine details. That is a mundane, technical kind of reason. But secondly I think the whole texture of a story acquires greater richness and depth if the details are accurate and carefully worked out, so long as they do not become overly obtrusive. Thirdly, though I do not, naturally, expect children to go along checking for accuracy as they read, I hope that some of these details will nonetheless remain in the minds and encourage a habit of thinking about such points, of noticing them, of asking questions about them. Because that is the way to lead a more interesting life; to acquire such a habit is surely one of the purposes of reading.

Writers are constantly noticing details. I have a number of writer-friends and, while they differ from each other as much as any bunch of dentists or insurance salesmen or engineers or farmers, they definitely have one factor in common, which is that they are very, very seldom bored. Left alone at a bus stop in a straight, empty street, a writer—if not absorbed in planning his next book—will be guessing about the inhabitants of the houses from their exteriors; he will be inventing reasons why the public lavatory carries a mysterious notice saying "Not to be used after dusk"; he will be noticing a broken test tube in the gutter and wondering how it got there; he will be unabashedly listening to the conversation of two men behind a wall; he will be making mental notes about the color of the sky, and the shape of a dead tree, and the odd juxtaposition of two dummies in two adjoining shopwindows who seem to be gazing earnestly at one another.

If children learn to look and notice and think about all the things they see, to speculate and ask questions, they will be able to spread themselves over a wider area of living, become more adaptable, which we have all got to be if we are to survive. Thinking about things as they are leads on to thinking about things as they might be, wondering what is going to happen next, deducing causes from effects, and predicting effects from causes. This is one great virtue of fantasy: to be able to put oneself outside reality and think, "If things were not the way they are, what might they be like?"

I read a book on advanced driving technique which said that the best drivers are so alert all the time that they are on the brink of actual fear, because their imaginations are at work every minute, predicting the possible hazards that may lie round the next curve or shoot out of the next side road. I think this is highly applicable to living; so was another technique suggested in that book, known as commentary-driving: "My speed is forty, the road surface is dry, I'm in a suburban area, speed-restricted zone, parked truck on my left with a pair of legs sticking out from under it, dog's tail visible behind that lamp-post, old lady with a basket crossing the road diagonally with back to me, fifteen yards ahead..."

When one first practices commentary-driving, just listing all the things in view seems enough of a strain to send one crashing into the next tree, but it's wonderful how one's ability to notice and record speeds up with practice.

So I like to put all these details in my books; although the setting is an invented historical period, I like at least some of the background to be correct. I had a letter from a boy in Maryland last year which asked: "Do your books have a point of view or are they written for the reader's enjoyment?" Emphatically, they are written for the reader's enjoyment. I don't write them with any kind of missionary intent, because I don't think that is the way books ought to be written. But I sometimes find, analyzing the plots afterwards, that they have more symbolic meaning than I'd noticed while I was writing them. For instance, that the long, subterranean journey in *The Whispering Mountain* is a kind of parable of the hero's process of self-exploration, of discovering his own identity. And that the separated twins in *The Cuckoo Tree* represent the kind of split, of insensibility, that can occur in a child when faced with adult unreason or wickedness.

On the whole, my books are concerned with children tackling the problem of an adult world in which things have gone wrong; I suppose this is a kind of exposition of a feeling that things in the real world have gone badly wrong, and our only hope is that our children will be able to put them right. I do have a great feeling of the responsibility involved in writing for children: that to enlarge their capacities is probably the most important thing one can do, and that it should be done with absolute integrity and concentration and care.

Talking about hope, I would like to tell you a dream I had. And, since I've been pretty derogatory about Lewis Carroll's use of his dreams, I can only apologize in advance. If it seems to you a great piece of impertinence that I should come to this august place and tell you my dream, all I can say is that my presence here at all seems just about as unlikely as a dream to me.

I had the dream just about a year ago. That phrase doesn't describe the experience very well—I didn't have it, it had me. Words won't convey its blazing intensity. I'd had a minor operation for deafness and after three days in the hospital I was spending a couple more days convalescing in a friend's house in London, being very lazy and relaxed. Just before, I had been working on some children's stories, which were set in an imaginary region of London that I'd christened Rumbury Town. It was supposed to be a kind of Poe-like slum, very wild and strange.

Well, I dreamed that I was in this region, or rather, that I was observing it, watching the story take place. It was about an old lady, a teacher, who made a very scanty living by giving lessons on the harp to a few children in the neighborhood. It was amazing that she made a living at all because if her pupils were no good she told them so baldly and dismissed them. Her character was an important part of the story: she was a dry, tart, austere spinster, completely uncompromising; she never made concessions to people's feelings. Years before, she had quarreled with the only man she ever loved, who was a poet, because she wouldn't praise his poems; she said she knew nothing about poetry and therefore wasn't qualified to judge. She had never seen him again. All this was background to the dream, which I was aware of before it began.

In my dream the old lady—her name was January (it was some time after I woke before I understood the symbolism of this)—having heard from a third party that the man she had loved was now critically ill, probably at the point of death, started walking through Rumbury Town, to try and distract her mind from thoughts of his condition. It was at night. And in the middle of the dark, wild, deserted region she got lost and, wandering through a maze of alleys, came upon a kind of Satanic orchestra, composed of skeletons, who were rehearsing their music in an untenanted courtyard. The leader of the group, in fact, was Satan himself, who gave her a very sinister welcome and invited her to comment on his orchestra's performance. And she, uncompromising as usual in spite of the frightening appearance of the musicians, said that she thought their playing was terrible. Whereupon Satan, very angry—both with her and with them—turned round and called for Hope.

This Hope turned out to be a kind of huge werecat, or puma, or saber-toothed tiger, who sprang at the players and snarled at them and terrorized them into playing much more energetically. Obviously Satan had expected that Hope would terrify the old lady too, but in fact, she was accustomed to cats and merely scratched him under the chin, at which he purred. Not only that—she walked off with Hope following her, leaving the Satanic orchestra quite baffled. They had thought that the old girl was in their power for good, but not a bit of it.

On her way she met one of her pupils, one of her undauntable pupils, who, seeing she was lost, led her out of the maze of alleyways. She went on, always with Hope trotting behind her in the dark, to the big, dingy block of apartments where this poet lived from whom she had parted so many years before. Although he had become famous, he had never left the district.

But when she got to his room, she found that he had just been taken away to the hospital in an ambulance and it was thought unlikely that he would survive the journey. On his dusty desk she saw, lying, an unfinished poem with the title "Hope," which began with the story of her evening's experiences.

So, she went down the stairs again, out the door into the dark street. And, in the final moment of the dream, just before I woke, I was aware of the tremendous strength and profundity of her hope—and it was my hope too, on her behalf—that Hope, the saber-toothed tiger, would still be there, sitting on the sidewalk, waiting for her.

When I woke up, it was wildly frustrating to be in somebody else's house. I asked if I could borrow the use of a typewriter, and it turned out that the only one my hosts possessed was locked, and nobody could find the key, and I felt too weak to struggle with writing my dream out in longhand, so I had to wait for two endless days, carrying it round in my mind like a redhot coal, before I could get home and put it down.

Well, that was my dream about hope. Please forgive me for ending with such a personal experience, but it seemed to me then, and still does, to have a kind of meaning. And I hope that you will have this feeling, too.

Erik Christian Haugaard was born in Copenhagen in 1923. He came to the United States as a teenager, attending Black Mountain College and the New School for Social Research. In 1942-45 he served in the Royal Canadian Air Force. For his book *The Little Fishes* he received the New York *Herald Tribune* Festival Award and the *Boston Globe-Horn Book* Award in 1967 and the Women's League for Peace and Freedom Jane Addams Award in 1968. In 1970 he was awarded the Danish Cultural Minister's Award and the Chapelbrook Fountain Award. He lives in Ballydehob, Ireland.

Books for children:
Hakon of Rogen's Saga (1963), *A Slave's Tale* (1965), *Orphans of the Wind* (1966), *The Little Fishes* (1967), *The Rider and His Horse* (1968), *The Untold Tale* (1971), *A Message for Parliament* (1976), *Cromwell's Boy* (1978), and, as translator, Hans Christian Andersen's *Complete Fairy Tales and Stories* (1974).

This lecture, given on March 5, 1973, at the Library of Congress, was part of the tenth anniversary program of the Children's Book Section. It was published as a pamphlet by the Library of Congress in 1973.

Portrait of a Poet

Hans Christian Andersen and His Fairy Tales

by Erik Christian Haugaard

If the drive for immortality were merely the vain wish to perpetuate one's name beyond the grave, then there would be better ways of doing it than through literature and art. History is filled with madmen and clowns whose names we are forced with shame to remember because of their foolish deeds. But what pleasure can there be in this? The eyeless sockets of a skull cannot read. We need the royal tombs in order to distinguish the skeleton of an emperor from that of his slave. No, it is present power, not future fame and honor, which tempts the Napoleons of this world. But the poet, the artist, why does he want immortality? What makes a man like Stendhal say that all his books are tickets in a lottery, the prize of which is that they will be read in a hundred years?

Art is not science. There are no laws, no scales on which a poem can be weighed and its value found. There is only time's test. The poet dies; his heart ceases to beat, and day no longer follows night; there is neither light nor darkness; but the passion of his creation may be such that it lives by itself. For immortal works of art not only exist, they are alive—this in contrast to material of historical interest which needs the custodian's care and enthusiasm to save it from oblivion. That a sonnet by Shakespeare was written four hundred years ago is not important, nor is the age of the bronze charioteer standing in the little museum at Delphi. We read the poem or look at the statue, and something within us is touched, almost physically, by them. It is our soul, alive because blood is coursing through our veins, that recognizes another soul, as alive as our own, in the cold metal and the printed word. For the greatness of art, music, and poetry is that it can contain passion and feeling; it preserves them, keeps them alive—it is the poet, not the poem, that dies.

We live in an age of toys; and toys are pleasant to own, especially when we invite a neighboring child for a visit. The greedy look in his eye we take

69

Pencil drawing of Hans Christian Andersen by Jean Hersholt. From the Jean Hersholt Collection of Hans Christian Andersen, Manuscript Division, Library of Congress.

as a compliment, forgetting that this same unpleasant expression has covered our own faces when we have visited those who have better toys than ours. In a world of toys, the toy rules and the purpose of man is to play. A work of art is the very opposite of a toy: it is alive, and anything alive makes demands on us. The point of the toy—the expensive motorcar, the yacht—is that it is ours alone. Art belongs to everyone who cares to make the effort to seek it out, and since we cannot own it, we share it willingly. "You must read this book!" we say to a friend. The book has touched us; now we wish genuinely, with all our heart, that someone else should have the same experience. If our friend does not like the book, if it fails to move him, we are unhappy and hurt, for we have exposed our soul and are defenseless. But if our friend does share our taste, then our pleasure is multiplied by his.

Can we live without art, without literature, without music? I cannot answer this question for all of mankind, for it seems to me that some men do. But for myself the answer is emphatically no! Religion, philosophy, or science might solve all the problems that I could phrase as questions. But I cannot bend my fears and sorrows into question marks, nor my joys. All the melancholy, all the sweet sadness, that I have felt would be locked in my chest forever if a piano concerto by Mozart did not have the key to it. And the loneliness of my walk on earth would be unbearable. But art in all its forms appeals to our feelings with feelings; a note is struck, and we are the sounding board. The artist, the poet, and the composer attempt to express emotional truth and make the unreasonable reasonable. Pity, fear, love—all the words which are so vague, so indefinable—through art suddenly become so clear, so real, that they eclipse the world around them. The moment of truth, of awareness, is brief—the curtain falls, the audience applauds, and it is gone. But because we have felt it, because we have experienced this inexplicable miracle, we are happy and at peace with ourselves. We have partaken in an act of creation, for the notes of the music, the lines of the poem, could only reach us if the emotions were there inside ourselves. That melancholy which Mozart touched was ours as well as his.

The written word is not a substitute for the spoken word, for conversation. The spoken word has a warmth that comes partly from the casualness with which it has been chosen. Written words are containers which hold for all eternity something as ethereal as thought and feeling. The great poet uses words so accurately that there are no other words that can take their place; there are no synonyms.

If it were only the sound of words that varied from language to language, then translating would be a mechanical task. But since our physical worlds and our cultures are not alike, even when we are describing the same things, we find different aspects more or less important, and more or less attractive. Andersen remarked that on the shores of the Mediterranean he learned to regard his old friend the sun as an enemy. But there are shades of meaning so subtle that they are seldom noticed by anyone but a native, for they depend upon intuitive knowledge which a stranger cannot acquire.

Yet contact with literature, art, and music from other cultures is enormously valuable. Without foreign impulses native art becomes provincial and self-satisfied and as often as not assumes its very faults to be virtues. A morality which views life differently makes us reevaluate our answers to elementary questions.

Unfortunately, in our time mass media tend to make our cultures alike; the contrasts are being eradicated. This amalgamation of all cultures into one has not been accomplished yet, and I am still hopeful that it won't be. But on one level it has taken place—a very superficial one, it is true, but a very influential one. A television producer or a journalist in Bombay may have more in common with his colleagues in New York or London than he does with his own countrymen who are living five steps from his studio or his office.

As the part of our culture that can be transmitted through tubes becomes more and more alike—and, therefore, more and more provincial—it will tend also to become more and more exclusive. Its very internationalism will convince it that it is broad and courageous, whereas it actually is timid and narrow. Since there will be no other cultures to measure our accomplishments and failings by—not because they do not exist, but because we shall not know about them—we shall have to seek them in time! Classical literature, the art and music of the past, must and will become more and more important! We cannot escape New York by going to Paris, or Paris by going to Rome. In Salt Lake City and Bombay the little galleries are exhibiting the same paintings; the little magazines are publishing the same poems and the same articles, which express the same opinions. Only in the world of the past do we meet daring ideas that may place question marks in front of our theories and dogmas. The work of translating Hans Christian Andersen's stories and fairy tales was, therefore, not only a labor of love; I felt it was a duty.

A translation of any work that has been translated before implies a dissatisfaction with the existing versions. It would be absurd, not modest, to claim otherwise. But this is not always a criticism, for the meanings of words do change. Some of the early translators of Andersen, however, were Victorians; and they were not afraid to censor and change according to their own taste. But now that I have completed this work and know how difficult it is to translate—how nearly impossible the necessary skills are to achieve—I no longer feel inclined to comment on any version other than my own. The success of a translation can only be measured in terms of its failure; it is a race without winners.

What are the skills needed to translate literature? A knowledge not only of the two languages but also of the two cultures. The linguistic intimacy should be so great that you should be able to dream in both tongues. Then an ability to write yourself, coupled with possibly the most difficult attribute of all: the humility to make that ability subservient to the author you are translating. You must be daring and unafraid, patient and careful—traits seldom found in the same person.

I certainly am not such a paragon. The only one of my own demands that I dare claim to fulfill is an intimate knowledge of both Danish and English—and that was the gift of chance. Until my seventeenth year I was a Dane. I spoke, thought, and dreamt only in Danish. Then the squeaking wheel of history turned, and I was forced to live in an English-speaking country. Had I been younger, I would have forgotten the Danish culture; had I been older, I should not have been able to acquire a new one; I should have remained a foreigner. But at the age of seventeen there was still child enough within me to learn another language in the same manner as I had the first.

A great writer is part of his native land, as if his name stood for something we could point to, like a mountain or a lake. This is the proof of our acceptance of his immortality. I could as little imagine a Denmark in which Hans Christian Andersen did not exist as I could believe that the island of Fyn or Odense, Andersen's birthplace, could vanish.

Andersen was woven into my childhood. I would quote him as an Englishman quotes Shakespeare, without knowing that I was doing it. It is this intimacy with my native land and its greatest writer which I hope has come across in my translation. Danish is a homespun language, and coziness is considered by Danes to be a most praiseworthy virtue. The vocabulary is small but rich in everyday, practical words. Today there are almost five million Danes; in Andersen's time there were probably fewer than half that number. An enormous family—but still, a family. Gossip flourished. The feather that became five hens must have been a daily occurrence. The conditions and the language were natural for the fairy tale. The farmyard was the setting, and the hens played the role of the Greek chorus.

I have tried to guard against modernizing Andersen's ideas and opinions. As for his style there were fewer temptations, for he wrote a clear, unassuming prose that he was much criticized for in his own times but that we in the twentieth century admire. Andersen never used dialect.

Cover illustration from The Complete Fairy Tales and Stories, *translated from the Danish by Erik Christian Haugaard, published by Doubleday & Company, 1974. Courtesy of the publisher.*

Everyone from kings to darning needles speaks an educated Danish, for he
never patronized his characters. Their tragedies were real to him, and he
made them real to us. He considered neither the fairy tale nor the folktale
unworthy of becoming literature. And when he tampered with his source
material, which he almost always did, it was never to make it more folksy
or quaint but to add that dimension which he hoped would give it the
dignity of a work of art.

The saint sets himself apart from the rest of mankind. He is different
because he is holier, nearer if not to God then to some concept of
perfection. The writer cannot be a saint. He must be subject to all, or
nearly all, the emotions other men experience. If he were not, he could not
write about them. His genius lies in his awareness and ability to express
and formulate this knowledge. The uniqueness of the poet is his
sensitivity, which can measure the depth of his feelings and place them in
proper perspective. In recreating something which has already happened
to him, the poet relives it outside himself. First, he partakes in the action
on the stage; then he becomes the spectator, watching the actors,
including himself, and that is the creative moment. Since the great writer
has faults as well as virtues, he undoubtedly partakes in much that is not
flattering, for such is the fate of all men. But the follies of most mortals are
buried with them, as are their accomplishments, whereas the immortal
bards have the mixed pleasure of knowing that their failings have been
given the same everlasting life as their good deeds. The poet is a figure
about whom we all can gossip; through his works he is alive to us and we
enjoy repeating all that we know, even the most malicious bits. Andersen
did many marvelously silly things; anyone who does not know about
them need only ask a Danish schoolteacher and he will be told them all.
But what the school teacher seldom tells is his source, which is usually
Andersen himself!

In his diaries Andersen has recorded a most amusing anecdote. A
foreign artist arrived in Copenhagen and announced in the newspapers
that he had come to paint portraits of the most famous Danes, and he
hoped that these great personages would come to the studio he had just
rented. The very next morning who should appear at his door but
Andersen and one of the actors from the Royal Theatre, a man known for
his self-love and conceit. Andersen looked at the actor and could not help
laughing, both at him and at himself. Later Andersen discovered that the
artist was a confidence man who made his living by appealing to men's
vanity. To write "The Emperor's New Clothes," one must be able to be as
foolish as the emperor—although I admit that it is more important to be
as wise as the child who saw that he was naked. But only the genius can be
both at the same time and, therefore, be able to write the story.

All artists are fascinated by their own kind; they cannot escape this
preoccupation, at least the artists of the last two centuries have not been
able to. Andersen is no exception to this rule. He wrote innumerable
stories about the poet. Some of the finest of them are almost unknown:

"The Gardener and His Master," "Psyche," "In the Duckyard," "The Bronze Pig." The most famous is that lovely fairy tale to which Andersen gave the title "The Nightingale," and I do think it is a little misleading to call it "The Emperor's Nightingale" when one of the points of the story is that the little bird belongs to no one.

Is the artist's interest in himself narcissism? I am not certain. But there have been eras when the artist was not so introspective and at least appeared to be almost at ease with his fate. Royalty, nobility, and the church treated the artist as if he were a clown, or as if he were a kind of precious jewel created by a whim of nature, which—like any other costly gem—was enhancing to own. In the nineteenth century the middle class became the patrons of the arts, and they had a far more complex and far less happy relationship to literature, art, and music. These new rulers claimed that their right to govern was based on moral and ethical principles. The kings, the dukes, and the pope had put their faith in God; and as we know, or ought to know, the ways of God are inscrutable. It was, indeed, a daring claim that power finally rested on the shoulders of those not only fit, but justly deserving of this glorious mantle. The artists in almost all cases belonged to the middle class themselves. They were being patronized in several senses of the word, and they spent their lives pointing out that, despite the claims of their parents, the pillars of this new temple were not made of Grecian marble but of plaster of paris. The only part of their heritage the artists embraced was the dream of the perfectly just society; and in the daylight of an unjust world they often became narrowminded and self-righteous. With wagging fingers they tried to improve their neighbor's character, as well as his life.

Andersen never engaged in politics. Once he said that politics was the most attractive of all the sirens but the one that led you quickest over the precipice. I think he was saved from following this maiden by his background. By birth he belonged to the group described as the poor—those so far beneath the rest of society that they are not judged by it. They escape censure and therefore are allowed as much freedom as the rich to become eccentrics.

Certainly Hans Christian Andersen's parents were not ordinary. There were books in the shoemaker's cottage and a puppet theater to play with. A common misunderstanding has cast a shadow over the memory of his mother. It was usually believed that she is the main character in "She Was No Good," the little story about the drunken washerwoman. But this is not true, although she did play an important role in the incident on which this story was based, but a quite different one from what is so often supposed. In his notes Anderson wrote:

The kernel of "She Was No Good" lay in a couple of words my mother said when I was a little boy. One day, on the street in Odense, I saw another boy on his way to the stream where his mother, who was a washerwoman, stood in the water rinsing linen. A widow, well known for her strict morality and her sharp tongue, screamed at the child from the window of her house: "Are you taking schnapps down to your mother again? It is disgusting! For shame! Let me never see you grow up to be like her, for she is no good!" When I came home I told about the incident, and everyone in the room agreed, "Yes, she drinks too much; she is no good!"

Only my mother was of a different opinion; she said, "Do not judge so harshly. The poor woman works so hard, she often spends the whole day standing in the cold water; and it is not every day that she gets a hot meal. She has to have something to fortify herself with. What she takes isn't right, that is true; but she does not know of anything better. She is an honest woman and she keeps her little boy neat and clean." I had been as willing as the others in the room to judge the washerwoman harshly; and therefore the mild and understanding words of my mother made a deep impression on me.

This is a picture of a woman who dares speak her mind; and it explains the rather unusual beginning of Hans Christian Andersen's long and painful education.

At the first school he attended, the teachers indulged frequently and freely in physical punishment. Hans Christian Andersen's mother did not approve, so she enrolled him in a private school for Jewish children. Certainly Hans Christian Andersen must have been able to attend it without payment, for this happened at a time when his family was desperately poor. Unfortunately, the school was disbanded the following year, and he had to return to the public school. To me this story reveals his mother as a remarkable woman; and it also tells much about the degree of integration of the Jewish community in Odense at the beginning of the nineteenth century.

We have a tendency to think too much in terms of economics, and the life of the poor we imagine as one long chain of miseries. But in reality there is such a thing as a rich little poor boy, and I think that this was exactly what Andersen must have been. He was seldom scolded and never hit. He was given all the time he wanted to dream, and he had the whole town to play in. At one point he presented himself at the castle in Odense, where the Crown Prince of Denmark and his family were residing. He knocked at the door and said he wanted to play with the royal children. He was allowed to come in and invited to return. We shall never know what the magic words were that gained him entrance to the castle, but like the hero of a folktale, he had a free, unbroken spirit and maybe that was the key which could unlock the gates.

Because one does not belong to a particular sect, be it religious or political or both combined, does not mean that one has neither morality nor ethical principles. Although the confines of Andersen's Christianity were vague, and within them was to be found the deist worship of nature, which he himself loved so passionately, Andersen believed in divine justice and a merciful God. He thought that man's redemption was always possible but only through personal suffering, as he shows us in "The Red Shoes" and in two lesser known but also very lovely stories, "The Girl Who Stepped on Bread" and "Ann Lisbeth." I think, however, the work that mirrors most clearly his faith and ideals is "The Bell."

In the narrow streets of the city, at dusk, just as the sun was setting and painting the clouds above the chimney pots a fiery red, people would sometimes hear a strange sound like the knell of a great churchbell. Only for a moment could it be heard; then the noise of the city—the rumbling of the carts and the shouting of the peddlers—would drown it out. "It is the vesper bell, calling folk to evening prayers; the sun must be setting," was the usual explanation.

To those who lived on the outskirts of the town, where the houses were farther away from each other and had gardens around them—some places were even separated by a field—the sunset was much more beautiful and the sound of the bell much louder. It seemed to come from a church in the depth of the fragrant forest; and it made the people who heard it feel quite solemn as they looked toward the darkening woods.

As time passed people began to ask each other whether there wasn't a church in the woods. And it was not far from that thought to the next: "The bell sounds so beautiful, why don't we go out and try to find it?"

Now the rich people got into their carriages and the poor walked; but to all of them the road to the forest seemed very long. When they finally reached some weeping willows that grew on the edge of the woods, they sat down under the trees to rest; and looking up into the branches, believed that they were sitting in the middle of a forest. One of the bakers from town pitched a tent there and sold cakes. Business was good, and soon there were two bakers. The second one to arrive hung above his tent a bell, which was tarred on the outside to protect it from the rain, but its tongue was missing.

When the people came back to the town, they said that their outing had been romantic....

Andersen goes on to tell us of the efforts of several persons to find the bell without success.

At last the emperor heard about it, and he promised that whoever found out where the sound came from would be given the title of "Bell Ringer of the World"; and that, even if he discovered that it wasn't made by a bell.

As one would suppose, this increased the traffic to the forest; and, indeed, someone finally claims the prize.

He had been no farther than any of the rest—and that hadn't been very far—but he explained that the bell-like sound came from a great owl who was sitting inside a hollow tree. It was the bird of wisdom and it was incessantly knocking its head against the trunk but whether the ringing was caused by the bird's head or the tree trunk he had not yet decided. The emperor bestowed upon him the title of "Bell Ringer of the World," and every year he published a paper on the subject, without anyone's becoming any wiser.

One Sunday in May a group of children who have just been confirmed decide they will look for the bell; they set out together, that is, all except one of them, a poor boy who has attended church in borrowed clothes and therefore must go home first. But the children are not much more tenacious than the adults who went before them; either they give up or accept some flimsy explanation for the sound.

They came to a house made of branches and bark. A huge wild apple tree towered above it, and roses grew in such abundance up its walls that they covered the roof of the little cottage. On one of the ramblers hung a little silver bell. Was that the bell they had heard? All but one of the boys agreed that it was. He claimed that this bell was too small and delicate to be heard so far away; besides, it did not produce the kind of music that could touch a man's heart.

"No," he said. "It is an entirely different bell that we heard before."

But the youth who had spoken was a king's son, and one of his comrades remarked, "Oh, his kind always wants to think themselves cleverer than the rest of us."

They let him go on alone. When the cottage and his friends were lost from sight, the great loneliness of the forest engulfed the prince. He could still hear the little bell, which had pleased his friends, tingle merrily and from far away—borne on the wind's back—came the sound of the people at the baker's tent, singing as they drank their tea. But the knell of the great bell of the forest grew stronger and stronger; then it seemed to be accompanied by an organ; the king's son thought the sound of it came from the left where the heart is.

Leaves rustled, twigs snapped; someone else was making his way through the woods. The prince turned; in front of him stood another boy. He had wooden shoes on his feet, and the sleeves of his tunic were too short because he had outgrown it. He was the youth who had had to return the clothes he had worn at confirmation, as soon as the ceremony was over. The landlord's son had got his finery back, and the poor lad had put on his own old clothes, stuck his feet into his clogs, and set off in search of the great bell whose deep clang had called on him so powerfully that he had had to follow it.

"Let us go on together," proposed the prince. But the poor boy looked down at his wooden shoes and pulled at the sleeves of his tunic to make them a little longer. His poverty made him shy, and he excused himself by saying that he feared he could not walk as fast as the prince. Besides, he thought that the bell was to be found on the other side of the forest, on the right, where everything great and marvelous is.

"Then we shall not meet again," said the prince and nodded to the poor boy, who walked into the densest part of the forest, where brambles and thorns would tear his wornout clothes to shreds and scratch his face, legs, and hands till blood streamed down them. The prince did not escape being scratched, but the sun did shine on the path he took, and we shall follow him, for he was a good and courageous boy.

"I will find the bell," he declared, "if I have to go to the end of the world."

The prince was wrong in assuming that he would never see the poor boy again. They were engaged in the same search and were bound to each other, for that which separated them—the wealth and royal name of the one, and the poverty and mean background of the other—counted for little when compared to the greatness of their common quest.

Listen to the last page of the story.

Just before the sun set [the prince] reached the summit. Oh, what splendor! Below him stretched the ocean, that great sea that was flinging its long waves toward the shore. Like a shining red altar the sun appeared where sea and sky met. All nature became one in the golden sunset: the song of the forest and the song of the sea blended and his heart seemed to be part of their harmony. All of nature was a large cathedral; the flowers and the grass were the mosaic floors, the tall trees and the swaying clouds were its pillars, and heaven itself was the dome. High above, the red color was disappearing for the sun had set. The millions of stars were lighted: the millions of little diamond lamps. The prince spread out his arms to embrace it all: the forest, the ocean, and the sky, and at that moment from the right side of the cliff came the poor boy in his ragged tunic and his wooden shoes. He had arrived there almost as quickly by going his own way.

The two boys ran to meet each other. There they stood, hand in hand, in the midst of nature's and poetry's great cathedral; and far above, the great invisible, holy bell was heard in loud hosanna.

Very touching, very romantic, and very easy to make fun of. It is a dream, and dreams are fragile. If they are not treated gently, they will break and only cynicism can glue them together again; but then they are less than worthless, they are dangerous. The dream has a part to play in reality; it is not its opposite nor is it even separate from it. This is something only puritans believe; but they think that the sleep of the virtuous is as dreamless as death.

The dream enables us to live, for it is its strength which makes it possible for us to bear our sufferings. If Hans Christian Andersen had not had an idealized picture of the artist and the importance of art, would he not have ended his life as a shoemaker? We do not know the answer to this question, but I do not think it improbable, for certainly the obstacles which blocked his path to fame must have seemed almost insurmountable.

That one has ideals and dreams does not mean that one is so starry-eyed that one stumbles over reality. After all, one need not be a cynic because one knows the world and, what is even more depressing, oneself. Andersen certainly did worship the artist, but this does not mean that he did not realize that the "ugly duckling" and the swans had weaknesses.

In a story called "The Philosopher's Stone," he tells how the devil traps the poet. In the castle that stands in the crown of the Tree of the Sun, which grows in Indialand that stretches east to the end of the world, lives the wisest of all men. He has four sons, and they all beg to be allowed to go out into the world to find the philosopher's stone. Each of the young men has one sense that is supremely developed, and the devil makes use of it to ensnare them one by one:

"Now it is my turn," said the third brother. "I have a nose for the work." That was not the most elegant way to express oneself; but that was the manner in which he usually spoke, and one had to take him as he was. He had a cheerful disposition and he was a poet; a real one, who could say in verse what couldn't be said in prose. He perceived many things long before other people could.

"I can smell a rat," he would boast; and in truth, it was the sense of smell that he had especially developed. This made him an expert on beauty, he felt. "Some love the smell of apples, others the odor in a stable," he said. "Each region of smell in beauty's realm has its adherents. Some feel most at home in the smoke-filled atmosphere of cheap cafes, where tallow candles smoke rather than burn, and the odor of stale beer mixes with the stink from cheap tobacco. Others like the pungent perfume of jasmine flowers, or they rub their bodies with oil of cloves—and that smell is not easy to get rid of. Some seek the clean air of the seashore, and others climb mountains to be able to look down upon the trivial life below!" This he said before he had left his father's house; one would think he already knew the world of man, but he didn't. It was the poetical part of him that had spoken: the gift of imagination that God had given him, while he lay in the cradle.

He bid goodby to his father's house in the Tree of the Sun. He did not ride away on a horse; no, he mounted an ostrich, for that could run faster. But as soon as he saw the wild swans, he picked out the strongest among them and rode on that instead, for he liked a change. He flew across the ocean to foreign lands, where great forests surrounded deep lakes, and there were huge mountains and proud cities. Wherever he flew, the sun broke forth from behind dark clouds. Every flower, every bush smelled more fragrant, as if they wanted to do their very best while such a friend and protector of odors was near them. Yes, even an ill-tended rose hedge that was half dead unfolded new leaves and bloomed. Its single flower was particularly lovely; even the black slug saw the beauty of the little rose.

"I will put my mark on it," the slug said. "I will spit on it, for more I cannot do for anyone."

"That is the fate of beauty in this world," said the poet. He composed a little song about it, and he sang it himself; but no one listened to it. So he gave the town crier two silver coins and a peacock feather as payment; and he shouted the song, accompanied by his drum, through all the streets and squares. Then people listened and said they understood it—it was so profound. Now the poet composed other songs about beauty, goodness, and truth. They were listened to in the cafes, where the tallow candles smoked; and they were heard in the fragrant meadow, the forest, and on the boundless sea. It seemed he would be more successful than his two other brothers.

This did not please the devil. He came at once, bringing with him large portions of incense. There were all kinds; royal and ecclesiastical, and the very strongest that the devil distills, which is brewed from honor, glory, and fame. It is potent enough to make an angel dizzy, not to speak of a poet. The devil knows how to catch everyone, and the youngest brother was caught with incense. He couldn't get enough of it, and soon he had forgotten his quest and his home, as well as himself. He went up in smoke, incense smoke.

This is a most honest picture of the poet and shows how well Andersen knew the weakness common to them all. For it is certainly in this craving for praise that the poet is most easily corrupted. This strong wish, or even demand, for approval seems from the essential loneliness and uncertainty of creative work; it is a logical part of it. Between the dream and the reality—the conception of a poem or a story and its finished form—perfection is lost. Compared to their intention, all works of art are failures; and this all poets, artists, and composers know. Is it any wonder, then, that they need praise to keep them working? Andersen, with his usual naivete, never hid how much it meant to him. "I was praised, and I thrive on it!" he wrote in a letter to a friend. And as much as applause pleased him, so much was he enraged and made downhearted by criticism—he might even burst into tears. His fury was foolish and his fear exaggerated; but he was a very lonely man whose talent was his only security, his sole passport to the world in which he liked to live.

Andersen claimed that his life was a fairy tale, and I am inclined to agree with him. There is an element of magic in everything that happened to him; but this was partly of his own making, for he believed that he was fated to do something great. There is an old legend that the most beautiful of all gems is locked in the head of the ugliest of all animals, the toad. I think Andersen knew that he possessed this jewel, and this gave him, even as a child, an almost unbelievable self-confidence and made him strangely attractive. This explains, too, why that old woman known in the town of Odense for her occult powers could prophesy that the ragged urchin would grow up to be such a famous man that his native city would be illuminated in his honor. When she looked at little Hans Christian, the reflection of the jewel was shining in his eyes; she saw it and guessed what it meant.

What distinguishes the fairy-tale world from the other world of fiction? First of all, the most obvious: its universality. The same plots appear again and again; it is only the physical environment that is changed; for the fairy tale is so simple, so sparsely told, that the more refined and complex aspects of society cannot be included. A king is a king; a pauper, a pauper; and a rich merchant, a rich merchant: archetypes all and as such recognizable. Its philosophy is simple and pragmatic, learned from hard knocks rather than intellectual pursuits. This unbookishness makes the reader secure: this is a friend telling him a story. No one questions that it is better to be born a rich man's son than a pauper's; and if one is so unfortunate as to be born poor, then it is advisable to try to marry a princess. People are divided into good and bad, but this very division means that these qualities exist and are recognizable. Women are often shrewish and mean, men brutal and hard; but love is possible and so is happiness—even ever after.

"Once upon a time" is no time, just as east of the sun and west of the moon, or the end of the world, is no place. In reality, however, it means "at all times, in all places." It is a declaration, announcing that what you are now going to hear is the truth—both in time and space. And we must, to a certain extent, all agree or we would not love the fairy tale so much.

Lost as we are in our own particular problems, locked in a world all too unique, we draw comfort from the fairy-tale world, finding in its simplicity, if not solutions to our private troubles, then at least a momentary respite from them. For the purpose of the fairy tale is to let out a little truth in a world of lies. It is a safety valve and a necessary one.

In a very short tale by Hans Christian Andersen called "The Little Green Ones," Dame Fairy Tale herself exclaims: "One ought to call everything by its right name; and if one does not dare to do it in everyday life, at least one should do it in a fairy tale!"

I think Andersen took this advice very seriously indeed. What ought to surprise us is the applause and the praise this truthfulness gained him; for what could have resulted in a jail sentence for insulting the king, had it been written in the form of a political pamphlet, was honored instead. Andersen criticized all and everyone—both children and grownups were mirrored with exactly the amount of favor they deserved. And everybody loved it! But why? Because they all, from beggar to king, agreed with Dame Fairy Tale. They wanted everything called by its right name—so long as it was only done in a fairy tale!

Our century has been more cruel. During the Nazi occupation certain Danish actors who publicly read aloud some of Andersen's fairy tales found out from their prison cells that tyrants have no sense of humor. Our times are not pleasant; some of the best among us live in fear and the worst, as often as not, in public glory. Our values have been eroded; when we hear of a murder, we ask who the victim was before we condemn it. We are, indeed, so sophisticated that we are able, with the ease of the Romans, to laugh when we should cry, and cry when we should laugh. Our children are grappling with fundamental moral questions, and we are not helping them.

I belong to the generation that called themselves materialists and yet worshiped such phantoms as paradise without free speech, and justice which was only to be ours when we learned to bow to despotism. I have no solutions to offer. I do believe that stupidity and evil are eternal but that beauty and goodness cannot die either.

My hope is that the fairy tales of Hans Christian Andersen will be read, especially by the young of today. For in his deep understanding of the ways of the world, there is wisdom to be found; and the fact that an innocence as tender and beautiful as his could live beside such knowledge gives both comfort and hope.

Ivan Francis Southall was born in Canterbury, Victoria, Australia in 1921. He attended Box Hill Grammar School and then served in the Australian Army and the Royal Australian Air Force, winning the Distinguished Flying Cross. In 1974 he gave the May Hill Arbuthnot Honor Lecture. In 1971 and 1976 he received the Australian Children's Book Council Book of the Year Award and in 1974 the Australian Writers Award. He lives in New South Wales, Australia.

Books for children:
Hills End (1963), *Ash Road* (1966), *The Fox Hole* (1967), *To the Wild Sky* (1967), *The Sword of Esau: Bible Stories Retold* (1968), *The Curse of Cain; Bible Stories, Retold* (1968), *Let the Balloon Go* (1968), *Sly Old Wardrobe* (1969), *Finn's Folly* (1969), *Chinaman's Reef Is Ours* (1970), *Walk a Mile and Get Nowhere* (1970), *Josh* (1971), *Benson Boy* (1973), *Head in the Clouds* (1973), *Matt and Jo* (1973), *Seventeen Seconds* (1973), *Fly West* (1973), and *What about Tomorrow* (1977).

For adults:
A Journey of Discovery: On Writing for Children (1976).

Ivan Southall delivered this lecture at the Library of Congress on November 12, 1973. It was first published in the *Quarterly Journal of the Library of Congress* for April 1974.

82

Sources and Responses

by Ivan Southall

When I set out to write a lecture—or a book—it is a journey into unknown places; hence each day has its own tension, its own suspense, its own fortunate or negative consequences. It could be called a disorganized way of life, and for a family man a hazardous way of life, not knowing what is coming next, not knowing whether any working day will earn wages or turn into a dead loss. This same method—or lack of method—is why I refuse deadlines. Deadlines fill me with panic and empty my brain and conflict with my way of life, of never doing today what I can conceivably delay. Yet to be here this November evening I accepted a deadline, so I am not immovable on the point, but I have paid the price, I have suffered my blackouts, despaired to my panics, endured the lot with my customary lack of fortitude.

I prefer, simply, to sit and dream across my valley. The large window of my room is as far as I need to go—no pollution out there, none to see or hear or sniff at, just distant mountain peaks and nearer hills, flower farms and forests and flights of dazzling parrots and cockatoos, snow white, and one morning, three wedge-tailed eagles in company against blue sky and cloud wisps at a great height.

Electricity came down our road only twelve years back; the water for our taps is caught from the skies off the roof and stored in tanks. If it doesn't rain we run dry and telephone the volunteer fire brigade and eager young men in their handsome red truck with brass bells to ring come heavyfooted with a thousand gallons pumped from the creek. If the wind blows, down comes a tree somewhere and the power goes off. Candles are always ready on the shelf, though in the dark they move mysteriously, eluding your grasp. Difficult roads and slopes a little too steep and thousands of acres of densely, darkly timbered temperate rain forest insulate us from the less uncivilized rigors of life. There is a sign on our road, the envy of all Australians not similarly blessed: *Drive Carefully, Lyrebirds Cross.*

From Benson Boy *by Ivan Southall, pictures by Ingrid Fetz. Copyright© 1973 by Macmillan Publishing Co., Inc.*

People say, what an idyllic place. What a place to work. All that peace. But I am the father of four, the grandfather of two, the husband of a wife. Our chaos is built in. We take it from place to place. No matter where we have lived, the seeds we have planted have come up as kids—the core of what this hour is about.

I think this lecture has grown largely from second thoughts and afterthoughts and manages to give a vague direction to my disordered lack of method. I think it tries to say something about books for children as I see them, and as I would like more to be, yet it is a personal statement; it does not set out to persuade or convert; it is my own view of my own road; but because I am a writer I address much of what I say to writers and to people who are interested in what writers do and how writers of my kind might function. I have tried to look at the creative process as I know it without burning into it to depths that might destroy it or inhibit its future functions. I also chuck a few bricks through a few windows because Australians are supposed to be wild and intemperate colonial lads and I would not wish you to suspect, through any lack I might demonstrate, that they had turned soft.

So, to begin with, I chuck a brick through a window of my own house. There is a continuing tendency in my country to regard the writing of books for children and the various professions and vocations arising from the original creative act as occupations suitable for minor-type, mouse-sized humans whose passions bubble at less than normal adult heat. Nowhere is this view more often aired than in the "world of literature." Writers, publishers, critics, lecturers, and pressmen, too, not actively occupied in the creation or appreciation of children's literature *as* it is, go on failing to comprehend *what* it is. Echoes of the same attitude probably go on reverberating everywhere else.

The viewpoint mystifies me—that works for children must necessarily be minor works by minor writers, that deliberately they are generated and projected at reduced voltage, that they evade truth, that they avert passion and sensuality and the subtleties of life and are unworthy of the attention of the serious artist or craftsman.

The sensitive child, the core of everything that I, for one, wish to write about, is the direct antithesis of this milk-and-water proposition. Adult scaling-down of the intensity of the child state is a crashing injustice, an outrageous distortion of what childhood is about. Physical frailty is not weakness, gentleness is not spinelessness, delicate sensitivities are not sentimental trivialities, apart from those aspects of childhood that are as rumbustious as run-away bulls. As we grow older we look back more and more, not, I suspect, because a mature person really wishes again for the agonies and ecstacies of youth in the immediate sense, but because he has the need to recall the enormous impact, the enormous importance, the sheer magnitude of childhood events to compensate for the lower key of subsequent adult life. I am sure they are recalled because they are the most worthy of recall, because little else in life surpasses them.

I suggest it is possible to extend the intensity of a sensitive childhood into maturity without wearing yourself out or giving yourself ulcers or coronaries or other undesirable side effects, although it may add to the daily anguishing of your heart. But was there ever a joy worth having that did not exact a price? Children's literature, so-called, the creation of it and the appreciation of it at a significant level, is one way of charging adult life with some of the extrasensual dimensions of childhood. Someone long ago, in different words, made a related statement and it *is* the key, from where I look at life, to being alive from the tips of your toes to the hair on your head and to every nerve-end in between.

Some do not share this partisan opinion.

I recall a literary function in Sydney during one of my visits there. Members of P.E.N. were the hosts, I was the guest, and *To the Wild Sky*, a book I wrote in 1965, had just been named Australian Children's Book of the Year, 1968. A lady novelist ran me into a corner. They come in two varieties, lady novelists, the sweet ones and the others. This lady may have lifted me by the lapel—I do not swear to it, but I swear to what she said: "I can't understand, I can't you know, how a grownup adult with literary equipment can waste his talent writing nice little stories for children when the world is full of man-size problems demanding all the enlightenment the novelist can shed upon them."

It's an interesting viewpoint and I have gone on thinking about it, gone on considering it, but only critics have ever come near to convincing me she might have been right—yet not for the reasons used by them to discipline me.

Out on the fringes of the field of the writing game, way out where the vague boundary line between player and spectator begins further to diffuse, are those people, those numerous people, who write for children the stories they are sure children will enjoy, because they have told them to children gathered round them to the sound of crackling wood fires or to the beating of moth wings against wire screens on long summer evenings. Mistakenly, they attribute the glow of those occasions to the magic of the story and forget the crucial contribution of the warmth of voice and smile and body and glance and that bedtime was being effectively deferred. Their success was a human success growing out of the aura of love—and that should have been enough. Upon the cold page in cold print the magic is not there. Human love is no longer present to overwhelm the defects. Sadly, for themselves, they are misled as to the quality of their talent and wastefully go ahead to misuse their own precious time, and wastefully to expend the time of publishers and others, and wastefully to inflict the subsequent bewilderments and agonies of their wounded egos upon people like me who generally are too polite to protest.

Manuscripts come to me for my *honest* opinion—something I would never dare give whilst valuing friendship or the quiet life. I learnt quickly that the word *honest* is used strictly as an illusionary sense. Hell hath no fury like the writer seeking honesty, and who gets it.

These manuscripts come through the post or through friends or are delivered by hand—after every publisher in the country has rejected them—all too often accompanied by letters running something like this:

The enclosed story is adored by my grandchildren. Everyone says it should be published. No one can understand why it has not been published. Every publisher who has sent it back was enthused about it. I enclose photostat copies of 17 of their letters for you to read. Don't you agree it is a shame for this beautiful story to be wasted? It is because I am not known and am without influence and do not have friends in the right places. Why don't you put it into a book with your name on it? No one will pick the difference and hundreds of thousands of children all over the world will be as happy as my grandchildren.

Sometimes those letters send my blood pressure up. It depends upon the day. But why do people go on being so ignorant of the craft they pretend to practice when an hour of honest self-scrutiny in the reflection of what children's literature is would surely convince them not only of their weakness but of their unreasonable vanity? But they do not judge themselves by the best; they shut their souls to that; they read the worst and say, "I can do better than that." And so the worst goes on propagating itself like a geometric progression of splitting cells, yet upon reflection these people sadden me and I cannot bring myself to hurt them. Life is more than blunt reaction. Life goes farther than what we know to be simple, obvious common sense. There they lie, naked, already hurt

The illustration "Miss Elaine Godwin" from Hills End *by Ivan Southall is reproduced by permission of Angus & Robertson Publishers.*

enough, so I add my own little white lie to the rest and sometimes bring upon myself most complex human complications that have taken months of my life to put straight, but I doubt if at heart I have regretted it once.

Here I would like to frame a definition, an explanation, a statement; call it what you wish. It is my response to lady novelists who do not understand and to others who should understand: I do not regard writing for children as a minor subdivision of literature. I do not regard it as a special subdivision of literature, I reject the term *subdivision*. When as a writer I address myself to children's literature, as now, I address myself to literature; and when as a writer I address myself to children I address myself to equals. I see no conflict of definition, and if I have a philosophy as a writer for children that is it. We will come to the clauses in smaller print later.

Let me make clear this has little to do with the nature of my relationship with children face to face—as in a classroom or assembly hall situation where I often meet children—or in family or personal situations. As most of us are, I am split in parts; one part is obviously a parent, sometimes straight-laced, sometimes compassionate to the point of indulgence; in another part I am obviously an uninhibited entertainer; and in another I am wholly *with* the child, in the pages of a book my heart beats with the pulse of a child, I become a child. It is upon that fact, the valid artistic achievement of identification, that I see children's literature as literature in its own right, yet I admire the need for the organized world of books for classification. Children, for instance, should know where the books most likely to please them are kept, or else libraries become disorderly houses, though many books that belong where the children browse belong also where the grownups browse, even if it is not common for them to be found in those areas. Children's librarians are imaginative people, not reluctant to pick the flowers from the fields where adult books grow; but the other way around—sadly, I think—it is a less catholic tale.

I suppose I regret the touchiness or the sensitivity (and certainly the need) that leads me to say this sort of thing. There is the risk of sounding truculent, or defensive, or apologetic, and I have been through all these emotions and should remember the struggles I have had to grow out of them when holding up to a form of ridicule viewpoints that do not coincide with those I express now. There was a time, and not long ago, when I regarded writing for kids as a fit and proper occupation only for a bandaged left hand. Is it surprising that others not sharing my background or commitment should think of books for children generally as being beneath the serious attention of the writer and unworthy of serious consideration as literature in an adult world—the great works of the past excepted? A letter from a friend this very day, received almost at this word, deplores the standard of children's books going into braille in her particular part of the world. Very low literary standard, she says, entirely visual books, action books, twee books, nothing that breathes of the soul and the spirit, nothing that stirs to the sensuality of smell and sound and touch, and are they not the qualities to give the child who has no sight? It is not that the right books do not exist; it is simply that the people who choose are ignorant. Choice in their terms is chance in our terms.

A well-known journalist, respected for her perceptive interviews, expressed with irony her surprise during our one short conversation that I appeared to be implying that significant writers were seriously involved in the creation of books for children. I think she felt she was operating at less than her proper capacity by giving time to me. Her irony was still evident in the patronizing piece published later; there she used it to cut me down to size. Yet people of her kind, involved with literature, do not snatch barbs like these out of the air. Her mind was closed, it is true, but why? Certainly not because the children's books she knew had impressed her with their grandeur or beauty or elegance. I would suggest she had not read any in a long time or had come to books for children in an unkindly selective or unsympathetic or hostile frame of mind. Of my own books, I doubt if she had scanned more than the publisher's blurb of two or three. Sometimes I say to people: "I know there are not enough hours in a day or enough days in a life to read everything you should not miss, but can't you come once in a while with an open heart and an open mind to a good children's book about childhood that reputation tells you has made the grade? You might be surprised by the substance you take away."

How much has society's labored misreading of a well-known biblical text cut off adult man and woman from many of the sensual wonderments of life or, at best, muted the appreciation or diluted the appreciation of emotions and sensations and events that should have *excited* them to the bloodstream. The young person is forever being urged to grow up, and there is a carryover of this unthinking indoctrination into adult life that desensitizes people. *Immature* is the word I read on a school report in 1968 referring to one of my daughters then nine years of age. What does God have in mind for a girl to be at nine years of age?

Putting away childish things, surely, has nothing to do with putting away the child. It is a total distortion of terms. The child should go on inside you helping you to reach out to each new emotion, helping you to excite to each new encounter, helping you to delight unconditionally to each new experience of the senses. Why should it be considered an unendurable or unacceptable strain? Given good health, are 70 or 80 years too many to handle when it has taken 4 billion years to prepare the place where you stand?

Life can be a rugged experience—I am aware of it. I have live through generous rations of fear and poverty and sorrow, but I have come through, I think, with the child in me relatively intact. It is an inner quality, not worn externally, not always visible externally, a very personal matter. Perhaps it is why I write for children, though I prefer to say it has happened to me *because* I write for children, and this I would wish for other writers of serious intent to enjoy. It comes so close to the core of all creativity, and this brings me to the threshold of thoughts I am anxious to express well: how is it that an adult of mature years and tastes and appetites can sustain the state of mind and emotion that writing about children for children obviously requires? Is it an agony? Is it worth it? Is there a measure by which one may say it is a proper activity for a serious writer? Or does one come to it simply because there is nowhere else to go; does one home in upon one's metier instinctively? Each to his own?

Creative writing for children does require a particular facility, but the writer is not likely to dig it out of himself roots and stalk and blossom fully grown. It is a discipline of specific subtleties arising out of awareness most laboriously sought but joyously found, and the best of it stands unblushingly as literature beside the best of anything. The worst of it should be sunk with a millstone in the sea.

I become irritable and intolerant when confronted by the smooth-tongued purveyors of the blatantly commercial second-rate. "We are giving them what they want" is the alleged doctrine of these people. I believe *they* do not want it for a moment and would never miss it if it were not there. The blatant second-raters dish up what is easiest to concoct or what careless or unthinking or ignorant adults are prepared to accept without question or exercise of discernment for their children or grandchildren or nieces or nephews or, Heaven forbid, for their students.

The pulp trade for kids is gigantic. It prospers on apathy and sells by the truckload because it sets up in the marketplace where the public gathers with the payday dollar. And people get what they bargain for— the superficially pretty book, the lazy book, the formula book, the patronizing book—and someone is making a wad of money out of it, though I doubt if much of this finds its way to the initial creators. In my view these people, both creators and publishers, are the ultimate cynics.

The producer of the honest second-rate is another matter. Time and persistence and conscience may yet make something of him, though not necessarily.

I would like to define, from my narrow viewpoint, what a good children's book is not. I am not implying that bad or dishonest children's books will cripple the finer instincts forever and will not give some poor little innocents their modicum of moderate pleasure, but good children's books available at the same price—or less, in paperback—would have given the same children so much more. And I do not mean *more* in the sense that these children know it from the corruptive, insidious, and sickening materialism of much mass-media advertising and virtually all mass-media giveaways, those daily doses of perversion administered in the privacy of their own homes.

A good children's book is not an imitation of something else, not an imitation of last year's Newbery or last year's Carnegie, not an imitation

Ray Plumtree, falling from the balcony, lands on Typhoon Trudy. From Head in the Clouds *by Ivan Southall, illustrated by Richard Kennedy, with permission of Macmillan Publishing Co., Inc., and Angus and Robertson Publishers, Sydney. First published in Great Britain by Angus & Robertson (U.K.) Ltd. 1972. Copyright © 1972 by Ivan Southall.*

of Walt Disney, not an imitation of Lewis Carroll, not intellectually or emotionally or artistically shoddy. It does not inevitably sugar the pill of life. It does not manipulate or indoctrinate. It is not public relations copy for anybody or anything, or sooner or later it is the sick victim of its own infection. It does not necessarily begin with *once upon a time* or necessarily end with *happily ever after.*

It is, as you can see, demonstrably easy to string a list of negatives together but much more difficult to define what a good children's book is. Bluntly, it is or it isn't, and over it almost certainly hang controversy and passions of difference that comparable literature intended for adults rarely provokes. Thank God, it is almost impossible to define the positives, or some smart aleck would long ago have programmed a computer. It remains an intensely human matter of creation and choice and approval, and original works for children, like exotic flowers, are springing up all over the world. Never before, as far as I know, have writers succeeded so often with brilliance.

It is possible then to define the writer who can reach children? May we come closer to a definition of a good book by swinging in from another angle?

Any writer who considers himself too sensitive or too subtle or too mature or simply too brilliant to write for children is undoubtedly a person of keen self-perception. And any writer who has discovered that the big, bad, man-size world is a bit beyond him and feels that the time has come to set his sights a little lower would be better digging a hole and jumping into it.

I would suggest that the writer for children can identify with children, consciously or subconsciously, and can project his images through the written word in such a way that children can identify with him. Here we run into a problem of word usage. *Identify.* The term *identify* and *identification* have become clichés. The inference of their true meaning has degenerated to a kind of second-rate emotional twitch. I am talking of a genuine emotion, a genuine and huge transformation of one's personal attitudes as an adult back into a genuine reexperience of one's personal attitudes as a child.

The children's writer does not write for all children any more than the writer for adults writes for all adults. You reach those and please those who tune in on your wavelength. It is a very personal matter. Rapport, no less and probably no more. If it is not there the reader is wasting his time. If it is there it's something like a love affair, and even children fall in love. It is an absurdity of much criticism that one adult person can declare the judgment that a book will not appeal to children—in the plural, in the mass. There are factors involved here, there are vanities and assumptions that perturb me, because the influence of some of these people is out of all proportion to their stature. Children have sent their love to me for giving them stories that adult authorities have declared no child would understand or want to read.

It is fashionable where I come from, and probably elsewhere, to deny that one writes for children specifically, to assert that one writes for people, but I cannot hang my hat on that hook. I believe one *does* write for children in a certain difficult-to-define way. There is, as you know, a strong school of criticism directed against some writers because they write about children rather than for them. The subtlety of this distinction has always eluded me. I have to say that the writer for children, as I know him, is very much committed to writing about children.

In a *Times Literary Supplement* of five years ago, in what I assume was meant to be a major critical article, a full page of it about books I have written, I read, and I quote, that "most children have fantasies of their own, but do not particularly relish a description of other people's." This generalization typifies the nature of the article—generalizations one after the other. And what is a generalization? It is the taking-away of individuality from human experience and human response. In this case it is psychology gone mad, the closed adult mind out of touch with the open child mind. It is the ivory-tower mind no longer in communication with the soul of story or storyteller or listener. What do people build these opinions upon and how by preaching them do they acquire stature for themselves and disciples to follow them? Often they go further and state that this writer or that writer is trapped in the discipline of this branch of psychology or that branch of psychology and develops his plots in detail beforehand in accord with this theory or that theory or some other brand of categorical declaration.

The creative writer, as I know him, does not function this way. He is intuitive. His raw material is life. He is not shaped in a jelly mold. He is himself, instinctively following the light and the radiation of his own star. Immediately he opens a textbook or tunes into the limitations of a theory, he is someone else and less than himself. So I know nothing of what social scientists have declared. Their work belongs in its proper and rightful place. That place is not in the mind of a creative writer. I have never read a textbook on psychology and will not rectify this abysmal lack even to prove a critic right.

I must say something about criticism. It is a fact of life for the writer and I doubt if any writer is completely immune to its effects. Only once have I followed the advice of a critic and that was a mistake. Over the last seventeen years I have ignored the critics, in that sense, though they continue to try my patience very sorely. You know I do not mean all critics or all criticism. I'm human, I enjoy a pat on the back, I blossom where there is understanding; but I wither where there is injustice and malice. So I try not to read destructive criticism, but sometimes it creeps under the guard, appearing where one does not expect to find it or coming as a shock from a formerly sympathetic source.

These are matters perhaps peculiar to the criticism of children's books. Some critics forget that literature is literature and that a serious work of fiction has its own personality, its own morality, its own soul, and the writer has passed through an experience gathering from it all that he can whether it reflects his own soul or not. There is a type of critic who forgets this under pressure or does not know it and proceeds to impale the author upon the hot little sticks of his own personal hangups, condemning sturdily all matters with which he does not or feels he should not concur. He attacks the author personally though he knows nothing of the author's private life and would not recognize him on the doorstep of his own house. Histrionics run out by the yard, often so wide of the world that children actually live in that one wonders—as I have said on one other occasion—whether some of these people are born six feet tall with boots on. Sometimes it seems to me that *anyone* may call himself an expert on children's literature and may nail up his plate and proceed to pontificate, no matter what he does to the reputation, public or private, or to the emotional state of the writer's inner life.

The writer, be it understood, must never reply in print—or orally in a voice too loud—and must never name these people; goodness, that would be ill-bred. If he breaks this rule he will be strung up by the toes a second time while inches of his spirit are publicly hacked off. There are limits to how far mere mortals can stand this treatment before something is seriously hurt. Yet I do know of private apologies from critics for various scurrilous utterances. I do not know of public apologies in print for anyone else to hear about.

Any writer who believes he can stand up to this kind of thing uncomplainingly, even joyously, and doesn't run too fast for cover at the sight of a living, red-blooded kid, and can accept the judgment of a substantial bloc of his fellow writers that he has found his proper level, then he's in, he's the man for books for kids, though perhaps he should look in a general way at what is already lying about. He might not have done this in a long time. Except for the enduring classics, much of what he read years ago and even remembers with affection may look less than monumental in present company. There is a difficulty here, however. One feels one should say, "Yes, do look at what others have done," yet this advice I have not taken myself. I know what other writers are doing only by reputation. For me that is enough. For others it might not be enough. There is a philosophy in this, not to be expressed in half a dozen words; it comes back to the nature and objectives of the writer's talent.

The survival of the classics is interesting. Most were written for adults. Children adopted them. Is it a thought to be hurried over as irrelevant?

Present-day literate children, under the guidance of sensitive teachers and librarians, helped by the reactions of responsible critics, expect more than the old sentimental sweetness, the old superheroes, the old exploits of middle or upper class children solving crimes and accomplishing deeds beyond the intelligence or courage or capacity of grownups. We are writing now for what is the largest literate openhearted audience in the history of the world. I would not try to calculate how many of these children I have met in recent years face to face or through correspondence. I begin most working days by answering their letters. We are not committed to a noncaring, uninterested, apathetic, brassed-off audience. At the risk of sounding trite, we are committed to the hope of the world— and should never for a moment doubt it.

As for the *ill*-literate children I regret that it appears there is not much the serious writer can do. I have anguished over it, I have been asked to write in simplified English, to confine myself to set vocabularies, to limit themes and avoid abstracts, but I have always in the end refused, not able

Hugh shining a flashlight on the army tent. Illustration from The Fox Hole *by Ivan Southall, illustrations by Ian Ribbons. Copyright © Methuen & Co., Ltd. in original edition. Courtesy of Methuen Children's Books Ltd., publishers.*

to convince myself that the specialist editors and educationalists concerned were beyond challenge in their views. I stick to my instinct that the person who is not going to read is not going to read, and that the person who *is* going to read, eventually, will get there on his own terms. The experts can probably produce masses of bullets to shoot me down; they're welcome, that's their privilege; but I keep to my instinct that we are trying to turn uncomplicated people into what they are not, and we go on adding to their lives tensions and anxieties and pressures they do not need and would be much happier without.

The serious creative writer cannot and must not reduce his standards to a lowest common denominator. I know some are trying to do this, from high motives, but I believe they are in error. Immediately the creative writer stoops he loses his stature. His disciplines collapse. The good writer, despite himself, can produce a load of rubbish. It is the responsibility, however difficult, of the teacher to bring the marginal child up to the writer, to whatever level the particular writer functions at. The writer cannot go down. But I repeat, I fear for the peace of mind and the emotional balance of the child who is driven uphill against his will. Who and what turns kids into split personalities and sick personalities? Too many of the kids I know who have gone this way have been pushed. Yet there are other children who never can and never will come up to meet the writer. To take an extreme case my own youngest child at home, now aged twelve, cannot write or read or speak and probably never will. We are not born intellectually or emotionally equal. Yet this child of ours will drag us by the hand across the garden to a flower, and for hours will watch the moon, her eyes radiant.

The only way the writer can reach the marginal children is by going out to meet them, to meet *all* children, indiscriminately, and people such as I often do, but to acquit oneself adequately takes years of practice, of disciplining nerves and self-consciousness, even of subduing one's proper modesty, but I do see it as an exciting and rejuvenating part of the life of the writer, even though in the immediate sense it can be an exhausting ordeal. I go out, certainly twice in every year, into culturally deprived or geographically remote areas for the Australian Literature Board, supplied with a government car and a driver-escort, to meet up with schoolchildren by the score or by the hundred several times in every school day over two or even three successive weeks, usually speaking to their parents at night, and traveling in between in stages probably several hundred miles in each day.

One goes out to these kids to stir them up, to entertain them, to bring them something they haven't seen before, and this sort of stimulation given only once can set the gifted child on his way, or bring the backward or reluctant reader finally to the printed page, but there that lass or lad has to discover that the writer on paper is not the same as the writer who clowned in the classroom or on the school stage. To the novelist, as such, I fear, vast numbers of children are lost and if he tries to reach them in print he does so at peril. If he reaches them by striking a responsive chord, hallelujah, but that is another matter. We each live in a different world, there are as many worlds as persons, and as many needs, every consciousness and every encounter is unique. No one knows what is waiting to be found, even in his own mind, until he explores.

I cannot see how the writer for children, for his own sake, can consider the risk of consciously compromising an intellectual principle, or of committing the patronage of consciously contriving character or incident, or of consciously considering the boy or girl who is to read him as other than his equal. You are aware of him as a child, but never as an iddy biddy little kiddie. He can always go back a page and pick you up again if he's in doubt. If he can't be bothered to go back a page, then clearly in his case it doesn't matter anyway.

As I see it, the writer is on his honor to extend his creative capacities always to the limit. If he does not, he is betraying himself. Talents grow from stretching, not from being compressed. The writer may use language as he wishes, grandly or daringly or experimentally. He may be as *different* as his star directs. He is deluded if he believes he is creatively inhibited or caged or finds himself wondering whether his genius is going to waste on pint-sized mentalities. The kids in tune with him will be up there with him. Critics may tell him he is writing over their heads. Children will send letters with love to say, "Thank you for opening my eyes." If some children *are* left confused or wondering or frustrated by what he has given them it is simply a foretaste of life.

Think on the complexities of your readership. Every day someone coming to you for the first time. Always someone growing, evolving, as you draw him into your creation. A readership not set in its ways, its tastes not formed, its opinions not determined. Oh, tread with care. This at times becomes an all but daunting challenge to creativity and decision, yet I do not see that the closed roads and detours impose restrictions that are unacceptable to a free, creating spirit. They provoke him. They stimulate him. Certainly the mainstream of present-day writing for adults might indicate that novelists are superbly liberated, or possibly it indicates something else, a sort of uncaring, unthinking, undisciplined pitching of paint at a wall that later generations may scrape off.

What I wish for the writer for children, what I wish for myself, is the ultimate compliment—the return of the child in maturity to read the same book with new insight, new discovery, new joy. I would not wish for the writer for children, or for me, that the child in maturity should come back with the accusation: "You deceived me. You sold me short. You did not write from your heart. You wrote in a hurry off the top of your head."

What does one write for children?

I hesitate to accept that there can be a significant difference, at heart, where it counts, between modern children and the rest of the kids who have gone swarming across this planet since men and women long ago started waking up to the miracle of being. We all have in common our childhood, this extraordinary, overwhelming occurrence, this progress of the pilgrim seed through years of gathering awareness. And most of us have in common a tragic capacity to forget what childhood is about. We leap into the luxury of grownup liberty and allow the impact of life and events upon children to sink at once into a shadowed pit. We ignore the truth (until violently reminded) that anything that can happen to a grown person can happen to a person not grown. We forget the vividness and brilliance and breathtaking wonderment of the world a kid finds each morning when he slams the door and rushes out. We forget its terror, its violence, its bewilderment, except in the sense that children should be shielded and sheltered, that voices should not be raised in anger or serious dispute in their presence. There is a certain irrationality about this. We rear them upon impossible simplicities that must confuse them profoundly, that life consists of opposites; dark, light; dull, bright; bad, good; wrong, right; and that parents are all-wise and all-knowing and sinless.

I choose my characters and to this group of people rarely add. Those I glimpse first of all usually see me through to the end. Almost always they grow from reality, from adults I know pictured as children, or actual children about me now or known way back. Some are born out of fragments, fragments of other people, fragments of myself, and create themselves, create their own lives. A name has its own generating power, so I know the meanings of names or can refer to their meanings in appropriate dictionaries. This can take days, the choosing and naming of characters, with care, with anticipation, with expectation, even with excitement.

I select the scene. (These initial steps are deliberate steps.) Is it to happen in a city, or a country town, on a mountain, beside the sea, down a hole, up a tree? The pleasurable toying with alternatives. Scene influences character. Bill under tension is different from Bill at ease. Jane on a mountain is not the same as Jane beside the sea. Fascinating.

My book is still a mystery, an unexplored land. It can be anything of a thousand million things; that's how many books there are out there waiting to be found. But little by little, by luxuriously daydreaming, I am narrowing the choice down; more often than not drawing closer unawares to the story that will invite me in this time. Twelve hours a day it might hold me for a week or two weeks or more, just looking for the door, with little to show, but I have learnt not to rush, not to push hard. Better to relax, to enjoy myself, slowly swinging my chair, deleting all uninviting possibilities, or grossly improper ones (that can happen, you know), discarding all stupidities and irrationalities, until the moment is there. "Eureka." The door! It happens. It's there. A mood, a word, a certainty that from *here* I go on into the unknown, that inexhaustible source of originalities from out of which comes excitement that I wish all could enjoy. The unknown is a word ahead of me all the time, word by word I move out into it, a patient, wondering questing exploration. A contemplation of the word.

Why are so many writers in a hurry? Out of haste comes mediocrity, comes the cliché, comes the predictable situation and word, comes the usual old story. I know there are exceptions, I know there are times when the fire burns brightly and furiously, but it is uncommon for these times to be built in significant terms upon other than the pure excitement of preparatory meditation and considerable choice. To writers who ask me, I say, "Give yourself a chance. Allow your story to find its way. Discover your story day by day. Exercise your control of it by rejecting the false. For every right way there are innumerable wrong ways. Your quality as a writer depends upon your talent for making choices." Discovering a good story day by day is an enormous joy. It is like living another life. Everything you have is committed, your entire intellectual and emotional and spiritual resources.

Out of this contemplative approach comes the wisdom that surprises you, comes the poetry you have never heard before, all the themes that build your book, the innumerable themes that arise unexpectedly, the mood, the tone, the depth, the breadth, the humanity—all these qualities are born from contemplation of your own word. Not from reflections of what others have done, not from great poetry or great prose subconsciously recalled, not borrowed, not stolen, not strayed in because the fence was down. This is the peculiar joy that belongs to the slowly grown, self-cultivated writer who with deliberate intent or from the compulsion that time is only for rest or creativity, has denied himself the pleasures of the great literature of the world.

I have no scale against which to judge except the rhythms of the Bible, the King James, sown during faraway hearings of childhood when the groundwork was done, rhythms from the pulpit, rhythms from readings at home. The back pew with my mother and father and young brother was my college, oldtime nonconformist preachers were my lecturers, the only serious lecturers I have ever known. There was a depression and my father died and there was work to be done. At just fourteen years of age school was gone, suddenly, in a day.

Fulfillment is not the acclaim. Fulfillment is the work as it goes, as it leaves you at the end of a long day, or a long year, trembling, glowing, warm.

Ursula (Kroeber) Le Guin was born in Berkeley, California, in 1929. She was educated at Radcliffe College, where she was elected to Phi Beta Kappa, and received an M.A. in 1952 from Columbia University. She was a faculty fellow and Fulbright Fellow in France in 1953 and that same year married Charles A. Le Guin. They have two daughters and one son. She taught at Mercer University and conducted writing workshops at Pacific University, University of Washington, Portland State University, Melbourne, Australia, and Reading, England. She received the *Boston Globe-Horn Book* Award in 1969; the Science Fiction Writers of America Nebula Award in 1969 and 1975; The Hugo Award in 1972, 1973, and 1975; and the National Book Award in 1972.

Books for young people:
The Wizard of Earthsea (1968), *The Tombs of Atuan* (1971), *The Farthest Shore* (1972), and *Very Far Away from Anywhere Else* (1976).

Novels and collections of short stories for adults:
Rocannon's World (1966), *Planet of Exile* (1966), *City of Illusion* (1967), *The Left Hand of Darkness* (1969), *The Lathe of Heaven* (1971), *The Word for World is Forest* (1972), *The Dispossessed: An Ambiguous Utopia* (1974), *The Wind's Twelve Quarters* (1975), *The Water Is Wide* (1976), *Orsinian Tales* (1976), and, as editor, *Nebula Award Stories II* (1977).

Verse for adults:
Wild Angels (1975).

Nonfiction for adults:
From Elfland to Poughkeepsie (1973).

For National Children's Book Week, this lecture was given at the Library of Congress on November 11, 1974. The article based on the lecture was first published in the April 1975 issue of the *Quarterly Journal of the Library of Congress*.

The Child and the Shadow

by Ursula K. Le Guin

Once upon a time, says Hans Christian Andersen, there was a kind, shy, learned young man from the north, who came south to visit the hot countries, where the sun shines fiercely and all shadows are very black.

Now across the street from the young man's window is a house, where he once glimpses a beautiful girl tending beautiful flowers on the balcony. The young man longs to go speak to her, but he's too shy. One night, while his candle is burning behind him, casting his shadow onto the balcony across the way, he "jokingly" tells his shadow to go ahead, go on into that house. And it does. It enters the house across the street and leaves him.

The young man's a bit surprised, naturally, but he doesn't do anything about it. He presently grows a new shadow and goes back home. And he grows older, and more learned; but he's not a success. He talks about beauty and goodness, but nobody listens to him.

Then one day when he's a middle-aged man, his shadow comes back to him—very thin and rather swarthy, but elegantly dressed. "Did you go into the house across the street?" the man asks him, first thing; and the shadow says, "Oh, yes, certainly." He claims that he saw everything, but he's just boasting. The man knows what to ask. "Were the rooms like the starry sky when one stands on the mountain tops?" he asks, and all the shadow can say is, "Oh, yes, everything was there." He doesn't know how to answer. He never got in any farther than the anteroom, being, after all, only a shadow. "I should have been annihilated by the flood of light but I penetrated into the room where the maiden lived," he says.

He was, however, good at blackmail and such arts; he is a strong, unscrupulous fellow, and he dominates the man completely. They go traveling, the shadow as master and the man as servant. They meet a princess who suffers "because she sees too clearly." She sees that the shadow casts no shadow and distrusts him, until he explains that the man is really his shadow, which he allows to walk about by itself. A peculiar

101

arrangement, but logical; the princess accepts it. When she and the shadow engage to marry, the man rebels at last. He tries to tell the princess the truth, but the shadow gets there first, with explanations: "The poor fellow is crazy, he thinks he's a man and I'm his shadow!"—"How dreadful," says the princess. A mercy killing is definitely in order. And while the shadow and the princess get married, the man is executed.

Now that is an extraordinarily cruel story. A story about insanity, ending in humiliation and death.

Is it a story for children? Yes, it is. It's a story for anybody who's listening.

If you listen, what do you hear?

The house across the street is the House of Beauty, and the maiden is the Muse of Poetry; the shadow tells us that straight out. And that the princess who sees too clearly is pure, cold reason, is plain enough. But who are the man and the shadow? That's not so plain. They aren't allegorical figures. They are symbolic or archetypal figures, like those in a dream. Their significance is multiple, inexhaustible. I can only hint at the little I'm able to see of it.

The man is all that is civilized—learned, kindly, idealistic, decent. The shadow is all that gets suppressed in the process of becoming a decent, civilized adult. The shadow is the man's thwarted selfishness, his unadmitted desires, the swearwords he never spoke, the murders he didn't commit. The shadow is the dark side of his soul, the unadmitted, the inadmissible.

And what Andersen is saying is that this monster is an integral part of the man and cannot be denied—not if the man wants to enter the House of Poetry.

The man's mistake is in not following his shadow. It goes ahead of him, as he sits there at his window, and he cuts it off from himself, telling it, "jokingly," to go on without him. And it does. It goes on into the House of Poetry, the source of all creativity—leaving him outside, on the surface of reality.

So, good and learned as he is, he can't do any good, can't act, because he has cut himself off at the roots. And the shadow is equally helpless; it can't get past the shadowy anteroom to the light. Neither of them, without the other, can approach the truth.

When the shadow returns to the man in middle life, he has a second chance. But he misses it, too. He confronts his dark self at last, but instead of asserting equality or mastery, he lets it master him. He gives in. He does, in fact, become the shadow's shadow, and his fate then is inevitable. The Princess Reason is cruel in having him executed, and yet she is just.

Part of Andersen's cruelty is the cruelty of reason—of psychological realism, radical honesty, the willingness to see and accept the consequences of an act or a failure to act. There is a sadistic, depressive streak in Andersen also, which is his own shadow; it's there, it's part of him, but not all of him, nor is he ruled by it. His strength, his subtlety, his creative genius, come precisely from his acceptance of and cooperation with the dark side of his own soul. That's why Andersen the fabulist is one of the great realists of literature.

Now I stand here, like the princess herself, and tell you what the story of the shadow means to me at age forty-five. But what did it mean to me when I first read it, at age ten or eleven? What does it mean to children? Do they "understand" it? Is it "good" for them—this bitter, complex study of a moral failure?

I don't know. I hated it when I was a kid. I hated all the Andersen stories with unhappy endings. That didn't stop me from reading them, and rereading them. Or from remembering them...so that after a gap of over thirty years, when I was pondering this talk, a little voice suddenly said inside my left ear, "You'd better dig out that Andersen story, you know, about the shadow."

At age ten I certainly wouldn't have gone on about reason and repression and all that. I had no critical equipment, no detachment, and even less power of sustained thought than I have now. I had somewhat less conscious mind than I have now. But I had as much, or more, of any unconscious mind and was perhaps in better touch with it than I am now. And it was to that, to the unknown depths in me, that the story spoke; and it was the depths which responded to it and, nonverbally, irrationally, understood it, and learned from it.

The great fantasies, myths, and tales are indeed like dreams: they speak *from* the unconscious *to* the unconscious, in the *language* of the unconscious—symbol and archetype. Though they use words, they work the way music does: they short-circuit verbal reasoning, and go straight to the thoughts that lie too deep to utter. They cannot be translated fully into the language of reason, but only a Logical Positivist, who also finds Beethoven's Ninth Symphony meaningless, would claim that they are therefore meaningless. They are profoundly meaningful, and usable—practical—in terms of ethics; of insight; of growth.

Reduced to the language of daylight, Andersen's story says that a man who will not confront and accept his shadow is a lost soul. It also says something specifically about itself, about art. It says that if you want to enter the House of Poetry you have to enter it in the flesh, the solid, imperfect, unwieldy body, which has corns and colds and greeds and passions, the body that casts a shadow. It says that if the artist tries to ignore evil, he will never enter into the House of Light.

That's what one great artist said to me about shadows. Now if I may move our candle and throw the shadows in a different direction, I'd like to interrogate a great psychologist on the same subject. Art has spoken, let's hear what science has to say. Since art is the subject, let it be the psychologist whose ideas on art are the most meaningful to most artists, Carl Gustav Jung.

Jung's terminology is notoriously difficult, as he kept changing meanings the way a growing tree changes leaves. I will try to define a few of the key terms in an amateurish way without totally misrepresenting them. Very roughly, then, Jung saw the ego, what we usually call the self, as only a part of the Self, the part of it which we are consciously aware of. The ego "revolves around the Self as the earth around the Sun," he says. The Self is transcendent, much larger than the ego; it is not a private possession, but collective—that is, we share it with all other human beings, and perhaps with all beings. It may indeed be our link with what is called God. Now this sounds mystical, and it is, but it's also exact and practical. All Jung is saying is that we are fundamentally alike; we all have the same general tendencies and configurations in our psyche, just as we all have the same general kind of lungs and bones in our body. Human beings all look roughly alike; they also think and feel alike. And they are all part of the universe.

The ego, the little private individual consciousness, knows this, and it knows that if it's not to be trapped in the hopeless silence of autism it must identify with something outside itself, beyond itself, larger than itself. If it's weak, or if it's offered nothing better, what it does is identify with the "collective consciousness." That is Jung's term for a kind of lowest common denominator of all that little egos added together, the mass mind, which consists of such things as cults, creeds, fads, fashions, status–seeking, conventions, received beliefs, advertising, popcult, all the isms, all the ideologies, all the hollow forms of communication and "togetherness" that lack real communion or real sharing. The ego, accepting these empty forms, becomes a member of the "lonely crowd." To avoid this, to attain real community, it must turn inward, away from the crowd, to the source: it must identify with *its own* deeper regions, the great unexplored regions of the Self. These regions of the psyche Jung calls the "collective unconscious," and it is them, where we all meet, that he sees the source of true community; of felt religion; of art, grace, spontaneity, and love.

How do you get there? How do you find your own private entrance to the collective unconscious? Well, the first step is often the most important, and Jung says that the first step is to turn around and follow your own shadow.

Jung saw the psyche as populated with a group of fascinating figures, much livelier than Freud's grim trio of Id, Ego, Superego; they're all worth meeting. The one we're concerned with is the shadow.

The shadow is the other side of our psyche, the dark brother of the conscious mind. It is Cain, Caliban, Frankenstein's monster, Mr. Hyde. It is Vergil who guided Dante through hell, Gilgamesh's friend Enkidu, Frodo's enemy Gollum. It is the Doppelganger. It is Mowgli's Grey Brother; the werewolf; the wolf, the bear, the tiger of a thousand folktales; it is the serpent, Lucifer. The shadow stands on the threshold between the

conscious and the unconscious mind, and we meet it in our dreams, as sister, brother, friend, beast, monster, enemy, guide. It is all we don't want to, can't, admit into our conscious self, all the qualities and tendencies within us which have been repressed, denied, or not used. In describing Jung's psychology, Jolande Jacobi wrote that "the development of the shadow runs parallel to that of the ego; qualities which the ego does not need or cannot make use of are set aside or repressed, and thus they play little or no part in the conscious life of the individual. Accordingly, a child has no real shadow, but his shadow becomes more pronounced as his ego grows in stability and range."[1] Jung himself said, "Everyone carries a shadow, and the less it is embodied in the individual's conscious life, the blacker and denser it is."[2] The less you look at it, in other words, the stronger it grows, until it can become a menace, an intolerable load, a threat within the soul.

Unadmitted to consciousness, the shadow is projected outward, onto others. There's nothing wrong with me—it's *them*. I'm not a monster, other people are monsters. All foreigners are evil. All communists are evil. All capitalists are evil. It was the cat that made me kick him, Mummy.

If the individual wants to live in the real world, he must withdraw his projections; he must admit that the hateful, the evil, exists within himself. This isn't easy. It is very hard not to be able to blame anybody else. But it may be worth it. Jung says, "If he only learns to deal with his own shadow he has done something real for the world. He has succeeded in shouldering at least an infinitesimal part of the gigantic, unsolved social problems of our day."[3]

Moreover, he has grown toward true community, and self-knowledge, and creativity. For the shadow stands on the threshold. We can let it bar the way to the creative depths of the unconscious, or we can let it lead us to them. For the shadow is not simply evil. It is inferior, primitive, awkward, animallike, childlike; powerful, vital, spontaneous. It's not weak and decent, like the learned young man from the north; it's dark and hairy and unseemly; but, without it, the person is nothing. What is a body that casts no shadow? Nothing, a formlessness, two-dimensional, a comic-strip character. The person who denies his own profound relationship with evil denies his own reality. He cannot do, or make; he can only undo, unmake.

Jung was especially interested in the second half of life, when this conscious confrontation with a shadow that's been growing for thirty or forty years can become imperative—as it did for the poor fellow in the Andersen story. As Jung says, the child's ego and shadow are both still ill defined; a child is likely to find his ego in a ladybug, and his shadow lurking horribly under his bed. But I think that when in pre-adolescence and adolescence the conscious sense of self emerges, often quite overwhelmingly, the shadow darkens right with it. The normal adolescent ceases to project so blithely as the little child did; he realizes that you can't blame everything on the bad guys with the black Stetsons.

He begins to take responsibility for his acts and feelings. And with it he often shoulders a terrible load of guilt. He sees his shadow as much blacker, more wholly evil, than it is. The only way for a youngster to get past the paralyzing self-blame and self-disgust of this stage is really to look at that shadow, to face it, warts and fangs and pimples and claws and all—to accept it as himself—as *part* of himself. The ugliest part, but not the weakest. For the shadow is the guide. The guide inward and out again; downward and up again; there, as Bilbo the Hobbit said, and back again. The guide of the journey to self-knowledge, to adulthood, to the light.

"Lucifer" means the one who carries the light.

It seems to me that Jung described, as the individual's imperative need and duty, that journey which Andersen's learned young man failed to make.

It also seems to me that most of the great works of fantasy are about that journey; and that fantasy is the medium best suited to a description of that journey, its perils and rewards. The events of a voyage into the unconscious are not describable in the language of rational daily life: only the symbolic language of the deeper psyche will fit them without trivializing them.

Moreover, the journey seems to be not only a psychic one, but a moral one. Most great fantasies contain a very strong, striking moral dialectic, often expressed as a struggle between the Darkness and the Light. But that makes it sound simple, and the ethics of the unconscious—of the dream, the fantasy, the fairy tale—are not simple at all. They are, indeed, very strange.

Take the ethics of the fairy tale, where the shadow figure is often played by an animal—horse, wolf, bear, snake, raven, fish. In her article "The Problem of Evil in Fairytales," Marie Louise von Franz—a Jungian— points out the real strangeness of morality in folktales. There *is no right way* to act when you're the hero or heroine of a fairy tale. There is no system of conduct, there are no standards of what a nice prince does and what a good little girl doesn't do. I mean, do good little girls usually push old ladies into baking ovens, and get rewarded for it? Not in what we call "real life," they don't. But in dreams and fairy tales they do. And to judge Gretel by the standards of conscious, daylight virtue is a complete and ridiculous mistake.

In the fairy tale, though there is no "right" and "wrong," there is a different standard, which is perhaps best called "appropriateness." Under no conditions can we say that it is morally right and ethically virtuous to push an old lady into a baking oven. But, under the conditions of fairy tale, in the language of the archetypes, we can say with perfect conviction that it may be *appropriate* to do so. Because, in those terms, the witch is not an old lady, nor is Gretel a little girl. Both are psychic factors, elements of the complex soul. Gretel is the archaic child-soul, innocent, defenseless; the witch is the archaic crone, the possessor and destroyer, the

mother who feeds you cookies and who must be destroyed before she eats you like a cookie, so that you can grow up and be a mother too. And so on and so on. All explanations are partial. The archetype is inexhaustible. And children understand it as fully and surely as adults do—often more fully, because they haven't got minds stuffed full of the one-sided, shadowless half-truths and conventional moralities of the collective consciousness.

Evil, then, appears in the fairy tale not as something diametrically opposed to good, but as inextricably involved with it, as in the yang-yin symbol. Neither is greater than the other, nor can human reason and virtue separate one from the other and choose between them. The hero or heroine is the one who sees what is appropriate to be done, because he or she sees the *whole*, which is greater than either evil or good. Their heroism is, in fact, their certainty. They do not act by rules; they simply know the way to go.

In this labyrinth where it seems one must trust to blind instinct, there is, Von Franz points out, one—only one—consistent rule or "ethic": "Anyone who earns the gratitude of animals, or whom they help for any reason, invariably wins out. This is the unfailing rule that I have been able to find."

Our instinct, in other words, is not blind. The animal does not reason, but it sees. And it acts with certainty; it acts "rightly," appropriately. That is why all animals are beautiful. It is the animal who knows the way, the way home. It is the animal within us, the primitive, the dark brother, the shadow soul, who is the guide.

There is often a queer twist to this in folktales, a kind of final secret. The helpful animal, often a horse or a wolf, says to the hero, "When you have done such-and-so with my help, then you must kill me, cut off my head." And the hero must trust his animal guide so wholly that he is willing to do so. Apparently the meaning of this is that when you have followed the animal instincts far enough, then they must be sacrificed, so that the true self, the whole person, may step forth from the body of the animal, reborn. That is Von Franz's explanation, and it sounds fair enough; I am glad to have any explanation of that strange episode in so many tales, which has always shocked me. But I doubt that that's all there is to it—or that any Jungian would pretend it was. Neither rational thought nor rational ethics can "explain" these deep strange levels of the imagining mind. Even in merely reading a fairy tale, we must let go our daylight convictions and trust ourselves to be guided by dark figures, in silence; and when we come back, it may be very hard to describe where we have been.

In many fantasy tales of the nineteenth and twentieth centuries the tension between good and evil, light and dark, is drawn absolutely clearly, as a battle, the good guys on one side and the bad guys on the other, cops and robbers, Christians and heathens, heroes and villains. In such fantasies I believe the author has tried to force reason to lead him where reason cannot go, and has abandoned the faithful and frightening guide he should have followed, the shadow. These are false fantasies, rationalized fantasies. They are not the real thing. Let me, by way of exhibiting the real thing, which is always much more interesting than the fake one, discuss *The Lord of the Rings* for a minute.

Critics have been hard on Tolkien for his "simplisticness," his division of the inhabitants of Middle Earth into the good people and the evil people. And indeed he does this, and his good people tend to be entirely good, though with endearing frailties, while his Orcs and other villains are altogether nasty. But all this is a judgment by daylight ethics, by conventional standards of virtue and vice. When you look at the story as a psychic journey, you see something quite different, and very strange. You see then a group of bright figures, each one with its black shadow. Against the Elves, the Orcs. Against Aragorn, the Black Rider. Against Gandalf, Saruman. And above all, against Frodo, Gollum. Against him—and with him.

It is truly complex, because both figures are already doubled. Sam is, in part, Frodo's shadow, his inferior part. Gollum is two people, too, in a more direct, schizophrenic sense; he's always talking to himself, Slinker talking to Stinker, Sam calls it. Sam understands Gollum very well, though he won't admit it and won't accept Gollum as Frodo does, letting Gollum be their guide, trusting him. Frodo and Gollum are not only both hobbits; they are the same person—and Frodo knows it. Frodo and Sam are the bright side, Smeagol-Gollum the shadow side. In the end Sam and Smeagol, the lesser figures, drop away, and all that is left is Frodo and Gollum, at the end of the long quest. And it is Frodo the good who fails, who at the last moment claims the Ring of Power for himself; and it is Gollum the evil who achieves the quest, destroying the Ring, and himself with it. The Ring, the archetype of the Integrative Function, the creative-destructive, returns to the volcano, the eternal source of creation and destruction, the primal fire. When you look at it that way, can you call it a simple story? I suppose so. *Oedipus Rex* is a fairly simple story, too. But it is not simplistic. It is the kind of story that can be told only by one who has turned and faced his shadow and looked into the dark.

That it is told in the language of fantasy is not an accident, or because Tolkien was an escapist, or because he was writing for children. It is a fantasy because fantasy is the natural, the appropriate, language for the recounting of the spiritual journey and the struggle of good and evil in the soul.

That has been said before—by Tolkien himself, for one—but it needs repeating. It needs lots of repeating, because there is still, in this country, a deep puritanical distrust of fantasy, which comes out often among people truly and seriously concerned about the ethical education of children. Fantasy, to them, is escapism. They see no difference between the Batmen and Supermen of the commercial dope-factories and the timeless archetypes of the collective unconscious. They confuse fantasy, which in the psychological sense is a universal and essential faculty of the human mind, with infantilism and pathological regression. They seem to think that shadows are something that we can simply do away with, if we can only turn on enough electric lights. And so they see the irrationality and cruelty and strange amoralities of fairy tale, and they say: "But this is very bad for children, we must teach children right from wrong, with realistic books, books that are true to life!"

I agree that children need to be—and usually want very much to be—taught right from wrong. But I believe that realistic fiction for children is one of the very hardest media in which to do it. It's hard not to get entangled in the superficialities of the collective consciousness, in simplistic moralism, in projections of various kinds, so that you end up with the baddies and the goodies all over again. Or you get that business about "there's a little bit of bad in the best of us and a little bit of good in the worst of us," a dangerous banalization of the fact, which is that there is incredible potential for good and for evil in every one of us. Or writers are encouraged to merely capitalize on sensationalism, upsetting the child reader without themselves being really involved in the violence of the story, which is shameful. Or you get the "problem books." The problem of drugs, of divorce, of race prejudice, of unmarried pregnancy, and so on—as if evil were a problem, something that can be solved, that has an answer, like a problem in fifth grade arithmetic. If you want the answer, you just look in the back of the book.

That is escapism, that posing evil as a "problem," instead of what it is: all the pain and suffering and waste and loss and injustice we will meet all our lives long, and must face and cope with over and over and over, and admit, and live with, in order to live human lives at all.

But what, then, is the naturalistic writer for children to do? Can he present the child with evil as an *insoluble* problem—something neither the child nor any adult can do anything about at all? To give the child a picture of the gas chambers of Dachau, or the famines of India, or the cruelties of a psychotic parent, and say, "Well, baby, this is how it is, what are you going to make of it?"—that is surely unethical. If you suggest that there is a "solution" to those monstrous facts, you are lying to the child. If you insist that there isn't, you are overwhelming him with a load he's not strong enough yet to carry.

The young creature does need protection and shelter. But it also needs the truth. And it seems to me that the way you can speak absolutely honestly and factually to a child about both good and evil is to talk about himself. Himself, his inner self, the deep, the deepest Self. That is something he can cope with; indeed, his job in growing up is to become himself. He can't do this if he feels the task is hopeless, nor can he if he's led to think there isn't any task. A child's growth will be stunted and perverted if he is forced to despair or if he is encouraged in false hope, if he is terrified or if he is coddled. What he needs to grow up is reality, the wholeness which exceeds all our virtue and all our vice. He needs knowledge; he needs self-knowledge. He needs to see himself and the shadow he casts. That is something he can face, his own shadow; and he can learn to control it and to be guided by it. So that, when he grows up into his strength and responsibility as an adult in society, he will be less inclined, perhaps, either to give up in despair or to deny what he sees, when he must face the evil that is done in the world, and the injustices and grief and suffering that we all must bear, and the final shadow at the end of all.

Fantasy is the language of the inner self. I will claim no more for fantasy than to say that I personally find it the appropriate language in which to tell stories to children—and others. But I say that with some confidence, having behind me the authority of a very great poet, who put it much more boldly. "The great instrument of moral good," Shelley said, "is the imagination."

Notes

1. Jolande Jacobi, *The Psychology of C.G. Jung* (New Haven: Yale University Press, 1962), p. 107.
2. Carl Gustav Jung, *Psychology and Religion: West and East*, Bollingen Series XX, *The Collected Works of C.G. Jung*, vol. 11 (New York: Pantheon Books, 1958), p. 76.
3. Jung, *Psychology and Religion*, p. 83.

Virginia Esther Hamilton was born in Yellow Springs, Ohio, in 1936. She was educated at Antioch College, Ohio State University, and the New School for Social Research. She married Arnold Adoff in 1960 and they have two children. In 1969 she received the Mystery Writers of America Edgar Allan Poe Award, in 1974 the *Boston Globe-Horn Book* Award, and in 1975 both the National Book Award and the American Library Association Newbery Medal. She lives in Yellow Springs.

Fiction for children:
Zeely (1967), *The House of Dies Drear* (1968), *The Time-Ago Tales of Jahdu* (1969), *The Planet of Junior Brown* (1971), *Time-Ago Lost; More Tales of Jahdu* (1973), *M. C. Higgins, The Great* (1974), *Arilla Sun Down* (1976), and *Justice and Her Brothers* (1978).

Nonfiction:
W. E. B. DuBois; A Biography (1972), *Paul Robeson: The Life and Times of a Free Black Man* (1974), and, as editor, *The Writings of W. E. B. Du Bois* (1975).

Virginia Hamilton presented this lecture at the Library of Congress on November 17, 1975, in observance of National Children's Book Week. It was published by the Library of Congress as a pamphlet in 1976.

Illusion and Reality

by Virginia Hamilton

What I do for a living and what I do daily as, generally, a most pleasurable pastime are one and the same. I make up people and places. I write fiction. Occasionally, I write a work of nonfiction, which is no less important to me. But I am predominantly a fiction writer.

The best definition of fiction I've come across is a dictionary definition which states that fiction is "an assumption of a possibility as a fact irrespective of the question of its truth." Put another way, the fiction writer works within the realm of illusion. Without the benefit of visual aids or even background music, the writer uses a single system of language to create the illusion of reality.

The most frequent question asked of fiction writers is "Where do you get your ideas?" I've yet to find a satisfactory answer to that question, but usually I reply rather lamely, if not desperately, "Well, they just come into my head." It's obvious from the ensuing silence that the questioner might well be thinking "Why do they come into your head? Such ideas certainly never come into mine."

I think it can safely be said that there is no one answer and no one place where a writer gets ideas. Rather, there are many answers and many places, perhaps as many as there are writers. What I'd like to suggest is the particular direction I take in uncovering the scope of an idea as it relates to reality and illusion in fiction, and also in biography. For ideas do just come into my head and I create fictions out of them, often long before I uncover their source.

Anyone who has been asked by a child whether what he or she views on television is real or unreal is familiar with the confusing elements of reality and illusion. Before the most recent restrictions on the depiction of violence on family–hour television, my own son was mightily confused when the bad guys fell mortally wounded. "Are they actors?" he asked. "Are they acting dead? Will they get up after the show? How can they be shot and get up after the show? How do you *know* they will get up after the

115

From Zeely *by Virginia Hamilton, illustrated by Symeon Shimin. Illustrations in* Zeely, *Copyright © 1976 by Symeon Shimin. Courtesy of Macmillan Publishing Co., Inc.*

show?' I never convinced him that the actors did indeed get up. But unknown to me, my young son had gathered evidence for the proof, himself. For in all those dramas in which bad guys fell down dead, there had been one element of truth missing.

A few years ago, when suddenly the horrid scene flashed on the air of a prominent individual being shot and falling seemingly mortally wounded, my son happened to see it. He covered his eyes. "It's real!" he whispered and ran for the room. Later I asked him how he had known it was real, for he had come in the midst of the scene and not at the announcement of a special bulletin. "Because," he said, "there was blood on him. There was blood on the ground." My son had noticed what I had missed when the bad guys fell on Saturday-night television. Earlier restrictions had cleaned up some of the violence. Blood was never shown.

This example is, of course, a much too vivid and tragic way for a child to learn the difference between the real and the unreal. My own children now often watch the evening news and documentary programs because I think it's important that they understand the difference between reality and illusion in life, in entertainment, and in books as well.

A work of fiction is an illusion of life in which characters attempt to transfer a basic reality by casting their desires and their subjective view upon it. In essence, the attempt creates internal conflict between elements of the real and the unreal. Characters must sort out the conflict through experiences that enable them to discover what truths finally exist.

In *M. C. Higgins, the Great,* an environment of plot and characters is based upon the supplanting of reality by the wishes and dreams of one main character. M. C. Higgins desperately seeks escape for his family through a single misconception which becomes for him the only reality: his mother will become a great singer, acquiring enough money for them all to leave their ancestral home on a threatened mountain. Within the misconception, M. C. is able to sort out certain truths by means of experience. Finally, he sees there is no way for him to rid the mountain of its spoil through illusion. At the end, the scarred land, the spoil heap, and the immense mining machines remain to be dealt with by means of whatever reality is left to him.

The two books of Jahdu stories I've written fall outside the realm of the reality-illusion principle of the novels and delve, instead, into the rich vein of American black folklife, both past and present. These tales are based less on a fantasy tradition and more on African prototypal folk myths of animal heroes. The African jackal, hare, tortoise, and hyena were translated on the American continent into the fox, rabbit, terrapin, and wolf. The shaman/hero of Africa is here transformed into the trickster/hero, who personifies the wit and cunning of individuals once condemned within a slavocracy. The amorphous Jahdu of the Jahdu tales, born of no woman but in an old oven, suggests the transcendental nature of present-day black experience in America.

Aware as I am, and was, of the limitations imposed upon purveyors of black literature in this country, perhaps I sought through the Jahdu tales to expand and elevate concerns beyond real and imagined limits of nonwhite American experience. From this, some few critics have deduced an eccentricity of character delineation and definition within my fiction.

Virginia Hamilton's characters are said to deviate from the recognized or usual. They are variously described as peculiar, odd, and queer— strange, columnar figures fixed somewhat off center of known human orbits. They are detached, as was Zeely, separated by her very height; or Mr. Pool in *The Planet of Junior Brown*, barred from his professional group by a self-imposed disengagement; or Mr. Pluto in *The House of Dies Drear*, isolated because of the locals' superstitious belief in his supernatural activity; or Junior Brown, rejected because of his ugly fat; or M. C. Higgins, literally risen above mere mortals by means of a forty-foot pole. These are some of my eccentrics. But why the need for them? Why are they created with this quality of spiritual isolation, of other-worldness, when I, their originator, feel so normal within, having no mental aberrations that obsess me?

We find a clue in my past. Back in college, I tested "normal" as part of the control group in a series of psychological experiments. Translating "normal" to mean that I was average, I came to detest the term. In vain, I searched within me for a secret hate, a trauma. But it seemed that all of my conscious and unconscious fears and "bumps in the night" were boringly within the limits of normalcy, if we are to believe the results of the tests. Even my childhood anemia and bed-wetting were blandly attributed to the zealous but normal strivings of an overly protective father ambitious for his children.

Later on, I was amused and, ultimately, relieved to discover in the writings of Gertrude Stein that while at Harvard Annex (now Radcliffe) and a student of William James's, she was a subject of a student project in experimental psychology. Another student complained to Professor James that Gertrude Stein had no subconscious reactions; therefore she invalidated the results of his experiment. "Ah," said Professor James, "if Miss Stein gave no response I should say that it was as normal not to give a response as to give one.... "

Gertrude Stein always disliked the abnormal, which she felt was so obvious. And she believed that "normal" was "so much more simply complicated and interesting," a statement which gives us an insight into her writing of objective subjectivity. For Stein is the focus and center of all of her own work. Writing only of what she was hearing, feeling, and seeing at the moment, she nevertheless always viewed herself with complete detachment.

As a student, then, fortified by my reading of Gertrude Stein and her mentor William James, I came to accept my condition of being normal less as a terminal disease and more as something solid, like bedrock, upon

From Zeely by Virginia Hamilton, illustrated by Symeon Shimin. Illustrations in Zeely,
Copyright © 1976 by Symeon Shimin. Courtesy of Macmillan Publishing Co., Inc.

which some individual mark might be made. Coming to the present, I wonder whether eccentric creations in fiction are not as normal for me as totally conscious but seemingly automatic writings were for someone like Gertrude Stein.

Few writers are as un-self-conscious as was Stein, with the ability to write alone, as it were, with no involvement with the past. Most writers work within and through a framework of myths, delusions, dreams, and realities of the group to which they bear allegiance. This may hold true for black writers more than for other American groups, for the survival pattern of their group pervades the generations as though it were an inherent collective trait. Black people, who in recent history were born into bondage as property, had to be different from other people. Even for those born free within the bonded group, slavery must have become a stigma that bled their hearts and marked their minds.

My own grandfather had to be different. Born a slave, as an infant he was sold away with his mother, never to know his father. The years he lived as part of my child life, I knew him as this old friend, chewing tobacco, barely five feet tall, who at eighty could jump from a standing-still position into the air to click his heels together three times and land still standing. Never ever could I do that.

One of grandpa's hands was forever maimed to an inch of being closed tight. He had been employed in a gunpowder mill near Xenia, Ohio. One day, the explosive mixture caught fire; the mill burned to the ground. There were great flames, and for some reason grandpa reached out for the fire. In a moment of confusion, perhaps he thought the flame would melt away the stigma. His hand was burned hideously. It was bandaged shut and it healed that way, a closed fist from which the generation of his grandchildren, from which I, would hold tight and swing.

How eccentric an image is that fiery hand with the closed fist! How easily it becomes symbolic, even for me. How eccentric is the total history of blacks in America, imbued as it is with the spiritual isolation of the fugitive alone and running, with weird tales which are true tales handed down from one generation to the next. The characters I create are descendants of slaves and freemen. All carry with them the knowledge of former generations who were born in livestock, as property. That sort of knowledge must corner reality for them and hold it at bay. It must become in part eccentric and in part symbolic for succeeding generations. So it is natural that I try through fiction to break down the symbols and free the reality.

As an example, simple curiosity caused me some time ago to attempt to discover the depths of the term *the Street*. Trusting my instinct, I felt there was more to the inordinate use of the term in the lexicon of subculture language than mere ambience.

I had made use of the term in *The Planet of Junior Brown*, where both Junior Brown and Buddy Clark are involved in some way in the Street.

From The House of Dies Drear *by Virginia Hamilton, illustrated by Eros Keith.*
Illustrations in The House of Dies Drear, *Copyright © 1968 by Macmillan Publishing Co.,*
Inc.

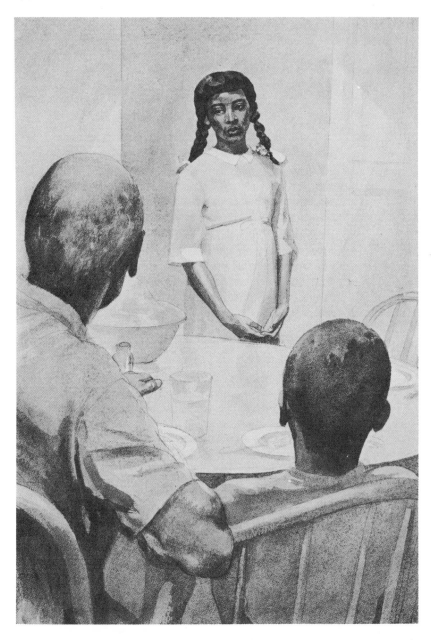

From Zeely *by Virginia Hamilton, illustrated by Symeon Shimin. Illustrations in* Zeely, *Copyright © 1979 by Symeon Shimin. Courtesy of Macmillan Publishing Co., Inc.*

Buddy is a street youth, having no home and no normal family as we know family. He lives by his wits in the Street, and he takes from the Street, as he learns from it, only as much as he needs for survival. However, Junior Brown is the opposite of a street youth. He has a home, he has family, but these do not nourish him as the Street nourishes Buddy Clark. Thus, Junior creates the illustration of the Red Man to fill his emptiness, in which he paints the Street—all of the people he sees as free and together, sharing all, even misery. It is interesting that Red Man is the name of a well-known tobacco and that my grandfather was the only one of my relatives who chewed tobacco. The Street also refers back to my grandfather, although I was not conscious of this when I wrote the book.

Many times, my mother had told me of the song her father sang to her while she swung from his closed fist, as I did in my youth. "Dad would tell about the Rag Man," she said. "Coming down the street, the Rag Man would sing his song: 'Any rags, any bones, any bottles today,' he'd sing. 'The big black rag man's coming your way. Any rags, any rags,' he'd sing, all along the street."

I loved that street cry and often sing it to my own children. It's only recently I've wondered at the phrase *the Street* as referred to by my mother in relation to the Rag Man. For there were no *streets* as such in our rural country a hundred years ago when my grandfather was a boy or eighty years ago when my mother was a small child. Was the term *the Street* a simple accident, the result of an unconscious shift to a more modern expression? I asked my mother about it. Now that she thought about it, she said, the Rag Man came down the road or the lane, but they always said he came down the street. She insisted on that "Even grandpa said the Street?" I asked. "Yes," she said, "always."

Occasionally, I wondered about the expression, not actually aware that I had begun to search for something. I knew that in the forties Ann Petry's novel *The Street* had been published. And I made a note when Mordecai Richler's book entitled *The Street* was published in 1975 here in Washington by New Republic Book Company. I remarked to myself how many different cultures view the Street as a particular reality. So it was with Richler's Street and Petry's Street in Harlem. Was it the same with my grandpa's Street, and if so, what particular place or reality did it represent, and in what period of time?

Things do fall into my hands rather unexpectedly. I have a habit of seeking the old, old curios and old people whose long memories I admire. I even follow old roads in the country which twist and turn, change names suddenly, and end just anywhere. One of my favorite old roads leads to a stupendous shopping mall, acres and acres of it out in the middle of nowhere. Surprisingly, the mall has turned into a gold mine for old things.

Perhaps all over, but certainly in my part of the Midwest, the great shopping malls built in the sixties and still being built have fallen on hard times. With lines of sleek stores opening onto one gigantic enclosure of fountains, potted palms, and rest areas, these monstrous malls are hit hard by a depressed economy. Consumers, suffering through long periods of unemployment, have given up making the long drive out when they can save gasoline by shopping in town or not at all. Mall lights are dimmed, stores are uncomfortably chilly, and sales personnel have disappeared. Viewed from a distance, surrounded by huge, empty parking lots, my favorite mall is eerily quiet, like the giant launchpad for a dream ship that has come and gone.

I find it all very sad, for shopping malls have always seemed to me particularly American—our adventuresome, garish ode to good times— what with their massive promenades and thirty-foot display windows. We show off; like to think big. But I can envision a day when the whole extravaganza will fall into the hands of the populace. Displaced farmers will come forth on giant tractors to plow up acres of cement. Workers will plant boutiques of corn and wheat. Hired hands will lay out endless holding pens for Black Angus under massive skylights.

Yet, suddenly, something has happened out there in nowhere that is far more interesting than any future sight of fountains irrigating fields. These days one expects to see camels drinking at marble watering holes. For every inch of the spacious promenade has been taken over by incredible bazaars. Hawkers of every stripe and character are out selling Americana to America. They drift in on Harley-Davidsons, or in minibuses and campers like gypsies, and then melt away again. While they're out there, you can buy old coins, handwoven blankets, old oak furniture, handblown bottles, rolling pins, quilts, Kewpie dolls and carnival canes, and books. Area communes produce afghans and pure honey. One dude wearing chaps and a leather vest came strolling in leading a matched team of Leopard Appaloosas, but they threw him out. On weekends, we go out to the mall to be astonished and to pick over and fondle the past.

The first item my hand fell upon one Saturday was an album of old postcards. I can't say why I paused there, since I collect little of the past beyond that which I store in memory. But as I leafed idly through the album, I came to a section labeled "Negro Postcards." These were a ghastly commentary on an uncertain black history—painted portraits of toothy "pickaninnies" slurping watermelon or photos of ragged black children grinning and dancing. At once repelled and fascinated, I flipped over one card depicting a melon eater, to discover this message: "Dear Mildred. I am here where I was going. I was going no farther and Mildred, I hope to die here. I thought you would want to know. Alice."

Such a stunning, sad message. I stood there for half an hour reading other messages but the whole time wondering what kind of journey Alice had embarked upon. Were these cards with their stereotype portraits used solely by white wanderers? Would even white users of the cards believe that the crude portraits truly represented blacks? I thought of buying up all of the "Negro" cards to study them at my leisure. But in the end I left them there, every one of them. At the last, one intrusion into the privacy of the dead and gone was enough. I had learned all that I needed to know.

I did find something at the bazaar that day which I had to have, and which is the point of this long exposition. A slim paper volume entitled *Homes of the Freed*, published in the twenties and written by Rossa B. Cooley. Its cover illustration is a woodcut of a crude cabin with a figure seated before it, a clouded sky and a road winding by the cabin. Below the title is the notation, "The oncoming of three generations of women from the plantation street. . . ." Here was the Street again, but used in a wholly unexpected way.

Homes of the Freed hoped to demonstrate how "the purely academic character of the early Negro schools" started by northern teachers during Reconstruction could be thoroughly eradicated by means of domestic training and service programs and supplanted by "the self-dependent households of freedom and . . . what this has meant to the women at the race." It was a terribly biased approach to the education of black women, but interesting to me personally for the story it tells of the great transition from the black Street of slave days.

Homes of the Freed gives testimony of old black people remembering what their parents and grandparents told them. An elderly man relates the history of a row of slave cabins, always calling it the Street.

Women worked from "dayclean," as the dawn was called, until tasks in the fields were done. The fields were isolated, lonely places where, apparently, women often worked separately from men and were cut off from the comparative security of the cabins, from newborn babes, and from their very young children. A whole system of day care had to be arranged for these children in the Street. Black women too old to work the fields became the Maumas or nurses, and the newborns were carried out into the fields to be suckled by their mothers and then returned to the Street.

In the Street in front of the cabins, the Maumas built a huge fire and, in one great cooking pot, cooked the meals for the children, for themselves, and for the field hands. The food for the pot was supplied by the whole of the Street. The Maumas and babies all ate from it. When the workers had completed their tasks, they returned to the Street and they too ate from the pot.

They ate and talked quietly. They were tired to the bone now, but they gained strength again from one another and the communal life of the Street.

So it is that the Street down which came the Rag Man of my grandfather's song and the Street in *The Planet of Junior Brown* may both hark back to the old time in the plantation Street. The Street may well be that which the slaves gave up in order to be free. To flee from the only security they had ever known must have terrified many, but break away they did, from an old order, to discover a new reality. Still, the Street exists, not only in racial memory but in the daily lives of those who escape from mean rooms to the camaraderie, sometimes even the danger, of Petry's ghetto Street, or the stupefying drudgery of Richler's Street; in the lives of Street people, the voice of Street poets, the drama of Street theater and the prose of Street literature; also, in the lazy times on the street corners of boring small towns. The meaning of the Street in all ways and at all times is the need for sharing life with others and the search for community.

Knowing that the Street is so connected to past life in a special way which is personal to me makes the language of it richer and makes the past always present for me.

Every fiction has its own basic reality, as does the Street, through which the life of characters and their illusions are revealed, and from which past meaning often creeps into the setting. The task for any writer is to discover the "reality tone" of each work—the basis of truth upon which all variations on the whole language system are set. For reality may be the greatest of all illusions. We each know our own reality through which we seek a common ground of communication with others. The fiction writer seeks the common ground by relinquishing her own reality for the creation of a new one. No number of past successes helps this writer in the creative process of a new writing. For the very process must be created for each new reality. The way to do this is never mastered and never really learned.

It would be interesting to create a fiction in which reality and illusion are completely personified. The thought of attempting such a fiction came to me from observing my own children and their contemporaries. All seemed to be trying to find out who they really were through testing and by changing roles. I have watched them for days playing at being one another, using one another's language, walks, and hairstyles. When one Elodie D. Dangerfield from Little Rock, Arkansas, entered the seventh grade at the beginning of this year, a number of her twelve-year-old classmates began affecting syrupy southern accents. For a time, they discarded their blue jeans and talk of sisterhood for pink dresses and evening prayer meetings. I have nothing against Elodie D. Dangerfield— not her real name of course. In fact, I find her fascinating as I attempt to discover just who it is *she* is playing at being, or whether she is really being herself.

My observation of these young girls started me thinking. To write about a family unit in which some members are in the process of learning who they are and in which others are living a fiction they admire seemed to be the perfect sort of risk for me. Which of them would live a true portrayal and which would live an illusion? On what basis of truth can be measured the reality and the illusion personified? Moreover, it occurred to me that we all carry with us the somewhat tattered baggage of our pasts, so why not personify the past in the present as well? How does one accomplish this without reducing characters to symbols or creedal types? Add to this questions of racial identity and it becomes clear how diverse an environment of illusion and reality might be created.

The whole idea might sound rather complicated for children. Actually, it's the approach to the process of creation that gets complicated, not the idea or the manner in which it's to be written. Moreover, we've all observed children struggling daily with an incredible array of identity forms. One nine-year-old youth of my acquaintance who is white was asked what he wanted to be when he grew up and replied, "I want to be black." His father, telling me this, was pleased by his son's answer. I was not so pleased and I told the father so, for I believe it is poor mental health for a white youth to want to grow up to be black, as it would be for a black youth to want to grow up to be white.

Said the father, "David admires black athletes. He also sees black people living around him just the way he lives. He sees no difference."

"If he sees no difference," I said, "why wouldn't he want the group to be white, to admire white athletes as well? And suppose he weren't living in this middle-class community where most of what he sees includes only one class of black people. Suppose he were to see the hungry and out-of-work. What then?"

"But the truth is," said the father, "David's living here where black people are living in the same way he lives."

"You must never let him believe it is the whole truth," I said, finally.

We ended our discussion there, with the question of truth unanswered. But David nags my mind. My instinct tells me that he must be made to understand that being white is quite all right, as is being black. Perhaps he should be told that he can wish to be black if he so desires, but that the wish will not be fulfilled. Even as I say these words, they seem to melt in illusion. For me all are at least aware of the fact that there are whites among us who live as blacks, and blacks among us who live as whites. There are biracials and multiracials among us, such as my own children, who might more realistically be termed Other Kinds, or Composites, or Betweens. Can you hear children of the future saying, "I'm a 'posite. She's an 'okind. The others are 'tweens." I don't doubt anything.

Transracial peoples are nothing new in this country. The Shawnee Nation Remnant Band of the Tecumseh Confederacy has set up a nation house in my hometown, and although they appear to be white and do not seek recognition from the Bureau of Indian Affairs, they nevertheless live as Shawnee Native Americans. The Wesorts—a people who are probably Native American, but this is uncertain—live in large groups in the swamplands of southern Maryland. In the Piedmont and Blue Ridge areas of Virginia there are groups known as the "Amherst County issues," brown people who may or may not be Native American and who for years have intermarried. Many of us have long been familiar with those mysterious people, the Jackson Whites, living in New York and New Jersey, who number more than five hundred and whose origins are unknown.

We have yet to deal successfully with American transraciality in real terms, as we have failed to redefine race in light of the modern, twenty-first-century progress of human kind. Certainly, here is an arena for serious study by anthropologists, sociologists, philosophers, and, of course, writers of fiction.

Delineating such areas of a writer's thoughts as these may give an inkling of the difficulty in answering the question "Where do you get your ideas?" For ideas come from without as well as from deep sources within. They may just as easily come from my son's original knock-knock jokes as from quiet moments of contemplation in my study. They come from memory, from sight and sound. They come from living.

I've only made mention of a type of writing besides fiction and folktales which has given me a good deal of satisfaction. Although I've written just two biographies for young people, one concerning the life of W. E. B. Du Bois and the other the life of Paul Robeson, they are no less involved with the subject of reality and illusion.

I had hoped, by writing the personal history of a real individual through a disciplined presentation of facts, to create the illusion of total reality; to give readers the feeling that they walked along with the subject in his life; and through the creative use of source material, to allow the subject to speak as closely as possible in his own voice.

In this respect, of the two biographies, the Robeson biography is the more successful. The research and study of the Robeson material took a number of years. When that phase of the work was completed, I discovered it was possible during the day to evoke the Robeson spirit in my mind and to live with it as though the man were a guest in my house. I began to know Paul Robeson quite well, and slowly two aspects of him emerged to trouble me and to pose definite problems in the actual writing of the book.

The first problem, and the one easiest to deal with, was the problem of Robeson emerging not as a man but as a symbol. The same difficulty occurred in the writing of *M. C. Higgins, the Great.* In that fiction, I had to come to terms not only with the symbolic nature of mountains and rivers but with all the preconceived notions about blacks being in a state of nature or nearly so. In my Robeson research, it was almost impossible to find a single newspaper account that did not depict the man as somehow supernatural and larger than life. Take this one by a sportswriter when Robeson was barely eighteen and playing football for Rutgers: "He rode on the wings of the frigid breezes; a grim, silent and compelling figure . . . . It was Robeson, a veritable Othello battle." Or this one: "A dark cloud . . . Robeson, the giant Negro."

Hardly ever was Robeson described as a man. Rather, he was "this giant," "that great, noble prince," or "the original stuff of the earth." Individuals who knew him and whom I interviewed often seemed at a loss for words or struck dumb with awe, and when they *could* put their experiences into words, the superlatives would role forth in godlike descriptions.

Eventually, I learned to use these overwrought passages to an advantage. But it became necessary for me to write in a very tight, simple style; to write close up to the individual in the hope that a concise and straightforward revelation of his life would finally produce a composite of the man.

The second problem was more difficult and became clear to me only after I had written a first draft of the book. Then Robeson still seemed elusive. I could not get a handle on him. He stood alone, but he did not stand out in a way I knew he must. Something about him remained out of focus and out of time. It took months for me to realize that no simple, factual presentation of Paul Robeson's life was likely ever to reveal the man in his true stature. For the basic difficulty of writing about blacks in America was intensely a problem here: the origin of black American history is fundamentally different from that of traditional American history. I have said that that history is eccentric because it departs considerably from the usual or traditional. Because of slavery, because of continuing discrimination, segregation, and exploitation throughout the history, it was and is necessary for blacks to make extreme changes in their view of themselves in American life, in their evaluation of themselves, and in their institutions.

In order to understand Paul Robeson or W. E. B. Du Bois, it is necessary that we understand that what the majority viewed as radical in their time was quite a normal point of view for these men whose lives were profoundly restricted by a whole system of established mores. Thus, it was not possible to write about Paul Robeson without a thorough understanding of the political and social times in which he lived. Furthermore, it became necessary to go beyond the usual thorough and traditional histories having to do with political America, Europe, and the rest of the world, such as those written by Commager and Leuchtenburg, and to search for and find those revisionist historians, like Gabriel Kolko, whose historical truths emerge as radically different from what we have taken for granted as the truth.

In revisionist historiography, the alliance of Great Britain, the United States, and the Soviet Union at the time of World War II becomes not a matter of high ideals, deliberation, and choice but one of ruthless necessity to defeat an enemy. The European aid program instituted by the United States after the war becomes less a program of recovery for Europe from pain and suffering and more the deliberate attempt to take from Britain control of foreign markets and Middle East oil and to advance American investments and economic and military power by means of the extension of a capitalistic system throughout the world.

Paul Robeson's drift toward radicalism and the appeal radicalism had for him become understandable from the viewpoint of a colonized people. Robeson saw himself as a citizen of the world and identified himself, as did Du Bois, with the world's workers and colonized peoples, whom he deemed criminally exploited under capitalism.

Whether the view is wholly correct or partly inaccurate, it is not possible to write about either man without recognizing that they were in a position to make contact with the world, to travel it and study it, in a way few Americans other than statesmen ever had.

Writing these two biographies from a more radical perspective was quite a challenge, and the perspective is as justified as any other, if not more so, with regard to blacks. Curiously, my studies in radical history and research into black life and history have tended to radicalize me not so much in terms of world political views as in fictional terms. I would be a rather useless individual in any revolutionary situation. I hate violence and tend to view it as a human aberration—certainly not a very radical point of view. I also tend to view capitalism as an aberration which provokes extremism, which I suppose *is* radical. In any case, we must remember that radicalism is as American as apple pie. The men who wrote the Declaration of Independence were radicals who overthrew a great colonial power. American abolitionists were radicals who were not above trickery, rabble-rousing, rioting, and murder in aid of fugitive slaves.

For myself, I deliberately attempt a kind of literary radicalism in the hope of removing traditional prose restrictions and creating new ways to approach literary forms from a perspective other than that of the majority. It is a way of continuing to legitimize nonwhite literature, bringing it into full view to provoke curiosity and discussion. Many in this country are attempting to bring not only good literature but representative literature to the country's children. I don't believe that anywhere else in the world has such an attempt been made. Here it is not always successful; it meets with varying degrees and kinds of resistance. Still, few of us would deny the right of nonwhites to a literature reflecting their concerns. I am not talking about a literature that merely satisfies a need, though that's important; I'm speaking about a literature whose themes and philosophy may begin now and in the future continue to be entirely different from what is traditional. Indeed, it would be radical.

Tracking down the source of an idea and discovering the true components of a fiction are intriguing work. But they are work that is, in a sense, a sideline and after the fact. It is not necessary to know the source of an idea in order to expand upon it. For to get an idea and from it create a system of illusion we accept as reality is the most exciting prospect of all. Through the use of words alone, the writer creates sight and sound and emotional response. By reading words alone, the reader see, hears, and feels. Both are demonstrating an act of mentality, the connection of minds through which belief is suspended in the interest of illusion. One would be at a loss without the other. I for one would find it impossible to write indefinitely with only myself to read what I had written.

That is why, when eager young writers seek me out for help when they know their work isn't ready and I know it isn't, I understand so completely their impatience. It is not just the need to see their work and their names in print, although that is part of it always. It is the overwhelming desire to make that connection of mind with mind, to have demonstrated the act of mentality and to have communicated. For the writer, there is nothing quite like having someone say that he or she understands, that you have reached them and affected them with what you have written. It is the feeling early humans must have experienced when the firelight first overcame the darkness of the cave. It is the communal cooking pot, the Street, all over again. It is our need to know we are not alone.

John Rowe Townsend was born in Leeds, Yorkshire, in 1922. He was educated at Leeds Grammar School, 1933–40, and Emmanuel College, Cambridge, getting a B.A. in 1949 and an M.A. in 1954. He served in the Royal Air Force, 1942–46, as flight sergeant. In 1948 he married Vera Lancaster and they had two daughters and one son. He worked as reporter for the *Yorkshire Post* and *Evening Standard;* as subeditor and art editor for the Manchester *Guardian;* as editor for the *Guardian Weekly;* and, 1969–78, as children's book review editor for the *Guardian,* Manchester and London. He served as visiting lecturer, University of Pennsylvania, University of Washington in Seattle, and the Simmons College Center for the Study of Children's Literature. In 1971 he gave the May Hill Arbuthnot Honor Lecture and the Anne Carroll Moore Lecture. He received the *Boston Globe–Horn Book* Award and the English P.E.N. Award in 1970 and the Mystery Writers of America Edgar Allan Poe Award in 1971.

Books for young people:
Good-bye to the Jungle (1967), *Pirate's Island* (1968), *Hell's Edge* (1969), *Trouble in the Jungle* (1969), *The Intruder* (1970), *Good Night, Prof, Dear* (1971), *The Summer People* (1972), *Forest of the Night* (1975), *Noah's Castle* (1976), *Top of the World* (1977), *The Visitors* (1977), and, as editor, *Modern Poetry: A Selection* (1974).

For adults:
Written for Children: An Outline of English Children's Literature (rev. ed., 1975), *A Sense of Story: Essays on Contemporary Writers for Children* (1971; rev. ed., 1979), and *Twenty-five Years of British Children's Books* (1977).

This lecture, presented at the Library of Congress on November 8, 1976, during National Children's Book week, was first published in the April 1977 issue of the *Quarterly Journal of the Library of Congress.*

Under Two Hats

by John Rowe Townsend

The world was large and consisted entirely of streets. When Sam was very small, the long continuous rows of houses loomed over him like the walls of canyons. As he grew bigger the streets grew smaller, but they still stretched endlessly in all directions.

The part of the world Sam knew at five years old was a maze of perhaps twenty narrow streets with connecting alleyways. In most of these streets there were people related to him. With the last street that held any relatives, the known world ended. Beyond it were many more streets and alleyways, but they were foreign. It did not occur to the small Sam that there might be some far point at which the whole great network of streets came to a stop. And if it had occurred to him, he could not have guessed what might lie beyond. He only knew that the world was streets.

And the world was not round or flat; it was sloping. It sloped up to the Marigolds and down to the Violets. The Marigolds were Marigold Street, Marigold Way, Marigold Mount, Marigold Grove, Marigold Row, Marigold Terrace, and Marigold Avenue. The Violets were Violet Street, Way, Mount, Grove, Row, Terrace, and Avenue. In between them were the Daisies. Sam lived in the Daisies. The Marigolds, Violets, and Daisies were row upon row of back-to-back houses. They had been run up as cheaply as possible some time in the previous century by a speculative builder, but Sam didn't know that. Nor did he know that somewhere under the weight of concrete and brick and slate, of cobbles and paving stones, there lay what had once been a living hillside.

Along the edge of the Marigolds, Violets, and Daisies ran the main road. Both road and district were known as City Hill. At the top and bottom of City Hill were other foreign worlds, linked with Sam's by the tall two–decker streetcar known as the tram. The tram groaned painfully up City Hill toward the higher suburbs, then went into reverse and came

133

wailing and clanging back into town at twice the speed.

Up was good, down was bad. Sam had heard of heaven and vaguely thought of it as somewhere uphill beyond the Marigolds. He had heard of hell and supposed it lay in the black brick depths below the Violets. But Sam stayed in his own world. There was no need to leave it. You played— and in summer almost lived—on the street. At the junction of every street with City Hill was a pair of corner shops. Grocer, butcher, baker, greengrocer, post office, hardware, candy shop—all that a family could need was there at hand.

There were living things in the world besides people. There were grimy grasses and riotous dandelions on the trodden, brick-littered scraps of open ground where houses had been pulled down. There were cats around the trash bins and budgerigars in cages that hung in windows and a dog or two. You could tell the seasons apart by the coldness or warmth and by the length of daylight. On a sunny summer day the sidewalk was hot to your bare feet and the doorstep hot to your bottom. On freezing winter mornings men slipped and skidded in their booted, before-dawn descent to work at the clothing factory or the engineering works. Winter and summer there was laughter and singing, shouting and swearing and quarreling outside the corner public house on Saturday night. Then respectable folk like Sam's family closed their windows and wished they

Pen-and-ink drawing by Graham Humphreys, from The Intruder, *copyright © 1969 by John Rowe Townsend, is reprinted by permission of Oxford University Press.*

could move uphill to a better district. On every fine Monday the clotheslines were hung across the streets and blossomed with washing.

I have been reading to you the first two pages of what may someday be a novel or may not. You will be wondering why. I will give you part of the answer by telling you that, although fictional, this is a fairly accurate description of the environment into which I was born. And although the novel, if ever finished, will not be autobiographical, the young Sam who is its protagonist could very well have been the young John Rowe Townsend.

Let me continue just a little farther, and I hope you will begin to see the relevance of this account to the subject and also its relevance, perhaps, to the National Children's Book Week.

The world of Sam had two poles: Mom's house in Daisy Mount and Grandpa's in Marigold Way. Mom had been married young, a slip of a girl, motherless. Now she had Dad and Sam and a baby, but Dad was working away from home and Grandpa kept an eye on Mom. They were child and parent still. Mom went to Grandpa's house every day, trailing Sam by the hand and pushing the baby in its trolley. She told Grandpa her problems, and Grandpa told her what to do about them. And Grandpa always had something for Sam, if he'd behaved himself: an orange, or a handful of dates, or a cookie, or a couple of squares of plain chocolate.

Grandpa never gave him milk chocolate; he thought milk chocolate was too rich for children.

Grandpa had recently retired from work. He lived in an end-of-the-row house with a front parlor, which set him a little apart from—and above—his neighbors. He was round-faced with a fringe of white hair, and his spectacles had narrow steel rims. In any matter except religion he was a mild, kind, accommodating man; but where religion was concerned he was severe and unyielding. He was a devout chapelgoer. On the parlor wall he had a Lord's Prayer cut out of satinwood in fretwork, two feet wide and three feet deep, mounted on dark blue plush and framed under glass. He had designed and made it himself, and it had occupied the leisure time of three years. It had Gothic lettering surrounded by marvelously convoluted scrolls and flourishes. But as he neared the end of his task, Grandpa's fretsaw had slipped and taken the middle out of the final *e* in "for ever and ever." He was not dismayed and often pointed to this flaw as demonstrating the imperfection of all human achievement. "Only that which God does is perfect," he used to say.

On Sunday afternoons Sam would go with Mom to Grandpa's house, where several other relatives would have gathered. Grandpa was the recognized head of the family. He was a strict Sabbatarian and conversation was conducted accordingly. Jokes were few, and laughter was quickly hushed. As it was Sunday, Sam was not allowed to go out and play, and there was no other child to keep him company through the hours of droning adult small talk. But when he had learned to read, Grandpa allowed him to do so, provided the book was suitable. And Grandpa himself had an endless supply of suitable books, which had been carefully preserved from his own Victorian childhood.

There were long runs of the *Children's Prize* and *Chatterbox*, improving periodicals that had been launched in competition with the abominated penny dreadfuls. These were innumerable Sunday school rewards: prizes for regular attendance, good conduct, and knowledge of the scriptures—all virtues in which Grandpa had been a model of excellence. There were stories in which children of astonishing virtue suffered dreadful injustices in silence rather than betray the actual perpetrators of the misdeeds alleged against them, or in which children strayed from the straight and narrow path but were brought back to it repentant, or in which radiantly saintly children acted as beacons of light for erring adults. The only book with any claim to literary merit whose title Sam could afterward recall was *John Halifax, Gentleman,* by Dinah Mulock Craik. But the one that made the deepest impression was a story that ran as a serial through a large, thick, bound volume of a magazine called *Our Darlings.* It was called "Not a Sparrow Falls" and it was about the struggle for survival of two orphaned waifs on the streets of London. This Sam found totally gripping.

Such improving works constituted Sam's early literary experience. In his own home there were not above half a dozen books; and it is doubtful

Entitled "Hand Shadows," this engraving by an unknown artist served as a cover illustration for the December 15, 1869, issue of the Chatterbox.

whether there would have been any books in Grandpa's house had they not been prizes and, moreover, of value for moral improvement. To Grandpa, reading was not a pleasure, and pleasure in any case was suspect. Sam never heard of Beatrix Potter, though her best-known books were all in print throughout his childhood; he never heard of *Winnie-the-Pooh*, published when he was four; and as he grew older, he remained unaware of Kenneth Grahame's *The Wind in the Willows*, which had come out before he was born, and of Arthur Ransome's *Swallows and Amazons*, which appeared when he was nine.

This unawareness is not remarkable. Sam did not grow up in an educated family. He never went into a bookshop or even into the public library. As he got bigger, however, he did contrive to read a good many books besides those that were on Grandpa's shelves. Probably he read more than most children, but it was poor stuff on the whole: series books and comics, and vapid school and adventure stories. No doubt it was one of the latter, now long forgotten, that inspired him at the age of eight or nine to write his own first novel, in which a family of children made a boat from a hollowed-out tree, rowed it round the world, and had a series of encounters with pirates, sharks, cannibals, and other unfriendly creatures.

Yet it was Grandpa's books that stayed in Sam's mind; and although they formed an extraordinary literary background for a twentieth-century child, they were not without value. Grandpa's books, unlike the routine school and adventure stories just mentioned, were very much concerned with real life. And life in these books was not only real, it was earnest. Death and disaster were usually just around the corner, if not actually across the threshold; moral crises were real, serious crises.

I think you may have had enough of Sam by now. I will devote only one sentence to a school career in which he passed many examinations but remained a total stranger to the love of learning, and in which the English language was merely a subject. I will tell you only in one sentence how Sam was pushed by his parents into the humbler ranks of the civil service, which they saw as a safe job for life and, moreover, a step up in the world. Happily for Sam, the ill wind of World War II blew him some good—or perhaps I should say that, in a sense, World War II wiped him off the face of the earth. Sam disappeared into the Royal Air Force. He never flew an airplane—he was rejected for aircrew duties because his eyesight was not good enough—but he had momentous experiences of a kind he had not expected. Mixing with new people in new contexts, he discovered poetry, then plays and novels, then the visual arts; he discovered new countries, he discovered an unsuspected interest in people and places and the past; he began belatedly to see what education was all about. Back from the wars came a different young man who talked his way into Cambridge University and went from there into journalism on the Manchester *Guardian* and from there into authorship.

And here I am. I have talked about Sam's—or, with slight transpositions, my own—early life more than perhaps I should, but for what I think is a good reason, which will emerge in a minute. I have also given myself an opening to mention something that is never far from my mind: in my day there were many Sams—and Sallies too—who grew up in as great a state of ignorance as mine—if not greater—and who did not have the astonishing stroke of luck that gave me a second chance. And we all know there are many mute inglorious Sams and Sallies today. My parents did not read books or listen to music, nor do a very large percentage of parents in our two countries now. My elementary school teachers taught me reading and writing as basic skills. They were not concerned with reading as a source of enjoyment, and if they had been I doubt whether their efforts would have prevailed in an atmosphere which was overwhelmingly inhospitable to anything that smacked of culture.

In large areas of our two societies, that atmosphere remains today. No sensible person believes you can or should try to turn every child into a junior egghead, but we all know there are children in whom a love of learning, of literature, of the arts could blossom if only the seed were sown and nurtured a little until it took firm root. That, I suppose, is in a large degree what National Children's Book Week is about. It raises questions of the greatest importance which we all discuss endlessly but which I do not propose to examine further on this occasion.

The subject toward which I have been making my way by a somewhat circuitous route is the experience of being both author and critic in the children's book field: the springs from which the two activities are fed, the interplay between them, the different kinds of involvement with books and children that they imply, the effects on one's creative work of being critically engaged and vice versa, the relative value of and need for each of them, and whether indeed it is desirable that authors *should* be critics. Insofar as I shall refer largely to my own endeavors, I am afraid my talk may seem self-centered. But I am not as diffident as I used to be about talking in public about my own work, since it seems to me now that the principal thing a writer has to talk about that is of any interest to anyone else is what he does and how and why he does it. If he proposes to talk on any other subject, he should ask himself in what way he is specially equipped to do so and whether he would not be better occupied if he got on with his job and kept his mouth shut.

I have spoken of Sam and the metamorphosis of Sam because without them I could not begin to explain myself to myself, never mind anybody else. I said a minute ago that in a sense the Second World War wiped Sam off the face of the earth. A poor boy, an ignorant youth disappeared; an educated person began to emerge, though, alas, one whose education had and still has many fearful gaps in it. But, of course, inside myself, down at the deepest roots of being from which creation springs, Sam is not dead. I am still Sam. I shall be Sam until I die. The remembered back streets of

Dick Hart's frontispiece from Gumble's Yard, *copyright © 1961 by Hutchinson & Co. (Publishers), Ltd., is reprinted by permission of Hutchinson & Co. Publishers, Ltd.*

Leeds are to me as the blue remembered hills were to the poet A. E.
Housman. I say remembered because the streets I knew have all been
pulled down, replaced by high apartment blocks and grassy open spaces,
split up by throughways. A way of life has died; I suppose it had to die. But
that world still lives on in me and no doubt in many others. I have an
infinitude of recollections, and there are sights, sounds, smells, and
reminders of all kinds that bring it back to me still.

Meindert DeJong said in his Newbery acceptance speech twenty-one
years ago: "To get back to the essence of childhood you can only go down.
You can only go in—deep in. Down through all the deep, mystic layers of
the subconscious back into your own childhood. And if you go deep
enough, get basic enough, become again the child you were, it seems
reasonable that by way of the subconscious you have come into what must
be the universal child. Then, and then only, do you write for the child."
Well, I am not at all sure that when I am Sam, when I remember the things
I tried briefly and feebly to tell you about, I am the universal child. That
seems a big claim to make, and an impossible one to substantiate. Perhaps
Meindert DeJong meant something by the phrase that I have failed to
understand. But I do know that at those times I am most *me*. And I know
that inside, for ever and ever, I am a poor child, an ordinary poor child—
not an ill-treated child, not a hungry child, just a poor child.

And it is with poor children, ordinary children, that I identify. People
sometimes ask me, a propos of Kevin, the young narrator in my first book,
Gumble's Yard, or *Trouble in the Jungle* as it is known in America, "Is he
you?" No, he is not *me*, exactly. He is not a self-portrait, but I am *him*. He
is a poor boy, and I know the feeling of being a poor boy. In a later book,
The Intruder, there is a boy, Arnold, who is not so much poor as slow,
rooted to the point of immobility, unlearned in anything except the
vagaries of sand, sea, and weather that make up his environment. He is
helped in a struggle against an unwelcome newcomer by two young
people, Peter and Jane, whose parents and whose assumptions are those
of the educated, fairly well-to-do middle class. For years now, I suppose
that my family and I have been much closer to them in outlook and way of
life than to Arnold. But it is slow, inarticulate Arnold with whom I
identify—profoundly. I know Peter and Jane, I hope; I know them from
outside by observation, and I know them to some extent from inside,
because I think you cannot create any character without some
identification, some sympathy. But I know Arnold at the deepest level of
my being, in the part of me where I am still Sam.

So much, for the moment, for the springs of authorship. But the springs
of critical activity, what are they? What do they have in common with
those other springs? In me, I think the impulses that led toward criticism
were first felt neither in school days nor in the years as a somewhat
elderly—that is to say mid-twentyish—undergraduate at postwar
Cambridge but in the time in between that I have already mentioned. It all

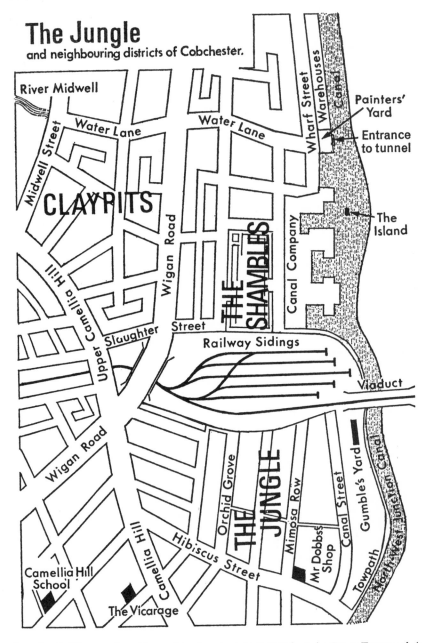

The Jungle
and neighbouring districts of Cobchester.

River Midwell

Water Lane

Water Lane

Painters' Yard

Entrance to tunnel

Warehouses

Wharf Street

Canal

CLAYPITS

Midwell Street

Wigan Road

The Island

Canal Company

THE SHAMBLES

Upper Camellia Hill

Slaughter Street

Railway Sidings

Viaduct

Wigan Road

Orchid Grove

Hibiscus Street

THE JUNGLE

Mimosa Row

Mr Dobbs Shop

Canal Street

Gumble's Yard

North-West Junction Canal

Towpath

Camellia Hill

Camellia Hill School

The Vicarage

Douglas Hall's map, from Pirates Island, *copyright © 1968 by John Rowe Townsend, is reproduced by permission of Oxford University Press.*

goes back to the twenty-year-old airman, discovering, off duty, that the world was full of adventures for the mind and spirit that he had never dreamed of. And for me then, and ever since, the essence of the thing has been discovery. I found that certain poems and paintings did things to me; I wanted to find out why. I found that some poems and paintings did more for me, or less for me, than others; I wondered why. I found that one thing led on to another, and that to another. I found that people had written about poems that I read and paintings that I looked at. I wanted to know what they had said and how their experience compared with mine. I wanted to go to university to extend these voyages of discovery. For me it has always been a matter of seeking, finding, identifying, exploring, and sharing the experience that works of art and literature can give. And because I came to this experience late, I have never taken it for granted; because it is something that through my formative years I never knew about, I have never ceased to feel a Miranda-like surprise at the wonders of this brave new world of the arts. But it is the world of my maturity; it is the world of John Rowe Townsend rather than of Sam.

As a student and as a beginning journalist I was not, however, greatly aware of children's books. I had missed out on the good ones in my own childhood, and they were not what had excited and stimulated me in air force days. The way I became both a writer of and a writer about children's books was a matter of happy accident. Some seven or eight years after I joined the Manchester *Guardian*, the literary editor of that time suggested to me that I should review children's books for the paper. The only obvious qualifications I had were two small children of my own, but I said I would do it, partly because it seemed quite useful to me in the role of parent, partly because I was more than willing to do some reviewing, and if that was what was being offered to me, very well, that was what I would do.

In fact I soon developed a keen interest, as I think nearly everybody does who becomes involved with children's books. Here was a new field of discovery, here was a new excitement, and here was a new and unique stimulus, because whereas the experience of other arts had led me back no farther than to my own awakening at the age of twenty, here was something that led me straight back to Sam. Here was something that brought my two selves together in what turned out to be a complicated creative tangle. Before long, either Sam alive in John Rowe Townsend was writing a book, or John Rowe Townsend was writing a book for Sam, or both. The result was *Gumble's Yard*. It is a story about poor children in a district not unlike the one I grew up in, fending for themselves after they had been abandoned by the grownups who were supposed to be looking after them.

In my time, I have listed the incidents that supplied immediate inspiration for that first book. Probably every piece of fiction ever written has a large number of major and minor external sources. I have actually

W. T. Mars's pen-and-ink sketch of Kevin (center) and two other characters from Trouble in the Jungle *(originally* Gumble's Yard), *copyright © 1969 by J. B. Lippincott Company, is reproduced by permission of J. B. Lippincott Company.*

noted a forgotten source of *Gumble's Yard* in the process of preparing this talk. Somewhere behind it there must have lain an unconscious or half-conscious recollection of *Not a Sparrow Falls*, that Victorian story about waifs on the streets of London.

While I was working on *Gumble's Yard* I thought—that is, I, John Rowe Townsend, university graduate, journalist, and reviewer thought— I was trying to write a book that would say something to, about, and on behalf of ordinary poor children, children like Sam. I thought I was producing some kind of counterblast to the bourgeois smugness which, rightly or wrongly, I found pervading a good deal of British children's literature at that time. And plenty of other people concurred with me in thinking that that was what I was trying to do. It was years before I realized that however worthy my conscious motives might be, they were not the heart of the matter. I wrote *Gumble's Yard* because it was there inside me, wanting to come out; and it was there inside me because of Sam. No Sam, no book. I suppose that without Sam I might still have written critical works, but I would never have written my early fiction, and perhaps I would not have written fiction at all.

So there we are. It is nearly twenty years since I first became involved with children's books and a little over fifteen since publication of *Gumble's Yard.* In these last fifteen years I have been at work fairly steadily, sometimes wearing one hat as author, sometimes wearing the other as critic, never putting either of them aside for very long. I should perhaps make it clear that in a professional context I use the word *criticism* as shorthand for a whole range of activities, some of which you may think ought not to go under so dignified a name. The critic's hat, so to speak, is a somewhat battered and shapeless piece of headgear, covering such activities as reviewing, review-editing, and the production of ad hoc newspaper pieces on children's books, as well as more formal critical writing. As an author I have produced about a dozen books of fiction; as a critic, besides writing regularly for the *Guardian,* I have done a book of essays on contemporary children's writers and a historical survey of English-language children's literature. I have also, under a third and smaller hat, edited an anthology of modern poetry, which was an outstanding instance in my life of doing something with enormous pleasure and getting paid for it in the bargain. For better or worse, I think I am the only person in England who writes a substantial amount *about* children's books and is also fairly well known as a writer *of* them. I think there are not many such hybrids in the United States either. Perhaps other authors have more sense than to be in business as critics, and other critics have more sense than to be in business as authors. It could be so.

So far, I have tried to take a brief look at the springs of creative and critical activities. My sketch of the early world of Sam was, of course, an effort to take you as close as I could to one of those springs. I have also attempted to explain how I became engaged in the two activities. In the space that remains to me I would like to discuss some other aspects, most of which describe the interplay between the two roles.

For myself, I find that in the actual performance of literary tasks—the writing of a novel on the one hand or a review or essay on the other—it becomes more and more necessary to prevent author and critic from getting in each other's way. I try to be one thing at a time. An author is an instinctual creature, a creature plunging into areas of deep and often disturbing emotion, a person making use of creative sources which can be very powerful and which in the nature of things he cannot fully understand. It does him or her no good—at least in the phase of primary creation—to stop and inspect himself, to pull himself up by the roots, so to speak, to see how he is getting on. It does him no good to compare his work in progress with the work of other people, which can be desperately discouraging, since there is always somebody who has done something rather similar much better.

No, the author must just be left to get on with it until the rough size and shape of the work are known. *Then* he must become his own relentless critic. But I think the self-criticism of an author getting his own work into shape is a quite different process from the critical appraisal of the work of others. It is still largely instinctual, because the author knows or should know in his bones what he can and cannot do; the solutions he is seeking are the right solutions for *him*, not the right solutions in any absolute sense. I know authors who perform this process of self-criticism and creative response with extraordinary brilliance but who are quite at a loss if they have to discuss the work of somebody else; their whole process of thought is directed to the practicalities of creation rather than to appraisal. And there is nothing wrong with this; it is probably a strength.

I myself, when venturing—I hope with due humility—to wear my critic's hat, try to achieve a kind of sympathetic detachment that would be impossible to me as an author. I know what authors are; I know they are often ultrasensitive, overemotional, too much involved with their work to see it clearly. I know this from experience, because it is how I am myself. I have feelings about my own work so strong and irrational that they might seem more appropriate to a jealous lover than to a novelist. I am breathtakingly vulnerable: I live my books fiercely while writing them, usually react against them as soon as they are finished, am immensely dejected or incensed by an adverse review, and am delighted by a favorable one, even if in any other context I might not greatly value the opinion of the reviewer (I feel he is showing promise at last).

As an author I suffer from the well-known disease of author's paranoia. I can easily convince myself that a large section of the book world is actuated by jealousy or malice toward me, and I am inclined to feel that if two reviewers both condemn my book it is a conspiracy and if the same reviewer pans two books in succession it is a vendetta. Yet as soon as I put my critic's hat on, I can and do switch off this turmoil. I truly believe— and I say this after searching self-examination—that as a critic I am dispassionate. The fact that I dislike John Doe intensely as a person, whereas Richard Roe has been a friend of mine for years, will not cause me to write less favorably about John Doe's book, or more favorably about Richard Roe's, or, indeed, the reverse. Impartiality is a matter of professional ethics, and after long practice, it becomes automatic, it does not have to be struggled for. But, of course, one has to have—and I would like to think that I have—a temperament which is capable of being dispassionate and at the same time receptive, capable of approaching every new book in a spirit of hope and excitement, of being always ready to enjoy yet never without discrimination.

You will have gathered from this and from my remarks made a few minutes ago that in my own practice I favor appreciative, exploratory, and expository criticism rather than the dissection, and far rather than the destruction, of books. I have never greatly cared for laying works of art out of the slab and taking them to pieces; it is all too easy to finish up with nothing but the dead remnants. True, one needs to grasp the anatomy of the work, rather as, if you will forgive an inexact analogy, a sculptor or a surgeon needs to understand human anatomy to know what he or she is about. Nevertheless, it is the living body that one is concerned with, the thing that breathes and moves.

There is not, in my opinion, only one valid critical style; I find it strange that so many people seem to think there should be. I think one needs different kinds of critics, and the kind I have mentioned is the kind I am. But I spoke at length about critical standards for children's literature in my Arbuthnot lecture five years ago, and I do not propose to go further into that vexed and confused subject now. I will only remark that I am still a little skeptical about theoretical critical frameworks. I am inclined to think that as with teaching so with criticism: just as almost any method will work if used by a good teacher and any method will fail if used by a poor teacher, so I believe that what matters in criticism is not the theory or even whether the critic has a theory but primarily the personal quality of the critic.

I suggested in my Arbuthnot lecture that a good critic of children's books would be sensitive, would have a sense of balance and rightness, would respond. He would, I said, "have a wide knowledge of literature in general as well as of children and their literature, and probably a respectable acquaintance with cinema, theater, television, and current affairs. That is asking a lot of him but not too much. The critic (this is the heart of the matter) counts more than the criteria."

I did not, incidentally, say that I myself measured up to this prescription; indeed, I knew all too well that I did not, and I know all too well now that I still do not. But I stand by what I said. I notice, however, that I did not say that the critic should be an author, or even that it was a good thing for him to be an author.

Well, should he be? Is it a good thing? Certainly there are some who think that authors should keep their fingers out of the critical pie. As it happens, the great critics of English literature at large have mostly been practitioners: Dryden, Dr. Johnson, Coleridge, Matthew Arnold, T. S. Eliot—all of these were no less eminent as creative writers than as critics. I cite them with great diffidence, aware that I am looking up to a level infinitely far above my own, but at least I think I may be allowed to mention them as a clear indication that creative writing and criticism are not actually incompatible. Indeed, although the roles of author and critic are quite separate, one should probably beware of constructing a false antithesis. The production of imaginative literature is clearly creative, but it should not be supposed that criticism is therefore uncreative. A good piece of critical writing is a good piece of writing.

On a down-to-earth, everyday level, I would say that at least a person who has written books should have an awareness of the methods by which technical problems are handled—an eye for the corner that has been cut or the chance missed—that I don't think he or she could quite have without this experience. I was reviewer before I was author, and I remember vividly how much more I felt able to perceive about the books I was reviewing when eventually I had written one myself. Yet, cannot the things that really matter about a book he grasped perfectly well by a sensitive, intelligent, well-read, aware person who is not an author? Only one answer is possible to that question. Yes, of course they can.

My belief, on balance, is that being an author is a great help, provided you have it in you to be a critic, but that it does not in itself make you one. You need the critical temperament, the critical sensibility. One thing I will risk saying, however, is that a good critic must be able to write. It is not necessary to be able to write a novel or a poem or a play, but if you cannot produce an effective piece of writing—if your review or whatever it may be is not itself an effective piece of writing—then to my mind you are disqualified. I do not feel that someone incapable of using language with precision and sensitivity is capable of judging its use by others.

Today, incidentally, the critic of children's literature requires, in addition to the qualities I have mentioned, a certain toughness of spirit to pursue his or her own independent and unspectacular line when faced with pressure groups demanding the application of very crude criteria indeed. The fact that a critic or, for that matter, an author or editor may have supported a cause all through his life will not avail him if he refuses to look at books with a propagandist's eye. He is likely to be branded as an enemy not only of the methods used to advance the cause but of the cause itself. Here I can only say we must hold fast to our principles. If we are swayed in all directions by the prevailing ideological winds, we shall receive and we shall deserve contempt rather than respect.

One advantage I myself find as critic in being also an author—and this is one that counts enormously in the matter of children's books— is that as author I speak to, hear from, and meet children. If I were only a critic, then, since I am not a teacher or a children's librarian, I would find it difficult to have regular contact with children other than my own children and their friends, all of whom are growing up rapidly. And although I think the critic of children's books must judge by his own standards and not by some specially modified standard, I also think he must judge, as the writer must write, with proper awareness that children are going to read the books. There are as many traps, both for authors and critics, in the ivory tower as in the commercial marketplace.

On the whole, for myself, I find the two occupations fit quite well side by side in one person's working life. There are advantages in the ancillary jobs—going around giving talks, editing a review page—not the least in that they get me out of my chair and into the world outside. There are, however, corresponding drawbacks. With the variety of jobs I perform as a critic, there always seems to be something requiring urgent attention, and it is very easy for authorship to become residual. My own book becomes the thing I am going to work on if and when I can ever clear my desk. As in fact authorship is demanding—and I personally need to plunge in deep and stay down a long time—it is possible to go far too long without getting around to it and thereby lose impetus. Even giving lectures can be self-defeating if taken too far. You are so busy going around and talking that you do not have time to do the thing that makes people want you to go and talk.

Which job do I regard as more important? This is a question I am asked quite frequently, and it takes various forms. Often people say, "Do you primarily think of yourself as an author or as a critic?" Sometimes I sidestep this one and say, "Neither; I am just that old-fashioned thing, a journeyman of letters." But when really pressed, I will admit that above all else I aspire to be an author. That is what gives me the greatest creative satisfaction. And in terms of literature in general, I feel very strongly that it is a higher calling to be a writer than to be one of the innumerable middlemen who come between writers—living or dead—and the public. Perhaps this is the author in me raising his paranoic head, but I do sometimes find it depressing that what I call the English literature industry can support huge numbers of academics and others in relative comfort, whereas the actual writer is lucky if he can scrape a living by working all the hours God provides.

In children's literature, however—at least in Britain—the position is by no means the same as in literature at large. I am not anxious that we should have an enormous children's literature industry. But the current problem is not overdevelopment of the machine; it is the opposite. We have, I believe, a great quantity of excellent imaginative literature for children being produced, but we are not very good at bringing it to the children. One of the main reasons is that most parents and many teachers know little about children's books and care less. And the reason behind that is that children's literature has no academic and not much educational status. So it could be argued that as a writer in Britain, unless you are producing masterpieces—and we cannot all be producing masterpieces all the time—you are merely adding teaspoonfuls to an already overflowing bucket. On the other hand, a person who is spreading awareness of children's literature among parents and others or who is educating people to take the subject more seriously is doing something more obviously needed at the present time.

I have used the words *critic* and *criticism* rather loosely today, but now I want to use them a little more strictly. I believe that the serious criticism of children's books today is an extremely worthwhile activity: first, for its own sake, because the books are there; second, to strengthen a consensus which is weak at present because there are not many critical minds at work

Beverly Brodsky McDermott's illustration from John Rowe Townsend's Forest of the Night, *copyright © 1975 by J. B. Lippincott Company, is reprinted by permission of J. B. Lippincott Company.*

in this field; third, as a discipline and stimulus to authors and publishers; fourth, to establish and make known the excellence of those books which are so good that they ought to be introduced to all children who could possibly be capable of enjoying them; and fifth, because if children's literature is to receive the recognition and acceptance which it desperately needs at higher educational levels, it will have to receive and be seen to receive the same kind of critical treatment as literature in general. Children's literature cannot expect simultaneously to be viewed with an indulgent eye and to be taken seriously. Incidentally, however, if children's books do come to face serious professional criticism, as I think they should, there will be shocks for many of us. At present, high reputations are frequently enjoyed by books which were written conscientiously and with good intentions but which possess no real literary merit. We shall have to accept not only that popularity is not enough—that is accepted already, to such an extent, indeed, that a popular book is apt to be unduly suspect—but that worthiness is not enough, either.

In summary, I get more pleasure, more creative satisfaction from being an author; my efforts as critic are directed more by a sense of what needs doing. I rate the critical function highly and am concerned that we have little in either of our countries that could be described as the serious criticism of children's literature. I would like to see more. So far as it is within my capabilities, I would like to contribute to it. And there *is* a satisfaction in criticism. As I said earlier, the distinction between creative and critical work is far from total. I am sure that a good critic is more truly creative than a bad author.

As for reputation, I really do not know, but I suspect from a selfish point of view that the attempt to be both author and critic detracts from one's standing as either. People do not quite trust a player in the capacity of referee; conversely, they do not really believe that the referee can be much use as a performer. And if the referee does appear as player, there are a good many around who remember past verdicts of his with which they did not agree and who would not be too sorry to give a verdict against *him*.

Yet, even as I say that, I feel the critic's hat sliding once more from my head. Is it not now the author who speaks, under the usual pressure of author's paranoia? Perhaps it is. Have I not been treated as generously as I deserve, and probably more generously? Perhaps I have. I must remember the golden rule which a former British prime minister, Stanley Baldwin, put before budding politicians: "Never complain. Never explain." And the still more golden rule—if it is possible to be more golden—for all who are serious about their writing, whether creative or critical: "Shut up and get on with it. You've a long way to go before dark."

Eleanor (Butler) Cameron was born in Winnipeg, Manitoba, in 1912 and moved to California as a young child. She attended the University of California and the Art Center School, Los Angeles. In 1934 she married Ian Stuart Cameron and they have one son. She worked in Los Angeles public and school libraries, 1930–42, and later as a reference and research librarian for business concerns. Mrs. Cameron won a *Boston Globe–Horn Book Award* in 1971 and the National Book Award in 1974. Her home today is in Pebble Beach, California.

Books for children:
The Wonderful Flight to the Mushroom Planet (1954), *Stowaway to the Mushroom Planet* (1956), *Mr. Bass' Planetoid* (1958), *The Terrible Churnadryne* (1959), *A Mystery for Mr. Bass* (1960), *The Mysterious Christmas Shell* (1961), *The Beast with the Magical Horn* (1963), *A Spell Is Cast* (1964), *Time and Mr. Bass* (1967), *A Room Made of Windows* (1971), *The Court of the Stone Children* (1973), *To the Green Mountains* (1975), and *Julia and the Hand of God* (1977).

For adults:
The Unheard Music (1950) and *The Green and Burning Tree: On the Writing and Enjoyment of Children's Books* (1969).

This lecture was given at the Library of Congress on November 14, 1977, in honor of National Children's Book Week, and was published in April 1978 in the *Quarterly Journal of the Library of Congress.*

Into Something Rich and Strange
Of Dreams, Art, and the Unconscious

by Eleanor Cameron

Full fathom five thy father lies;
 Of his bones are coral made:
Those are pearls that were his eyes:
 Nothing of him that doth fade,
Both doth suffer a sea-change
 Into something rich and strange.
 Sea-nymphs hourly ring his knell:
 Hark! now I hear them—ding, dong, bell.

Composed almost four hundred years ago, these words, for me, express symbolically how the unconscious absorbs our experiences, buries them, turns them through slow transformations over the years—during which time they may, in their original form, be entirely forgotten—into treasure which emerges from the depths to be used by the artist in ways he could never have foretold. So perfect is this symbolism, one would think that Shakespeare, that majestical sub-creator (to use Tolkien's word), knew precisely what is now known about the unconscious: how it is a fathomless sea, perhaps literally boundless, holding innumerable experiences, both individual and racial, knowledges, intuitions the conscious is not aware of, and how it nurtures them, turning bones into coral and eyes into pearls, before releasing them to the thinking mind.

Did he ever wonder, Mr. William Shakespeare, with a kind of awe, where it all came from, scene after scene that assaulted his imagination as if he had lived each one? Did he ever ask himself what there was in him that compelled this profusion and held him slave to it? For the writer, or any artist, literally cannot help himself. There would seem to be some ruling power in him that drives him to create and gives him the stuff of creation. Charlotte Bronte writes, in her preface to the second edition of

153

Wuthering Heights, when she was troubled over Emily's characterization of Heathcliff, "But this I know: the writer who possesses the creative gift owns something of which he is not always master—something that, at times, strangely wills and works for itself."[1] Consider Flaubert's sense of doubleness when he tells of having to get up and fetch a handkerchief because he had been so moved by his own writing that tears were streaming down his face. There was the Flaubert who wept, and the one who had made Flaubert weep, two deeply united and yet, as it were, separate entities, so that one could think of the other as Faulkner did of his creating self in writing to his friend Joan Williams: "And I now realize for the first time what an amazing gift I had: Uneducated in every formal sense, without even very literate companions, yet to have made the thing I made. I don't know where it came from. I don't know why God or the gods, or whoever it is, selected me to be the vessel. Believe me, this is not humility, false modesty; it is simply amazement."[2]

Flaubert and Faulkner must often, I should think, have reflected on "where it came from," the source of their art. Whether Shakespeare did or did not, we shall never know, or know what he called his teeming storehouse, but we can at least say that he did not call it the unconscious.

From The Court of the Stone Children *by Eleanor Cameron, illustration by Trina Schart Hyman. Courtesy of E. P. Dutton and Co., Inc.*

When did that word come into use, I asked myself, and picked up the book lying by my side and opened it at random to page five, where my eye lit at once upon the reply. "Each of them (sleep, the imagination, dream, the Unconscious, art, genius, death) has been an agelong problem; for even the term, the Unconscious, used for the first time in this sense so recently as 1909, was only thereby made specific."[3]

I use Jung's term *the unconscious* rather than Freud's *the subconscious*—for Freud a dark basement of repressed desires—because like de la Mare, who told me so instantaneously what I wanted to know, I responded to Jung's concept. For Jung, the unconscious was a world as vital and real as the conscious world of the individual, at least half of his total being, and far wider and richer than that of his thinking ego. From the unconscious, says Jung, comes advice and guidance that no one or nothing else can give; its language and its protagonists are symbols, and its way of communication is through dreams, or the creations of artists, or the fairy tales, myths, and legends that have come down to us over thousands of years from the memories of our race. All are connected. Carson McCullers spoke of writing, for her, as the flowering dream. "After months of confusion and labor," she said, "when the idea has flowered, the collusion is Divine. It always comes from the Subconscious and cannot be controlled."[4]

Dreams like art, like myth and legend and fairy tale, speak in poetic images. For example: My husband has been ill, and because of a doctor's mistaken prescription for therapy, which has resulted in increased pain, he says, "He has ruined me." That night I dream that I am in a ruin and turn to speak to my husband but he is no longer there; he has vanished, and I go over to a fallen wall to hunt for him, but I have lost him. I then see him on my right in front of a fireplace in a long, narrow, roofless room. He is sitting in a yoga position as if given over to contemplation. I go to him and he turns into a small oriental figure of fired red clay like the Japanese figures on top of my bookcase, still sitting in a position of calmness and serenity, of meditation, as though trying to attain wisdom. But now suddenly he becomes a little girl of nine or ten and I realize that she is to be my child, and that I have been given her in place of my husband. We are going along a crowded street in Los Angeles and she looks around in amazement and says that she somehow recognizes this street though she cannot remember ever having been here before. I tell her that of course she recognizes it, as she is in reality my husband, who used to live and work here in Los Angeles. She bursts into tears and I try to comfort her by saying that I will love and care for her and that she is not to worry about anything. And I myself know that only through my own patience and devotion will she be transformed back into my husband.

What does it remind you of? Yes, a fairy tale. In the true fairy tale, as in the true dream, says Edward Book in his life of Hans Christian Andersen, there lies always the force of a dark message.

I have felt for a long time that my dreams are a significant part of my life, and have written down those I could recall with startling clarity. Some have stayed with me since childhood; the earliest I have remembered in every detail since I was nine. And I can see now how two series of dreams point, each series in its own way, to what must be an unconscious preoccupation: a sense of lostness, of which certain dreams of de la Mare's also spoke to him. I was comforted to know that he too had had this sense, though why he had it he never told, so far as I know, and I am mystified about myself. In my conscious life I have never felt overwhelmingly lost, only as if I am continually searching. At times struggle is involved (or is this only in connection with writing? I can't be sure; but then writing can be a search for meaning, which can go deeper and deeper as the years pass), so that possibly this is my "lostness": not having yet found what it is I am searching for. But I would add that I need the struggle and the search; life would be pale without them, and I am accustomed to living with uncertainty.

Cathy, in *Wuthering Heights*, says, "I've dreamt in my life dreams that have stayed with me forever after, and changed my ideas; they've gone through and through me, like wine through water, and altered the colour of my mind."[5] De la Mare says that that is surely the voice of Emily Bronte herself, and that with some qualifications, it had been his own experience. Yes, and mine, though I had not realized how much dreams meant to me until I remembered how often I have introduced them into the texture of my books, not as embroidery, something that could be picked out, leaving the weave intact, but as a necessary part of the whole. There are two premonitory dreams in *The Court of the Stone Children*, inextricably knit into the pattern of meaning because of the central idea that if time is an eternal present, as I believe it to be, precognition is inevitable for those whose narrow human slits of awareness are widened on certain occasions so that they know ahead that which, according to human time sense, still has not happened. There is, also, near the beginning of the book, Nina's dream of lostness in which, trying again and again to telephone home, she exclaims to the telephone operator that time is passing, to which the cool voice replies, "Time is a river without banks. If there are no banks, there is nothing for time to pass." Chagall's painting *Time Is a River without Banks* hangs in the museum where Nina has seen for the first time the girl who has come out of time to fulfill her own dream of precognition and to inadvertently bring about Nina's. And when Helena Staynes, one of the curators, says to Nina, "And what do you make of the painting?" Nina answers, "I don't know. I wish I knew what it meant. It's like a fairy tale— or a dream...." And Mrs. Staynes says, "Yes, it is. You've hit it exactly.... If you try to make sense of it by means of logic, you can't because Chagall is always remembering his childhood and so, probably, his childhood dreams, and the feeling of losing himself in fairy tales."

A Room Made of Windows, *illustrated by Trina Schart Hyman. Copyright 1971. By permission of Little, Brown and Company in association with The Atlantic Monthly Press.*

To the Green Mountains begins with a dream, Kath's, of coming back in summer to a mountainside on which—and now, even as I sit here writing these words, the repetition strikes me for the first time—"she has an intimation not only that she is alone in this vast solitude but that she is lost." Here I am again. I keep saying it and keep saying it, in one way or another: I seem to make opportunities for saying it. "An intimation that she is lost," but "that she has climbed this path before and has come to her longed-for destination. No, she cannot say that. Rather, she has looked down upon it, though always the moment of actual arrival has been denied her." And with Kath once again looking down on her grandmother's house, down there in the valley, and the loved figure she can never seem to reach, she wakes as always, just before beginning the descent.

Two more dreams come into the book, both, now that I come to think of them, of lostness: the first of Kath being abandoned in a city theater by Tiss, the black girl whose valued friendship she has lost at the time of the dream, and the second of finding herself at her grandmother's house at last but realizing that there is no one there: "The garden was all gone to seed. There were no curtains, not even any blinds, and the porch was dusty and littered with old papers and dead leaves, and nobody answered the door." A terrible kind of lostness: to reach a place after years of effort where someone much loved has been waiting, only to find that that person has not been there for a very long time, died, or gone away, and no one has told us when, or where, or why.

Near the beginning of *A Room Made of Windows* twelve-year-old Julia takes from her desk drawer an unfinished story, a dream she has written down and now tries to continue as best she can, but it will not round itself out. It ends, simply because it will go no further, with the man she feels she knows in some intense and personal way going out of the tall, dark house into which she and a mob of unknown people have pursued him. He turns and hands her his mask, whereupon she takes it and in terror slams the door against him, but cannot lock it because the lock has been broken by the mob who forced it open to follow him with some evil intent. At the book's end, Julia realizes the man was her dead father and it is Rhiannon Moore, the musician who lives next door, who interprets her dream and tells her what will be meaningful to her later as a writer—having been handed on her father's complex qualities of willfulness and passion and persistence and intensity in the symbolic form of his mask.

This dream of Julia's is based on an exceedingly long and complex one I had as a child only a little older than Julia, and that I wrote down and still have in my possession. A simplified version is given in the novel because my dream would have taken up a disproportionate amount of space and I did not want to obscure the essential details. At the end of my youthful account of it, I noted: "I cannot explain the plot—for there *is* a distinct plot woven therein. . . . I can think of nothing in the past that has happened to me to connect with this strange dream."

What has astonished me in connection with my own discoveries of a preoccupation with lostness is the case of the dreams of Walter de la Mare, surely one of the kindest and gentlest men who ever lived. Yet, as one discovers upon reading his stories and poems for both children and adults, there is more often than not a haunting sense of the powers of evil, an obsession with death and ghosts and graveyards, with people like Seton's aunt who prefers the company of the dead and who absorbs the living as a mantis absorbs insects, and others like the dreamy, absentminded grandmother whose old oak chest swallows up the seven children in "The Riddle" and they are never heard of again.

De la Mare dreamed that though he had no reason for murdering her, he had killed his sister, then claimed that he had not. When he went back to the upstairs room where the murder had taken place, he did not recognize it; yet he went immediately to a chest, opened the bottom drawer, and groped about for the clothes he had been wearing to prove they were clean and that he was therefore innocent. But when he withdrew his hand, it was sticky with blood. He related also dreams of two other murders, both of which he committed. In the second he saw an old woman sitting in a chair. To the side of the chair was a door with a space beneath, and he knew that beyond was a hall where there were people who would hear any audible movements. Nevertheless, with no sense of revulsion, he leaned forward and plunged a knife into her, then noticed, when the blood began to flow, that it would run along the sloping floor toward the space under the door. At once he found a cloth and a leather bucket (why a medieval object, one wonders) and began to sop it up, then turned abruptly at some sound and knocked the bucket over. Now he looked out at the apparently drawn sky beyond the tall Gothic windows and noted the red in it—precisely the color of the spilled blood making its way toward the door—whereupon the dream ended. How could anyone explain that dream, demanded de la Mare. Who had constructed a story at once so complex and so coherent?

There you have it again, the intimation of some power at work, in this case giving the dreamer his dream; the ghostly provider for the creating mind as Faulkner implied concerning the novelist and what he writes: some larger unconscious, possibly, as Jung believed, speaking to the individual unconscious. Graham Greene asks, in his novel *The End of the Affair,* "I say 'one chooses' with the inaccurate pride of the professional writer who—when he has been seriously noted at all—has been praised for his technical ability; but do I in fact of my own will chose that black wet January night on the Common in 1946, the sight of Henry Miles slanting across the wide river of rain, or did these images choose me?"[6] The Bushman, cocooned in his ancient wisdom, says of human life that "There is a dreamer dreaming us," and Joan Aiken, at the end of her 1971 Library of Congress lecture, tells of a marvelously complex and coherent dream of which she says, "I didn't have it, it had me. Words won't convey its blazing intensity."[7]

Three experiences of Graham Greene's are curious exceptions to Jung's belief that dreams are extremely personal expressions of the unconscious, meaningful to the dreamer alone, rather than artistic expressions, and that only the conscious can, through the process of discrimination, turn what the unconscious gives us into art. Greene notes of his story "The Root of All Evil" that he dreamed the entire thing and woke laughing, and that he did not change a single incident, nor did he after dreaming "A Sense of Reality." In *A Burnt-out Case*, identification with character went so far that Greene actually dreamed Querry's dream, about which he is certain because the memories and symbols and associations of the dream belong specifically to Querry, so that the next morning Greene could put the dream without change into his novel, where it bridged a gap that for days he had been unable to close.

Jung believed that we do not dream our dreams, but that they happened to us, as experiences happen to us, which would perhaps explain the complexity and coherence and sophistication of that childhood dream of mine about the mask, seemingly too old for me, a version of which wound its way into *Room.* Does, then, what we create as novelists "happen to us" in the same sense if we draw upon the depths and not merely from the surface? Elizabeth Bowen has written of Katherine Mansfield that "there were times when [she] believed a story to have a volition of its own—she seems to stand back, watching it take form. Yet this could not happen apart from her; the story draws her steadily into herself."[8]

The question of what we create happening to us may find a response in several facts. First, what we ourselves write can instruct us, give us revelations about that which we were not previously aware of; symbols and themes can later be discovered that we did not realize were there; and the completed work can say something to us that we did not realize it would say. Second, characters are discovered. They are given, either gradually revealing themselves as the work progresses, or presenting themselves entire as though they had been waiting, existing like living beings "full fathom five." Only if one were to construct creatures to fit a plot, to be used purely for the purpose of plot, would one be aware of mechanically putting them together out of bits and pieces, all of which would have nothing to do with the unconscious. Third, like the dreams of Walter de la Mare and Joan Aiken and my child and adult self, what we write can seem to coalesce into amazingly complex and yet perfectly coherent patterns without conscious effort on our part—that is, the coherent complexity itself does not cause conscious struggle: all seems to weave together, sometimes with astonishing rapidity, as though the weaving had already been accomplished. Fourth, the unconscious has the ability to recall to the conscious mind, under pressure of the author's writing about a certain time and place, scenes and events long forgotten.

Concerning the ability of the writer's work to instruct him, one of the most remarkable instances of this is brought out by Mark Schorer in a few paragraphs on Emily Bronte. He makes no mention of the unconscious, however, Quite the contrary! He speaks of Emily's somnambulistic excess, generated by years of writing about a world of "monstrous passion, of dark and gigantic emotional and nervous energy,"[9] that was for Emily the ideal world. It was one she had lived in since childhood, the natural atmosphere of her most private being as set down in those interminable stories she called her Gondal Saga.

What Emily wanted to do in *Wuthering Heights,* according to Schorer, was to persuade us of "the moral magnificence of . . . unmoral passion."[10] She wanted us to accept at their own valuation such demonic beings as Heathcliff and Cathy. But then, says Schorer, because of a "mere mechanical device"—technique—and because "technique objectifies,"[11] the novelist Emily Bronte revealed to the girl Emily the absurdities of her own conception. Her technique, as the novel progressed, exposed those absurdities for what they are, so that in the end we are persuaded that it is not Emily Bronte who was mistaken in the estimate of her characters, but they who were mistaken in their estimate of themselves. Technique alone, Schorer believes, taught Emily that the theme of the moral magnificence of unmoral passion is a false one, and that it was not what her material meant as art.

Now I can well believe that Emily Bronte's novel instructed her as to the truth. But I am not willing to believe that it was merely technique, merely "a mechanical device" that persuaded Emily of the hopelessness of idealizing a world of demonic passions, together with its values, as she had at first thought to do.

The heart of the matter, it seems to me, the secret of what happened to Emily Bronte, is that her aesthetic intuition, her unconscious, call it what you will, chose as place for her novel not the imaginary world of Gondal she had lived in as child and adolescent, but Haworth country. And with that choice, because Emily knew Haworth country and Haworth people as she knew her own home and family, she was compelled to plunge into reality rather than, once again, into fantasy as she had done in the Gondal Saga. Whereupon the full force of her conscious and unconscious knowledge of the peculiar Haworth breed of human creature forced truth into the final pages of *Wuthering Heights,* despite the fact that Heathcliff remains a melodramatic figure throughout the novel. And that truth is that unmoral passion could not possibly call up a tale of moral magnificence, but could only resulve into, as Schorer puts it, the "devastating spectacle of human waste"[12] that *Wuthering Heights* turned out to be.

Glenway Wescott believes that writers of fiction learn from their material as the work unfolds, learn from "the phantoms of memory and from the powers and accidents of art."[13] They do indeed learn from their own material, but I think that a good many of "the powers and accidents of art" are flowerings of the creative unconscious, sudden, inexplicable revelations that can make the work of writing a novel an utterly absorbing adventure into hitherto unknown territory of the self. Ursula Le Guin wrote, at the time she was working on *The Farthest Shore,* "I finally finished a second draft last Friday, but have been fairly cross-eyed since. I have been working on a third volume—a trequel?—of the *Wizard,* and what happened was that Ged had the bit between his teeth, as it were, and started telling me things I didn't know, and doing things I hadn't intended him to do, and he changed the whole end of the book, and fouled me up good and proper. Damned strong-minded wizard."[14]

I myself have felt the power of what I can only call some kind of ordained pattern which had, apparently, worked itself out during the years *To the Green Mountains* was developing to that stage where it could finally be composed in words. At two points in the writing of the novel I felt the power of inevitability. Apparently there was one way to tell the story and one only, and I, the author, could not change it. Well, of course I could have changed it! I could have done anything I wanted with my own work, but my judgment, my self, knew that it would be unwise. First of all, I had thought that from the beginning (and that was about thirty years ago, when I wrote *Mountains* as a one-act play) that Tissie, the black woman, would come up to Elizabeth Rule's hotel room with a straight razor hidden in her pocket, intent, out of jealousy and hatred, on threatening Elizabeth and possibly in her rage doing Elizabeth actual harm. But what was my astonishment upon arriving at that chapter to find that Tissie was not going up to Elizabeth's room, Tissie having revealed herself to me as not at all the kind of woman who would threaten another human being with a razor or any other instrument. Yet all this time, for years, she had been supposed to. There were a good many things I realized I did not know about my novel, but that one thing I thought I knew. However, she could not possibly, could she? I said in answer to myself. No, she could not, the point being that the razor incident (something I had known about that actually happened) was an act I had taken for granted I could give Tissie. But it was not, I discovered, an act she had shown me she was capable of and would do, and there is a world of difference there. The Tissie given me, my Tissie (who must have been there inside of me the entire time as a completed person, so that she could gradually reveal herself in one aspect after another under the pressure of various circumstances), was a woman of high passion, yes; full of delight in living, prone to laughter, to dancing, imitating, acting, teasing, but with, nevertheless, a most private, withdrawn place deep within that complex self of hers, a place of dignified reserve. So that when the world of her husband Grant's wholehearted devotion to her becomes divided because of the lawbooks Elizabeth Rule, in an act of blind good faith, has given him, Tissie does not go up to Elizabeth's room with a straight razor. Once it becomes clear to her just how the books are going to affect her life with Grant, she simply never has anything to do with Elizabeth Rule again, nor with Kath, the child who loved her and who had loved, above anything else, being with her. A friendship, unquestioning, and trusting all these years, simply vanishes as if it had never been. That was the truth about Tissie, and she revealed it to me.

Second, I did not want Tissie to die. Before I knew I did not want her to, I had envisioned the train scene, where she is run over, with great vividness. I saw it; I heard the words of Kath and of Aunt Maud and Uncle Tede, who did not want her to come near Tissie, though Tissie wants to speak to Kath. I could have handled it, I believe, and without either sentimentality or crudity. There was no reason why there should not have been such a scene—children have been present at railway accidents times without number. But then I discovered that I did not want Tissie killed. Not necessary, I tried to tell myself, not at all necessary. But I could not change it, though I ran around mentally, like a squirrel in a box, trying to find a way out of my dread necessity. And this is what I mean by inevitability, a sense suddenly apparently lacking in William Mayne, usually a superb artist, when he wrote one ending for the British edition of *The Jersey Shore* and another for the American. Perhaps he had not waited long enough for his unconscious to tell him the right ending. Certainly, for me, the American (written later) is the right and good one. In fact, so strongly did I feel this that I somehow knew that the main character Art would be killed in battle after the written part of the story was over, so that I was not in the least surprised when I was told by his editor that Mayne himself had, in fact, known that Art would be killed beyond the novel's end. I never for an instant felt this in reading the final chapter of the British edition.

At any rate, Tissie had to die. And I cannot tell why except that partly it was the final piece in the pattern which I see now, on looking back, as one of "downhill all the way,' step by fateful step. And I could not bring Kath onto the scene of the train accident because Uncle Tede would not let me. He came toward Kath with his hands out and turned her and led her back the way she had come with Aunt Maud following after.

Another thing that was discovered was a second theme. I thought I had only one: that of the necessity for human beings to face what is, not to fool themselves, which was why, after finishing the book, I put Alfred Kazin's words at the beginning: "facing a fact until it divides you through the heart and marrow like a sword." Now I do not mean that I wrote *Mountains* in order to demonstrate this theme. I wrote the book because I had a story to tell and could not rest until I had told it, and told it in a certain way. Then as I went along, the theme became apparent. I felt it there. And also I began to feel something else, just as strongly, or even more strongly: that I was writing out my abhorrence of possession, writing out a deep belief in a personal eleventh commandment: thou shalt not try to possess another. No review brought out either theme, but they are there, and when a friend asked me, "But, Eleanor, what were you trying to *say?* and later began telling me that she had had to leave her husband because he had insisted on trying to control every detail of her life, she stared at me and laughed. Of course! But I had not seen, until quite some time after the book was finished, how many instances—in the case of couple after couple, husband and wife, sister and sister, mother and son—exemplified, each in its own way, various kinds of possession, successful, attempted, and failed.

It is my books that have shown me that this theme of possession or attempted possession of one human being by another, and the unhappiness and frustration and bitter resentment it can bring, is apparently a preoccupation of mine. In *Room* the theme grew out of place because it was in Berkeley that I, myself, was a selfish child. Julia, in her youthful blindness, tries to possess her mother, and it is not until she is faced with her mother's words—that for her, children are not enough— that Julia is forced into the knowledge that she must allow her mother her own life, must allow her to be her own person and not simply an extension of Julia, existing solely for Julia's comfort and satisfaction. I suppose you could say that it was necessary that the windows of Julia's room, where she made up her stories and looked out onto the public world from the isolation of her private one, become windows of the self through which she must observe others as individuals with desires as passionate and needful of fulfillment as her own. I did not see the symbolism of the windows until it was pointed out to me later, and it was my editor who saw the room as symbolic of Julia's closed self-centeredness. The fact is, I was simply writing about the kind of room I had had as a child.

Concerning possession in *The Court of the Stone Children,* the book has as its central event in the past the rejection of Napoleon's tyranny by Antoine de Lombre, because of which he is shot. But there turns out to be another proccupation, something which I had felt during the writing but had not consciously enunciated to myself, and which a friend told me was of central significance to her, an artist. Again, as in *Room* and certainly as in *Mountains,* whatever significance there is, indeed the very story itself, grew out of place, because place is something without which my unconscious cannot conceive a book, and I should think this might be the case with a good many writers. If the seed of story finds no particular place to fall, no particular environment to breathe in and get light from, it dies. But that is not put in the right way. Place makes story by making possible certain characters out of which story grows.

When I was a child, after we left the house with the room made of windows, our home on a hillside in Berkeley had a 180-degree view of

A Spell Is Cast. *illustrated by Beth and Joe Krush. By permission of Little, Brown and Company in association with The Atlantic Monthly Press. Copyright 1964.*

cities, bay, and ocean. Directly opposite our western windows stood the Golden Gate, where San Francisco Bay and the Pacific interchange their waters. For me, then, San Francisco was a magical place, with its enormous wooded park and museum, its cable cars, its swooping streets all giving views of islands, of Marin County across the Golden Gate, and of my own little city over there on the other side of the bay, minuscule with distance.

And the core of my fascination centered on the museum which evoked for me—though I did not realize it then, staring at the remains of mummies, at Sumerian and Egyptian and Greek and Roman jewelry, and the elegance of chateau rooms brought from France—the poignancy of human beings hundreds or even thousands of years gone who had made and used these things, smoothed gradually with their hands and their clothing these very objects—hand mirrors, boxes, tables, chests, chairs, cabinets—on which I fed my imagination. What I felt then eventually resolved itself into the firm conviction that the notion of the three tenses of time is an illusion of our necessarily limited senses, so that the concept underlying time fantasy became to me not fantastical at all but one having its basis in reality. In *The Court of the Stone Children* I combined this belief, one going back through the millenia and shared by black and yellow and red men alike, and only much later by white, with my intense and special childhood sense of San Francisco as at once a city like no other and the place where I had experienced the "Museum Feeling."

I gave that feeling to Nina and something else as well that I myself had had as a child from the wrought artifacts and the chateau rooms: a loving appreciation of a certain kind of beauty other than natural, that which is humanly fashioned, contained in objects shaped by cultivated perceptions, expressions of civilizations not engrossed simply in the pleasures of business and the body and society, but in making with patience and devotion what would be the revelation of an aesthetic vision. This was what spoke to my friend and had significance for her: the effect of art on the sensibilities of a child who had never been brought into contact with it before.

As for character creation and the unconscious, I have already touched on this in speaking of what Tissie as good as told me she would and would not do. And I suppose there is nothing more mysterious than the ability of the unconscious to present the writer with his characters. It had been insisted that characters are only the prototypes of people we have known, and I would be willing to admit this—but only to a degree, only in my own case, in certain instances. I continually mingle people I have known with those who seem to me wholly given, wholly discovered, and I am aware of no difference in the quality of their responses to the story they are causing to progress. But whoever I have known becomes a novelistic self.

My mother and I were very close, even though we sometimes got at loggerheads in our younger days and could not see the other's point of view because of the ways in which we were alike. She was a power in my life and at times I rebelled against that power until the time came when I no longer had any need to because I began to understand her and myself a little more clearly. At any rate, she has come into my last books as the mother of the child each novel is about, and this has perhaps been unimaginative of me except that it somehow could not be helped. These books came after *The Green and Burning Tree,* a collection of critical essays on children's literature, which has seemed to divide my work in two so decidedly that some have told me they were surprised to find it was the same Cameron who wrote the early books as the late. What has happened is that I have now been basing (but only basing) them on childhood experience, using an actual situation as the takeoff into events that never happened in real life, whereas the earlier books are wholly imaginative.

In each of the later books my mother is there in essence, though only a part of her is there in each of the three women. There was no need to make an effort to do this—it came about because of place. For me, as I said earlier, place makes story by making possible, indeed I could say by making inevitable, certain characters. The mystery to me is why place—and time—should have called up three different essences of the same woman. In *Room* she was one who was compelled to say to her daughter that, for her, children were not enough because she did not feel whole without a man to share her life; in *Mountains* one whose dominant quality was independence, the ability to manage, specifically to manage a hotel, and the desire to manage the headwaiter Grant's life to the extent that she would change it without discussion with anyone because she could see so precisely what ought to be; and in *Court* the kind of woman for whom responsibility comes first, responsibility to circumstance, to making something decent of life but only within dependable circumstance, so that Nina thinks of her as habitually saying, "We must— we must—one must always" do this, that, or the other. The sense of duty. And all of these qualities were present in my mother: the femininity that struggled out of my own possessiveness toward someone she loved, the spunk and the courage and the ability to direct affairs, and as well the eternal sense of responsibility to circumstance with a view to shaping it toward its best ends. And yet my three women, different from each other, are also different from my mother, because each novel magnified one central quality around which others coalesced so that each novelistic essence is her own person.

Virginia Woolf wrote of her mother: "It is perfectly true that she obsessed me, in spite of the fact that she died when I was only thirteen, until I was forty-four. Then one day walking round Tavistock Square I made up, as I sometimes make up my books, *To the Lighthouse;* in a great, apparently involuntary rush. . . . I wrote the book very quickly; and when it was written, I ceased to be obsessed by my mother. I no longer hear her voice; I do not see her."[15] That fascinated me because I have wondered at times if I have been similarly obsessed. Virginia Woolf says that she supposes she did for herself what psychoanalysts do for their patients. Am I, then, like her, expressing "some very long felt and deeply felt emotion," and in expressing it, explaining it and then laying it to rest? ("But what is the meaning of 'explained' it?" Virginia Woolf wonders.)[16] I do not think so. I have been haunted by my mother and the quality of her life, yes. But I have had no need to write her out of myself. I still see her, still hear her voice and laugh, and shall no doubt go on doing so. She is still with me though she died seven years ago; and I want that presence, the seeing and hearing.

As for those characters who have been given, who have no prototypes, I ask as many another writer must have done about his own visitations, where do they come from? Where did Tissie come from? I have never known anyone even remotely like her. Where did Rhiannon Moore in *Room* come from, someone else completely given. I had thought I was ready to begin the novel when one day I saw Julia, in my mind, go over to the fence at the back of the brown bungalow, where I used to live, to speak to a woman in a dressing gown with her long gray-streaked hair tied back. She had just come out of the two-story barn-red house next door and she and Julia met at the fence and started to talk, and from that moment were fast friends in the special way only the very young and the old can be. I saw this happen. It happened with complete unexpectedness, and from that moment Rhiannon Moore took a central place in the book.

I do not see how the fact can be other than that in the depths of the creative unconscious the whole, given character must exist, for the writer has never to wonder what that person would do under certain circumstances. One knows, infallibly and unerringly, without having to stop and think. And it has often seemed to me that if one did have to cast about in order to find the answer, then that character must not naturally and deeply be one's own and that a serious flaw is likely to be woven into the novel which could become increasingly serious—felt subtly at first but with increasing proof of artificiality as the novel progresses. For the writer would constantly run the risk of having that character, purely for the sake of imposed story, do something that would run contrary to his inmost nature. Unless of course (and this is most likely if he is a "made" character) he is presented so shallowly that he would have no inmost nature. But even minor characters in memorable novels have inmost natures. The writer perceives them, and even if they come into the novel only briefly, he will have a distinct feeling about their essences, as Walter de la Mare does about the old sailor, the Oomgar, who befriends little Ummanodda Nizza-neela in *The Three Royal Monkeys,* and in *A Wizard of Earthsea.*

I quoted, above, Virginia Woolf's words on the conception of *To the Lighthouse* in order, there, to bring out the ridding of an obsession through the author's writing the object of it into a novel. And the way the novel came to her, "in a great apparently involuntary, rush" brings me to the third way in which the working of the unconscious seems to the writer some arcane and mystic process. Virginia Woolf used the words "apparently involuntary" as if she knew that her sudden visitation was not, in fact, purely of the moment, purely of the mind's conscious making. And she goes on: "One thing burst into another. Blowing bubbles out of a pipe gives the feeling of the rapid crowd of ideas and scenes which blew out of my mind, so that my lips seemed syllabling of their own accord as I walked. What blew the bubbles? Why then? I have no notion."[17] In my own way, I have had that experience. I had thought that, having gone backwards from *Room*, where Julia is twelve, to *Julia and the Hand of God*, where she is eleven, that I was finished with this child. But I was reading Monique Wittig's *The Opoponax*, when suddenly I beheld the garden where Julia had played at the ages of six and seven, and the voices and the happenings began, "the crowd of ideas and scenes," one bursting out of another just as Virginia Woolf described it. And I believe that I am committed.

But despite the apparently involuntary quickness of conception of her novel in the case of Virginia Woolf, we know that it was not a visitation out of nowhere. She was forty-four when this happened, and when she was nine, on vacation in Cornwall at St. Ives across from the Godrevy Lighthouse, we learn from *The Hyde Park Gate News*, which she produced for her family, that Virginia and her two brothers Thoby and Adrian were invited for a sail to the lighthouse on a day of "perfect wind and tide for going there" and that "Master Adrian Stephen was much disappointed at not being allowed to go."[18] And so the thirty-five years that day of perfect wind and tide and of the keen disappointment of the little boy who had had to stay at home had remained in her unconscious. It must have been her unconscious, for she gives no hint in her account of the book's inception that she recalls the incident she recorded when she was nine; yet surely that day and its intense joy, for her, must have lain there weaving itself into a novel all that time, ready to break forth as if newly conceived by the conscious mind as Virginia walked around Tavistock Square. But why on that particular walk; why at that moment? She herself asks, "Who blew the bubbles? Why then?" and answers, "I have no notion."

When the first urge for a book comes rushing in, when it comes quickly like this, it is a kind of bliss (and I do not mean that this guarantees its goodness!). Then either the book is written immediately, as in the case of *To the Lighthouse*, or one goes about the daily business of living knowing now that the unconscious is at work and that over a period of time the book is getting itself ready to be written. Later, after writing has started, the presentations of the unconscious continue, sometimes in long, pouring spurts when the conscious and the unconscious seem in perfect harmony and the right tone, the right voice, is found without effort. Or with struggle,when the conscious strives to find the tone that will satisfy.

In fact, I often picture the self as objective editor or judge. True it is that self can only be objective to a degree because it contains the conscious and the unconscious. But the cooler the self is in listening and judging—in other words, the more aesthetic distance can be attained—the better the work. The material can be hot, but the judgment must be cool. And by hot I do not mean a scene of violence, but that the writer has been cutting into the bone of truth, when the scene be light or somber, comic or harsh. Cutting into bone is always the hope, rather than skirmishing over the surface because one has not the knowledge, the ability, the wisdom, or the patience to hit the bone itself. If I know I am skirmishing, then I know further that it is a matter of waiting in order to be given insight, which is the voice of the unconscious. And whenever it is a matter of waiting, I am depending upon and trusting to the unconscious to send its message. Is it, then, that the unconscius knows better than the conscious? It would seem to me that it does and when I go astray, when I am struggling, it is because I have not waited long enough, or have not kept the channel clear, or have misinterpreted.

And it is always a matter of waiting, never of forcing, because forcing is fatal. In fact I believe that forcing is fatal no matter what we do.

Katherine Mansfield felt that for her "each idea for a story had an inherent shape, that there could be no other for it, that it was for her to perceive that shape, and that it was far more a matter of perception than construction."[19]

Carson McCullers tells us that for a whole year she worked on *The Heart Is a Lonely Hunter* without understanding it at all. Each character was talking to a central character, but why she did not know. "I'd almost decided," she has written, "that the book was no novel, that I should chop it up into short stories. But I could feel the mutilation in my body when I had that idea, and I was in despair. . . . Suddenly, as I walked across a road, it occurred to me that Harry Minowitz, the character all the other characters were talking to was a different man, a deaf mute, and immediately the name was changed to John Singer. The whole focus of the novel was fixed and I was for the first time committed with my whole soul to *The Heart Is a Lonely Hunter*."[20]

Vladimir Nabokov has spoken of inspiration at work "mutely pointing out this or that, having me accumulate the known materials for an unknown structure. . . . I feel a kind of gentle development, an uncurling inside, and I know that the details are there already, that in fact I would see them plainly if I looked closer, if I stopped the machine and opened its inner compartment; but I prefer to wait until what is loosely called inspiration has completed the task for me."[21] He looked upon the structure of a book in process, "dimly illumined" in his mind, as comparable to a painting upon which he could work at any point, never

From Julia and the Hand of God *by Eleanor Cameron, illustrated by Gail Owens. Courtesy of E. P. Dutton and Co., Inc.*

from left to right or from top to bottom, but upon any part which involved him most strongly, and keep working until all the gaps were filled in.

Related to Nabokov's sense that the whole work must somehow preexist in the unconscious ("the details are there already") is Graham Greene's observation that in the course of writing a novel "somewhere near the beginning for no reason I knew, I would insert an incident which seemed entirely irrelevant, and sixty thousand words later, with a sense of excitement, I would realize why it was there—the narrative had been working all that time outside my conscious control."[22]

Lewis Carroll said of the waiting process, the slow coalescing of the final version of *Alice in Wonderland* and of taking only what was given: "In writing it out, I added many fresh ideas, which seemed to me to grow of themselves upon the original stock; and many more added themselves when, years afterwards, I wrote it all over again for publication; but . . . every such idea, and nearly every word of the dialogue, *came of itself.*"[23]

Mark Twain, too, firmly believed that a novel should come of itself, that his unconscious was vitally involved and that if it did not freely give him its material, there was no point in continuing. The case of *Huckleberry Finn* with relation to waiting and the work of the unconscious is surely one of the strangest on record. For it was not only the writer who waited, in the beginning, but later the unconscious that had to wait, when it wanted only to give.

Mark Twain began work on "another boy's book," as he called it, in 1876, but was not engrossed, indeed started the writing, he said, simply to be at work at something, liked it "only tolerably well," and intended either to pigeonhole or to burn it when he had finished. But long before he came to the end he had set it aside and continued to ignore it for four years. In 1880 he took it up again, remained unenthusiastic, and abandoned it once more. Then in 1881, following that memorable visit to the Mississippi that was to make the great river central to *Huckleberry Finn*, Mark Twain suddenly became imbued with such a frenzy of creative energy that the book flowed from his pen day after day. However—and this is the inexplicable part—even though the unconscious was at last working full force in a way that would have overwhelmed any other writer with gratitude, Mark Twain allowed the most unimportant projects to tease him away from his work, so that in full spate it was forced to wait while he vitiated the hot, rich energy that should have gone into it without interruption.

When at length *The Adventures of Huckleberry Finn* was completed, Mark Twain began to realize in some degree what his unconscious had granted him. Yet even so he could not have guessed that his book was to be one of the seminal forces in American literary history, a book that was not particularly valued by its author until the response to it began growing, and that had had to wait interminably upon second-rate affairs before being given its completed expression.

Finally, to speak of place and the unconscious, something I touched on earlier, childhood place specifically: *Mountains*, a book that waited so long to be written—thirty years, at least—rose out of the deepest layer of any book so far attempted; it came out of the years of very young childhood. Nothing that happened in it actually happened; only the place is as it was, and a certain situation, the fact that I lived in a hotel between the ages of three and six. It was a book that had a long, slow parturition partly because I was uncertain of how it should be written, from whose point of view. And some element of my uncertainty came from the fact of having left Ohio behind so many years ago. Could I relive my place? Of course at any moment I felt moved to begin the book, I could always go back and explore that little town for as long as was necessary. But somehow, I did not go, nor did I tell myself why, and only when it came to the possible moment of going was an answer given.

I was about to begin writing when, in the scheduled order of events, I had to go east and there was no reason why I should not stop off in Ohio and take the train to that tiny spot on the map I have called South Angela. I stood at the desk in the airport having, as I had thought, completely made up my mind as to what I intended doing. "But do *not* do it," something said. "Trust to the aesthetic impulse."

I may never realize my subtlest reason for not going, if there was a deeper one, but I believe I was right in obeying the advice given me, which meant, it seemed to me, that all of the impressions of childhood are still there in the depths and that creation can do its best work, the most aesthetically satisfying work, with what is part of the unconscious and can freely combine with imagination, rather than with what has been freshly observed and recorded. Whether I was right or not I shall never know. I know only that I could never have foreseen all that would rise to the surface in the actual act of writing—scenes, details of street and countryside and the interiors of houses, gestures, sounds, smells I had not thought of in all these years. Much had already come to me, but it was the act of writing that brought me, finally, what I needed for place.

To sum up: the unconscious would seem to give the novelist, if he will allow it to, the material of the novel—its characters, the voices speaking, its landscape, and its construction—while it would seem to be the work of the conscious to discriminate as to expression, though, as I have said, words will sometimes come in an apparently unpremeditated flow that seems like a blessing. However, these words must be looked at later with a cold eye to determine their rightness. For style *is* content; meaning subtly tilts from word to word, and each part of a novel—each word, sentence, paragraph—depends upon every other part like the cunningly stressed beams leaning together without nails in the tower of the cathedral at Ely. Only by the use of certain words, these and no others, can the writer express his private way of seeing. Only by working his way toward those words and not being satisfied until he finds them can he do justice to whatever the unconscious has given.

I said above, "the unconscious would seem to give the novelist, if he will allow it to. . . ." But how does the writer open himself to the offerings of the unconscious? If a seed has been planted, if within the novelist something is unfolding, I think he would do it by maintaining receptivity and a state of general and attentive awareness for as long as he senses it necessary, for years perhaps. By never forcing. By intellectualizing as little as possible. And if there is a block, by waiting in unparticularized expectancy. Intuiting the whole seems infinitely preferable to making aggressive determinations. For this state of mind means that thinking will take over when the novelist begins writing character sketches, drawing up schemes and outlines, making diagrams of plot structure, and writing out family histories. All of this is a far cry from the poetic process involved in the secret and silent, slow and natural growth which will eventually, in its own good time (if the work is right for the novelist) offer its own solutions. Yet I cannot be dogmatic about this as the only way, for John Rowe Townsend, a highly successful novelist for children, reveals himself in *The Thorny Paradise* as one who, in fact, does make all of the intellectual preparations. However, it may not have occurred to him to tell of his nonthinking phases, such as those Alan Garner underwent in his work on *Red Shift*, during which years went by between writing bouts while he waited to be given further enlightenment as to the way in which his novel should be told.

In discussing an essay by Mary Hanle, Silvano Arieti, in his study of creativity, quotes her as saying, "We cannot get creative ideas by searching for them, but if we are not receptive they will not come."[24] Creative work, she believes, demands both a passionate interest, in which ideas are actively welcomed, and a certain degree of detachment. This paradoxical state she sums up as one of "detached devotion," a phrase which seems to me to be precisely right.

Gerard Manley Hopkins's privately created word was *inscape*, a word that for him was charged with meaning just as, for him, the world was "charged with the grandeur of God." And because it was, he believed that the only way to do justice to it, in Conrad's sense of "doing justice to the visible universe," was to observe minutely, to take in and to express the inscape of every created thing, the essence of it. Slowly his word inscape, the central word in his vocabulary and the motif of his mental life, came to mean an inner country that required a devoted seeing into. It is the way in which he explored and expressed his private vision, his singularity, and nowhere has he written more poignantly of his belief than in the lines:

As kingfishers catch fire, dragonflies draw flame;
As tumbled over rim in roundy wells
Stones ring; like each tucked string tells, each hung bell's
Bow swung finds tongue to fling out broad its name;
Each mortal thing does one thing and the same:
Deals out that being indoors each one dwells;
Selves—goes itself; *myself* it speaks and spells;
Crying *What I do is me: for that I came.*

I believe that only by listening for the voice of the unconscious can the artist make something worth his highest effort, for only what he makes in this way will speak truly of his uniqueness, his own inscape, something no one else on earth can give. *"What I do is me; for that I came."*

Notes

1. Emily Bronte, *Wuthering Heights*, ed. William Sale, Jr. (New York: Norton, 1963), p. 12.

2. William Faulkner, *Selected Letters of William Faulkner*, ed. Joseph Blotner (New York: Random House, 1977), p. 348.

3. Walter de la Mare, *Behold, This Dreamer!* (New York: Knopf, 1939), p. 5.

4. Carson McCullers, *The Mortgaged Heart: The Previously Uncollected Writings of Carson McCullers*, ed. Margarita G. Smith (Boston: Houghton Mifflin, 1971), p. 275.

5. Bronte, *Wuthering Heights*, p. 72.

6. Graham Greene, *The End of the Affair* (New York: Viking, 1951), p. 3.

7. Joan Aiken, "Between Family and Fantasy: An Author's Perspectives on Children's Books," *QJLC* 29, no. 4 (October 1972):326.

8. Elizabeth Bowen, *Seven Winters and Afterthoughts* (New York: Knopf, 1962), p. 153.

9. Mark Schorer, *The World We Imagine: Selected Essays* (New York: Farrar, Straus & Giroux, 1968), p. 7.

10. Ibid.

11. Ibid.

12. Ibid., p. 8.

13. Glenway Wescott, *Images of Truth* (New York: Harper & Row, 1962), p. 159.

14. From a letter to the author.

15. Virginia Woolf, *Moments of Being: Unpublished Autobiographical Writings of Virginia Woolf*, ed. and with an introduction by Jeanne Schulkind (Sussex, England: Sussex University Press, 1976), p. 81.

16. Ibid.

17. Ibid.

18. John Lehmann, *Virginia Woolf and Her World* (New York: Harcourt Brace Jovanovich, 1975), p. 12.

19. Bowen, *Seven Winters and Afterthoughts*, p. 153.

20. McCullers, *The Mortgaged Heart*, p. 275.

21. Vladimir Nabokov, *Strong Opinions* (New York: McGraw-Hill, 1973), p. 31.

22. Graham Greene, *Collected Stories* (New York: Viking, 1973), p. vii.

23. Jean Gattegno, *Lewis Carroll: Fragments of a Looking-Glass*, trans. Rosemary Sheed (New York: Crowell, 1976), p. 20.

24. Silvano Arieti, *Creativity, the Magic Synthesis* (New York: Basic Books, Inc., 1976), pp. 345-46.

Jill Paton Walsh was born in London in 1939. She was educated at St. Michael's Convent, North Finchley, London, and at St. Anne's College, Oxford, where she received a Dip. Ed. and an M.A. in English with honors, and then she taught English for three years. She married Antony Edmund Paton Walsh in 1961 and they have one son and two daughters. Her awards include the *Book World* Spring Book Festival Award in 1970, the Whitbread Literary Award in 1974, and both the *Boston Globe-Horn Book* Award and a Creative Writing Fellowship in 1976. She lives in Richmond, Surrey.

Books for children:
Hengest's Tale (1966), *The Dolphin Crossing* (1967), *Wordhoard; Anglo-Saxon Stories,* with Kevin Crossley-Holland (1969), *Fireweed* (1970), *Goldengrove* (1972), *The Emperor's Winding Sheet* (1974), *Toolmaker* (1974), *The Huffler* (1975), *Unleaving* (1976), *Children of the Fox* (1978), and *A Chance Child* (1978).

Novel for adults:
Farewell, Great King (1972).

This lecture was presented in observance of National Children's Book Week on November 13, 1978, at the Library of Congress. It was published in the *Quarterly Journal of the Library of Congress*, Spring 1979.

176

The Lords of Time

by Jill Paton Walsh

It is as a writer for children that I address you, and the insights I offer are those of the workshop rather than the scholarly library. I was once, at the expense of the British taxpayer, rather well educated in the subject called Honours English; but that was long ago and I have not kept up to date with literary criticism. So I have chosen as my subject the one most suited to myself and hope to convey with the utmost possible candor something about the mysterious process by which my books are written.

There are few more vexatious and unprofitable questions than that of what differences if any distinguish books for children from books at large. Although what I say here may throw a sideways light on that controversy I do not want to confront it head on right away. Let me simply say that as a writer for children I see myself as a maker of "narrative fictions." I would not call myself a novelist; the novel can do some extremely nonnarrative party tricks and be greatly prized and praised for them by many critical modern minds.

Suppose we ask someone what a book they have just read is "about." One kind of answer might go: "It's about this boy and this girl, and they're hiding in this ruined basement, and then this bomb falls. . . ." That is the answer of a child. Or we might ask, "What's the new book about?" and get the answer, "It's about a dump in Birmingham, and there's this child crawling out of a cardboard box and going along this canal, and then there are these other children coming after him. . . ." That is the answer of a writer. It is remarkably similar.

Now the first thing to notice about these answers is that they are likely to be disapproved of in critical or educational circles. They'll get you naught out of ten in the English lesson. The book you have just read, or just written, is supposed to be about something other than its plot. The answer that will get high marks will be that the book is about the cost of

177

Illustration from the book jacket for A Chance Child *(New York: Farrar, Straus & Giroux, 1978), by Jill Paton Walsh. Copyright © 1978, by Jill Paton Walsh. Used courtesy of Farrar, Straus & Giroux, Publishers.*

Jacket design by C. E. McVean for Unleaving *(1976), by Jill Paton Walsh. The seaside home Madge Fielding inherits from her grandmother becomes the gathering place for two Oxford professors and eight philosophy students. Used courtesy of Farrar, Straus & Giroux.*

war, the beauty of doomed relationships, the price of industrialization, and so on. The preoccupations of criticism are theme, imagery, characterization, setting, and style. The plot is seen as a sort of coat hanger on which the fine garments can be hung up in view. Yet from the writer's seat the plot covers all, the plot is what you are thinking about.

Characterization is the great classic rival to plot for the attention of critics. Generations of students have written character studies of Elizabeth Bennet—none of them, it would be safe to say, as interesting as *Pride and Prejudice* or even as interesting as a paraphrase of the plot of *Pride and Prejudice*. One of the most frequently asked questions which writers confront is about their relationship with their characters: Where do you get your people from? Are they drawn from life? Do you put your own children in your books? My answer is that my characters are not drawn from life; they are drawn from my plots. I know, for example, that a child will be pushed from a cliff in the later part of my story. I ask myself what kind of a person will do that. When I have thought long enough, I have the character of Patrick in *Unleaving*, ready to perform the action of which I dreamed. But now I have him I see he will do other things as well; and the plot must give him life room in which to act as such a person will. And this relationship is very complex, for character is not only a possible cause in fictions, a possible trigger of events, it is also a *result*, a possible consequence of events. Premodern writers, interested in types more than in individuals, knew that well enough. The villainy of·Edmund in *King Lear*, for example, is presented as a cause of disaster and as a consequence of bastardy. Patrick's character at the end of *Unleaving* is seen, by me at least, as partly a consequence of what he has done. No doubt novelists relate character and action in this way, thus exaggerating the importance of free choice, stressing the consequences of personality, and understressing the personality as itself a result of some kind, because we would prefer the world to be under our control in a meaningful fashion. We would like to think that our free choices can do immense good or harm, because the alternative—that who we are and what we do makes no great difference to anything—is so terrifying and so demeaning.

In any case, whether or not the chains of causality in a story run through the characters, modern literary convention prevents any separation between character and plot. As late as Jane Austen, and later, it was possible to tell the reader in general terms about characters. When Mr. Knightley enters the room, we can stop for a paragraph to learn about him. But ever since Henry James sternly adjured us to show, not tell, it has been possible to display characters only in terms of what they do, think, or say: that is, in terms of the plot.

Then again there is the problem of comprehensibility, which is naturally enough very acute for writers for children. People often suppose that this is a question of choosing easy ideas, easy concordances. It isn't that. It is the problem of finding a clear and direct narrative movement— which is not to say that the meaning will be simple. Stories are excellent agents for the reduction of complexities. If a narrative is good enough, it will itself be a simple thing with a complex resonance, and anybody at all who has read it will in the sense that matters most have understood it. Thus anyone who has read the parable of the talents or the tale of the prodigal son has understood some moral questions of fairly stiff difficulty. Perhaps you will think I am cheeky to claim Christ as a colleague, but he was in fact a first-class maker of narrative embodying meaning! Perhaps you will be unused to the idea that literary significance inheres in the movement of the narrative because significance is so often presented as a kind of ghost in the machine, while the plot is seen as machine only. But narrative has been truly called a tool for exploring cause and time. A good tool.

I hope to have more to say about the cause and time relationship later on. For the moment I am going to invite your sympathy with the writer,

A jacket illustration showing the working of the locks on a canal in England, drawn by Juliette Palmer for The Huffler *(1975) (published in London by Macmillan & Company in 1975 as* The Butty Boy*), by Jill Paton Walsh. Used courtesy of the publisher, Farrar, Straus & Giroux. Copyright © 1975 by Jill Paton Walsh. Pictures copyright by Macmillan London Ltd.*

standing on the brink of a work about to begin. He or she has, I assume, an
area of excitement about which the book will be written. Without this
intellectual passion nothing would be produced. Something sets one's
mind on fire. I have been in such an inflamed state of consciousness, in my
time, about Anglo-Saxon England, the Second World War, the Greeks,
the fate of Byzantium, the nature of philosophy, lifeboats, canals, and the
Industrial Revolution, and I am now in a state of considerable warmth
about the American War of Independence. Enthusiasms of this kind are
by no means confined to writers but are commonplace experiences among
all who lead a life of the mind. However, being in an excited state about
lifeboats falls a long way short of having an idea for a book about them.

Jacket illustration by Robin Eaton from Children of the Fox *(1978) by Jill Paton Walsh,
with pictures by Robin Eaton. The story, set during the Persian Wars, follows the adventures
of the Greek General Themistokles. Text Copyright © 1977, 1978 by Jill Paton Walsh.
Illustrations Copyright © 1978 by Farrar, Straus and Giroux, Inc. Used courtesy of Farrar,
Straus & Giroux.*

Having an idea for a book means having a book-shaped idea; that is, it involves beginning to see a plot. The crucial difference between those who can and those who can't write books lies somewhere here. There are some whose casts of mind are such that they meditate the subjects they love by proposing narratives to explore them.

I would like to detain you a little longer considering the plight of the writer before this book begins. There has to be a plot, but the plot cannot be considered as a structure until it is complete. The writer's endeavor is more like route-planning, reading a map and hoping that it will be all right to go this way rather than that. And whereas the reader and the critic are confronted simply with the way the author did go, the author himself was confronted with an immensely elaborate network of interrelated choices. No one but a writer ever looks at literary problems in quite this way, because before the nature of such choices can be explained to any other person, the landscape and the proposed route must be explained, and when that has been done the choice is made and most possibilities are already excluded. Help can be given in making these decisions only when help is no longer needed.

At the risk of boring you with rather obvious remarks, I would like to point out some ways in which the simplest element, the despised plot, is complex, even in very simple examples. For a start there are the different but related time strands. There is a natural chronology of the events which will be mentioned or dwelt on in the book. Wickham and Darcy, for example, quarreled before either of them met Elizabeth Bennet—before the narration of *Pride and Prejudice* begins. And then there is the order in which the writer decides to tell us about these chronological events. There are very few stories which literally begin at the beginning, go on till they get to the end, and then stop. There is almost always an order of narration, which is in fruitful counterpoint with the order of events.

Of course the order of events is subject to a rigid naturalism; people must get born before they act and do murder before they are hanged. But the order in which such things are revealed is open to almost infinite choice by the writer, is strictly under his control, and will be carefully designed for effect—for clarity, for suspense, for impact on the reader's feelings. So that deciding what is to happen in a book is only a preliminary toward deciding how to organize the unfolding of what is to happen. One has of course intuitions about these things, but one needs a theory also. Every time one is struck with a book one is going to need tools with which to think about the problem; and because the tools are not those which will later be needed by critics to discuss finished works, and because nearly all the people who can afford prolonged meditation on literary problems are critics, chiefly academic ones, who are interested in analyzing finished work rather than in helping working practitioners, the thinking tools for the writer do not exist in any well-developed form.

In particular, the ordinary idea of plot as the more or less paraphrasable sequence of events in a story is too crude. It won't even deal, for example, with a story in which Little Bear thinks Mother has forgotten to bake his birthday cake when in fact she has remembered. What somebody supposes to have been forgotten is not an event, and the paraphrase of that example is going to go straight off at a tangent into someone's frame of mind. One can extend the idea of plot to include psychological events and frames of mind where necessary. But let me give an example, necessarily autobiographical, of a dilemma caused by too crude a conception of plot.

I got along for a good while as a writer with the idea that a children's book must tell a story, and no dallying about with character study, description, setting, and so forth. The children's book is a purely narrative form, I told myself. Rule one is: Get on with the narration. This sufficed until I began to work on *The Emperor's Winding Sheet*. It was an action-packed drama in its way, but I kept writing long passages about the architecture of Constantinople or the ceremonial surrounding the emperor. Wrote them; stopped; told myself they were not advancing the action of the book; and chucked them. Went into a profound depression; found myself unable to write. And that subconscious maker which constantly proposes material to the self-critic kept throwing up scenes of moonlight on lovely domes or of white and green flower petals cast on a cathedral floor. Eventually I perceived that I could not get on without the descriptions, because the descriptions did advance the action of the book. They did not (descriptions don't) advance the action of the plot. And one sighs, perceiving that one is writing a book that is not going to be as easy to read as one might wish. And, one tells oneself, the descriptions had better be good; they'd better be terrific. And then one needs a new theory, in which the forwarding of the plot and the forwarding of the action of the book can be different things.

In this way I hit upon the concept of trajectory, which I have found easy to explain to other writers and hard to explain to anyone else and which I am trying very hard to explain to you here. In the case of *The Emperor's Winding Sheet*, the descriptions advanced the action of the book because they were to the point. Knowing what kind of city it was that fell was absolutely necessary to the tale I was telling. And the ceremonies of worship that surrounded the emperor were necessary to the horror of the emperor's death, to the sense of *desecration* of his body without which I could not convince you that a little boy would struggle to swap the slippers on the emperor's feet.

There is, you see, such a thing as the plot of the order in which the writer unfolds his story: a kind of metaplot. Let us imagine this to ourselves as a trajectory, a flight path which must take the best, the most emotionally loaded, route through the subject to the projected end. You could imagine that area of excitement, the subject of the book, as though it were a real landscape—say a famous and interesting town, like Boston—and imagine yourself showing someone around it for the first

The Emperor's Winding Sheet *(1974), by Jill Paton Walsh, tells of Constantine, last emperor of the Romans, and of the fall of Constantinople. Copyright © 1974 by Jill Paton Walsh. Jacket design by Guy Fleming used courtesy of the publisher, Farrar, Straus & Giroux.*

time. You choose a route. You might start with the oldest buildings and follow the town's progress through to modern towers. Or you might look first at public and then at domestic buildings. Or you might go with a child from one ice cream parlor to another. . . . There is an infinite variety of journeys through the town,, and each journey will present things in a different pattern. The Freedom Trail is a trajectory marked out in red. And the route you choose will reflect your view of the world. Is it history that in your view shapes the world? Or is the present conditioned by other things? In just this way the author chooses a path through his area of excitement, and the path he chooses is loaded with significance for both himself and the reader. The answer to the problem with *The Emperor* was a rejiggered understanding: the descriptions delayed the plot if the plot was understood in the old way, but they did not delay the action of the book. They lay right on the trajectory, the essential action of the book, and

Chris McVean's jacket illustration for Goldengrove *(New York, 1972), a story by Jill Paton Walsh set at the seaside of Cornwall. Used courtesy of the publisher Farrar, Straus & Giroux.*

they therefore did not delay the true movement of thought and feeling at issue, because they were part of it.

Then I remembered an enthusiastic remark made to me by a very well-thought-of judge of children's books about *Goldengrove:* "You are such a marvelous storyteller. . . ." Never fear, I have not descended to mere boasting; this remark is actually on the trajectory of my argument! For it totally astonished me. I haven't space here to give you the whole history of the making of *Goldengrove,* but for various reasons I had written a book which I thought would be very hard for children, and one of the reasons why I thought so was that I thought it had a vestigial, involved, and almost static plot. So what was all this about my being a marvelous storyteller? And I reflected and decided that though *Goldengrove* doesn't have anything else I would associate with a decent story, it does have pace: it moves over its subject matter with speed and cogency and a sense of emotional drive. It doesn't have much of a plot, but it has an elegant flight path, a lovely trajectory. And perhaps as long as one doesn't stray too far from the trajectory one may be forgiven much.

At this point I began to wonder if perhaps the idea of trajectory casts light on another problem to which writers perforce give thought, and that is the problem of boredom. Now if only some academic egghead would cast some light on this one for us! For it is, isn't it, very mysterious what makes passages of great literature boring? It may well be more mysterious than what makes bad books boring. Of course, one of the things that make it hard to discuss is the emperor's-clothes effect: very few people, especially if they have much at stake in their reputation as intellectuals, are prepared to admit that they find any words of the great masters other than electrifying. But I do. I am often bored when reading good books. Frankly, though I admire Walter Scott, I skip constantly when reading him. It's the descriptions of Scotland that I skip, mostly. And yet I cannot be allergic to description as such, for I devour every word of description of the landscape in the novels of Hardy. And I am not about to claim that England is more beautiful, and a better subject for an author's pen, than Scotland. Not seriously, whatever I may feel in my heart. There has to be some other difference. And now I come to think of it—with my lovely new intellectual toy, or tool, the concept of trajectory in mind—of course I see that there is indeed a difference. The descriptions in Scott go far beyond what is needed to give the illusion of solidity to his tales. They are, one might say, only the setting of the action, and important though the setting may be to Scott himself, it is not *on the trajectory.* Whereas in Hardy the landscape is a shaping force. It is part of the action of the books, and it is fully on the flight path by which he leads his reader to the projected end.

I hope I have not by now lost you in the tangled thread of argument. Can I offer to define or redefine trajectory, before I elaborate ideas about it further? The trajectory of a book is the route chosen by the author through his material. It is the action of a book, considered not as the movement of

paraphrasable events in that book but as the movement of the author's
exposition and the reader's experience of it. And a good trajectory is the
optimum, the most emotionally loaded flight path across the subject to
the projected end. What we would usually think of as action—
happenings of some kind—is not the only kind of action. The
"meta-action" I am calling trajectory can be composed of other things, as
for instance in *The Emperor's Winding Sheet* I found it was composed of
ceremonials and rapt descriptions of rituals.

It is easy to see that the trajectory of a book can lie also in
conversations—even apparently long, irrelevant, and boring ones.
Consider for example the chat of Miss Bates in Jane Austen's *Emma*. Her
talk ought to be boring and to some extent it really is, and yet we find it
funny. We enjoy the discomfort of the characters forced to endure it. That
much has often been said. But isn't there more to it? Would we be equally
amused if farther down the street Emma met another village chatterbox
and the whole joke was repeated? The fact about Miss Bates is that both
her conversation and Emma's anguished boredom with it are on the
trajectory: they are leading us toward the important scene in which Emma
snubs Miss Bates and invites a justified rebuke from Mr. Knightley. Miss
Bates goes on and on, irrelevantly. But Miss Austen doesn't. She is taking
us toward a moral crisis by the shortest possible, the most elegant, route,
and that route leads through the interminable rambling of Miss Bates.

I would like to lead you now into a seeming paradox. I hope you have
agreed with me that apparently static description and apparently static
dialogue can in fact both be rapid advances along the flight path of the
book; but what about action in the ordinary sense, what about
happenings? It seems to me that happenings by no means always advance
the action, nor do they of their nature lie nearer the trajectory than other
things. Action can be static. There is of course a kind of book—and many
books for children are of this kind—in which the trajectory lies along the
plot line all the way. *Treasure Island* is a good example. No question of
morality ever disturbs it; it relishes situation danger, and turns of fortune.
It is a dream of action: the happenings in it are its point, and there is no
distinction in it between plot and trajectory. But Stevenson was a genius
and a very great writer, perhaps the best there has been at this particular
kind of tale—the plotmaker laureate. It does not, however, follow that
journeys, shipwrecks, apple barrels, and hidden treasure will always
make a story bowl along. For an action-packed, thrill-a-minute passage
can be off the trajectory, where it simply delays the true action of a book
and becomes boring.

Certain forms of writing, like the thriller or the children's book, where
the writer is very much aware of the need to get on with things, can be
plagued by irrelevant action of this kind. Coward as I am, I'll not give an
actual example but shall simply point out that if you are reading a love
story and are anxiously awaiting the point at which the hero puts his arm

round the heroine murmuring declarations of love, you may actually be so annoyed at the delay occasioned by the police descending on the house and turning it over for stolen goods—while the butler absconds through the garden carrying a large wicker basket in his headlong flight, thus in a thrilling, action-packed fashion delaying the arrival of the story at its projected end—that you may well skip the very bit that the author put in for excitement. Similarly, if you are reading a gripping thriller in which, just at the moment when you think the wicked butler may be about to be apprehended you and the police are delayed by a tender love scene taking place in the drawing room, it is just possible that you will skip every word the hero says and decline to pay attention while he puts his arms round the heroine, because you want to know if the butler makes it across the garden and away.

This brings me to the point that readers have an uncanny sensitivity to the trajectory of a book. Some sixth sense informs one that Scott is just putting in the moor because he likes moors, but Hardy is putting in the heath because it will overwhelm his characters with their destiny. This is surely true even of unsophisticated readers. Readers are rarely off, but what can happen if one does make a mistake is illuminating. For instance, suppose you pick up a paperback to read on the beach and you think it is a sparkling exposé of American society; and suppose it happens in a railway car, with long descriptions of all the other passengers riding with the heroine, right down to what kind of shoes they have on and the kind of old labels stuck on their baggage. You would, I should imagine, be pretty bored by it all. What's the point of all that? We aren't reading Balzac, after all. But then suppose you discover, belatedly looking at the jacket, that it is in fact a detective story you are reading. You will probably have to go back and start the book again, and this time you will have your antennae out and be reading all that detail on the alert, because you know it may include a vital clue to the identity of the villain.

So I propose an answer to the problem of boredom in literature. We are not bored by description and entertained by happenings. Instead, we are bored by any kind of writing in a book either when the author is off trajectory or when through our failings or his we have misunderstood the nature of the trajectory we are on. This latter mishap can occur at any level. The difficulty of reading Proust or Joyce or even, for some readers, Henry James is precisely that of understanding the nature of their trajectories.

Let me move on now to point out that like any other aspect of a book, the trajectory is itself potentially good or bad. It may be coherent or it may be disorderly—indeed its disorderliness can be turned into a joke against the author as it is in *Tristram Shandy*. It may be complex or simple or it may itself be beautiful, and, more important than all, it is itself *meaningful*.

For a book of any merit contains many kinds of image—images, perhaps, of moor and mountain and blasted heath, and complex images of the human personalities of the agents. But any good book contains predominantly a narrative image. Because, yes, narration too images the world to us, and in the most important way, for it offers us a linear image, an image of change extended in time.

Change and time are the true ecology of the human soul. We are immersed in them utterly, and they sweep us toward our projected end. Like an author at the beginning of a book, we know what the projected end will be; like his, our task is to find a trajectory which will make sense of the end, by finding the action of which that end is the appropriate conclusion. A narration offers us consolation of a certain kind, comforting our fear of the immense, chaotic contingent universe by finding a pattern which may make sense of the confusion and thus open a possibility of meaning in life. A permanent dialectic applies to this patterning: if the pattern offered is too simple and does not represent the contingent complexities of the world to us, it seems trivial in a special way. For we do not fear that there will not be pleasing patterns in the abstract to contemplate; we fear that here may not be a meaningful pattern in *the world*, in *our lives*. A narration has to come to terms with the disorder of which it offers us an ordering. But should the pattern be overwhelmed in detail, should it be too slight to be perceived, we shall find the tale meaningless, full of sound and fury. Narrative is thus a linear image: a device for making sense of cause and time.

The scope of this sense-making can hardly be overstated. For the kind of sense a narrative makes varies according to the concept of the universe entertained by those of whom and for whom it was made. This last claim is presented by Frank Kermode in his book *The Sense of an Ending*, which is only the second book of criticism to which I feel indebted as a writer, though as a reader I am indebted to many critics for many insights. The first book to which as a writer I acknowledge indebtedness is Aristotle's *Poetics*—which is also a book about the meaning of plots.

Professor Kermode's view of the meaning of plots is very grand. He relates the sense in fictional endings to beliefs about the end of the world and sees in narrative forms attempts to construct concordances between beginnings and endings which will give meaning to the lives of those always, in Dante's sense, in the middle of things: suspended, as we all are, between a beginning and an end. The traditional structure of narratives depends on traditional views of causality and on a world view in which the beginning was an act of creation by God and the end will be the Second Coming and the Judgment.

The Sense of an Ending is a very sophisticated and learned book, and you must read it for yourselves—I cannot adequately represent it to you in summary here. Let me pick up the web of Professor Kermode's ideas at the points where they particularly interest me and leave the rest for you to encounter in the book itself. I am profoundly interested by the perception

A canal boat carries Harriet far away from her home near Shipton, England. Jacket illustration by Juliette Palmer from The Huffler *by Jill Paton Walsh, published in 1975 by Farrar, Straus & Giroux. Copyright © 1975 by Jill Paton Walsh. Pictures copyright by Macmillan London Ltd. Courtesy of Farrar, Straus & Giroux.*

he opens up of the cultural content of plots. Not of themes, imagery, characterization, or setting but of *actions* in fiction. For by proposing a meaningful connection between any two events, a plot proposes a way of making sense of the flow of time and thus offers by silent implication to connect in a similar way the beginning and the end of the world. A whole moral universe is implicit in the plot of *Peter Rabbit*. Even a crude paraphrase of the plot of Henry James's novel *The Golden Bowl* implies a morally ambiguous universe—certainly not like the one in which Flopsy, Mopsy, and Cottontail got bread and milk and blackberries for supper. To understand a story is to see a possible ordering of the world.

Let me give you a possible counterexample to make this clear. The catalog for the Rosenbach Collection in the Free Library of Philadelphia records a title called *Triumphant Deaths of Pious Children* translated into the language of the Choctaw Indians. I have often wondered about that. What do you think the Choctaw could have made of it? Unless you were very thoroughly converted to Christianity and familiar with some of its odder movements of thought, do you think you could perceive any sensible connection at all between piety and death in childhood? Or you might make sense of it in such a way as to think that the author's view was that God punished piety. Most likely, I should think, the Choctaw Indian failed to see the amazing book as containing stories at all.

I would like now to make two asides on the subject of the vast implied resonances of story we are now discussing. One is that a simple story does not necessarily imply a simple concordance between beginning and end or a simple universe. The resonance of a simple tale can be of mind-blowing complexity, depending on the receptivity and subtlety of the mind that receives it. The parable of the laborers in the vineyard, for example—Christ was, whatever else he was, an exceptionally brilliant narrative artist—proposes a simple moral universe and then overthrows it to assert a far more difficult concordance.

My second comment is that it is precisely this potential for even simple tales to imply huge orderings of the whole world, should anyone take them far enough, that has always made literature seem subversive to those who wish to control human thought. From Plato onward the infinite freedom to *mean* has always seemed to bigots and zealots to need harnessing to facts or to rightmindedness. From Plato all the way to enthusiasts leveling a charge of sexism with fantastic ingenuity against *Peter Rabbit*, the side effects, the spin–offs, and the imperfections of writers' fragile proposed concordances have opened their tales to attack. The attackers have seldom felt impelled themselves to subject their own ideas to such a total and radical test.

But in whatever terms one defends literature, as I believe it must be defended, against attacks on the shortcomings of the world view implicit in this or that writer's works, one must not defend it on the ground that it does not mean anything much. A person who defends *Peter Rabbit* against a charge of sexism by saying that a simple charming tale about rabbits for children could not contain propositions about the fundamental nature of the sexes is a person who just cannot read fictions at all. Writers' deep and often unconsidered beliefs about the nature of the world simply do underlie the fictions they create, and these beliefs can often be teased out from the story and held up to ridicule or respect. It is hard to claim that the respect could be justified while denying that the ridicule could. What is wrong with many antisexist or antiracist attacks on works of literature is the extraordinarily narrow and self-interested nature of the moral concern brought to bear on the world: not the seeking of moral significance in stories, however simple. For the moral significance is always present if the story makes sense.

I have been talking so far about theory, talking in a very abstract way. Let me now recapitulate the drift of what I have been saying by describing to you a process of making in such a way that you can see what a concern for the trajectory and its meaning amounts to in practical terms.

A book written by me starts, as I said, with an area of excitement. Imagine me, if you will, in such an excitement about the Black Country. The Black Country is the large industrial area in the English Midlands of which Birmingham is the heart, and the state of excitement was generated by a journey right through it on a canal boat. Once one of the great prosperous areas of the Industrial Revolution, Birmingham is now in a state of dereliction, desolation, and decay which would make anyone, whether or not they had read Professor Kermode, think of the end of the world.

I began to want to write a book which would relate the state of England now to the Industrial Revolution, a book which would, very roughly, account for how large areas of England got to be like that. For that purpose, a historical novel about the Industrial Revolution wouldn't do—it would be confined to looking at the state of the world then, and I wanted the state of the world now to figure in it, too. Some six generations lie, I suppose, between then and now, and a multigeneration story—*The Whiteoaks of Solihull* or *Roots in Wolverhampton*—might have done it, but only at the cost of being grossly unwieldy. Such a subject as this can, however, be traversed by a plot based on time-shift. You take a "now" child and put him on her back in time, to encounter the past. Not, of course, a very original plot, but I will not be put off by that. For I am using the device to serve a purpose, and a better one than merely to make a frame on which to hang a description of history. I am trying to relate two epochs.

But there is a terrible snag to this projected story line. For a long time I am held up, worrying at the problem. The gist of the difficulty is this. When characters in a book visit the past and return safe and sound to the present, like tourists on a package holiday returning unharmed to the airport they departed from, it is impossible to give the full weight of

Illustration by Robin Eaton from the jacket of Children of the Fox *by Jill Paton Walsh. Illustrations copyright © 1978 by Farrar, Straus and Giroux, Inc. Used courtesy of Farrar, Straus & Giroux.*

reality to both time levels. The past has the nature of dream or of haunting if the present carries the emotional weight of the story, but the present is just roughly sketched if the writer is merely using a trick approach to the historical novel. There might for some subjects be nothing wrong with treating the past as diminished in reality, as a dream of some kind from which the travelers return. But if the subject is the Industrial Revolution there is something wrong with it—morally wrong, I mean. It is somehow frivolous. The subject includes chilling and widespread cruelty to children, of which the hideous thing is that it really happened. To frame the past and soften it, to show it as somehow appearing to characters in the present, is simply to fail to confront its horror. Presently a narrative solution to that problem occurs to me: the past is not visited; the story shall be that of someone who goes back in time and gets stuck there for good and all.

I ask myself now what kind of child could become lost in the past and could suffer, rather than merely witness, the fate of early industrial children, and yet remain calm enough to be a mirror to the reader of the world he finds himself in? A well-fed, loved, cared-for twentieth-century child would surely be unhinged by such a nightmare experience. And one wants a calm character at the eye of the story, not a hysterical one, because, as always when some very intense experience has to be conveyed, the writer's emotion is the enemy of the reader's and must be kept on a tight rein.

And then I realized that in supposing that a twentieth-century child would have to be all right and well cared for, I was propounding to myself an untruth. For while it is true that nearly everyone is better off than they were, it is not true that everyone is. Cruelty has not vanished from the world; and not every child sleeps safe at night and is educated at the state's expense by day. The child I need is one of those one reads of from time to time in the papers who are miserably treated now. He may not even himself realize that he has moved into the past. And by a crazy but right-seeming emotional logic, the way he is treated now will propel him back in time. And then, I think, because he is after all very exceptional among modern children, because nearly everyone is much better off now, he must have a brother and sister who are more or less all right. Have they then no hearts? Yes, they have; they will have done their best, and they will come in search of him. But if he has gone for good they can't find him, and that will make a cruelly gloomy book. I do after all write for the young reader, and one concordance, though I think it is a possible one, that I do not think one should offer to the young as a version of the world is a totally black and despairing one. And in this manner I come to see what the projected end must be: there must be a kind of surviving in the past and a kind of finding in the present. And I do not want to tell you any more about this book, which is called *A Chance Child* and is published by Farrar, Straus & Giroux, because I hope that if you read it you will do so in order to find out what happens.

This seems as good a point as any to say that one of the reasons why literary criticism undervalues narration as an element in literary art is that it undervalues the first reading. By the time people get around to deep discussion of a book, or going into print about it, or teaching it, they have always read it right through at least once and usually many times: what they are in effect discussing is a long retrospect of the whole book. Yet there is a special urgency, a special intensity about reading a book for the first time. And in first readings, "what happens next" is preeminent. Writers, struggling through the first writing of a book, tend to be working toward a first reading: should that fail there won't be any others. And so I do not want to tell you the whole trajectory of my book, lest that spoil your reading, but I have told you something about it to illustrate the way in which whatever truth an author has to offer must find expression in the narrative movement, in the trajectory.

A "meaningful account of changes" is what a narrative fiction contains. To read, or write, to see what happens and in the light of what happens to arrive at the projected end is the heart of the matter.

I promised earlier that what I had to say to you might cast a sideways light on what difference there may be between books for children and books at large. And I think that once we see narrative in this way— exploring cause and time and seeking to make coherent sense of our ends and our beginnings—we can see at least one difference clearly.

Children are not less intelligent than adults, or less serious, or less sensitive, or less disposed to laugh and cry. But they do unquestionably stand in a different relationship to the flow of time. They are nearer the beginning, however you figure it, and we speak to them from nearer the end than they. In this context the poverty of children, their tiny hoard of experience and touchingly short span of memory, is often remarked. But what really needs remarking is their wealth. They are the plutocrats of time, inheritors of immense unspent riches, whereas we are squanderers, falling slowly into hard times. And, having so much, they have not comprehended the finite nature of what they have. The young are all immortal. They live in the present moment. They are not very good at imagining themselves forward:

When I am grown to man's estate
I shall be very proud and great,
And tell the other girls and boys
Not to meddle with my toys.

That is the authentic voice of childhood. Children cannot imagine change and therefore do not yet know who they are.

Whereas we . . . Long vistas of past time haunt us, and we have constantly a subjunctive sort of consciousness. Wish, doubt, hope, and fear loosen our grip on the present moment. We can grow old in a subjunctive way, moment by moment, and never really experience the moments as we spend them. But at least we know about change. Having experienced change and continuity in ourselves, we know more than children do. In the perception of mutability and in discerning what patterns there are to lend meaning to the flux of the world, we have more to go on than they have. We write to teach them about change. We write to tell them about loss and death and sorrow; and about growth and joy as compensations. We write to teach them that actions have effects and that effects have causes. And a book that is really pitched for those whose span of memory is short and whose span of hope is long will have special qualities which will make it unlike a book for adults, which is not to say that it cannot speak to adults too.

That catalog in which I encountered the book in Choctaw Indian that I mentioned earlier contained also a title called *Little Truths for the Instruction of Children*. And surely the maker of this title had got it wrong. Children may need small examples, but they need larger truths.

London during the blitz of 1940 is portrayed by Jill Paton Walsh in Fireweed (1940) and depicted on the book jacket by Ron Bowen. Design used courtesy of the publisher, Farrar, Straus & Giroux.

The time for little truths is when you have got the great ones sorted out—the grandest view of the world has to be sketched in first. I will resort to an example here. That is the narrator's distinctive habit of mind—to find a concrete example to think about.

When I was young my grandfather tried to teach me to play chess, which he deeply loved and wanted to share with me. And he got me horribly confused. Like most good players, he was not really interested in opening games. No sooner did I get far enough to advance a king's pawn timidly two paces than he was telling me about six thousand possibilities in the middle game opened up by such a beginning and six thousand others by the same act excluded. The more he spoke the less I understood him.

How often I recollect that situation when I read adult novels. They are treatises on the complexities of the middle game, written by and for players of some skill. My grandfather was not wrong to point out to me the consequences of an opening game, which does indeed condition the middle game. But he had forgotten to tell me about checkmate, and you cannot play at all unless you know how the game is won and lost and what will count as an ending. That is why it is necessary in children's books to mirror death, to show a projected end, and to teach that nothing is forever, so that the child may know the nature of the game he is playing and may take a direction, make purposeful moves. It is the plain truth that human life is passing and that we must find what we will value in the world and how we will live in the light of that.

It is easy to think that books which are directed to such simple matters as change and time are less subtle, less deep, and less important in our culture than books about the magnificently complex middle game. It is similarly easy to think of writing for children as being like giving them presents: here are our perceptions and our carefully gathered costly insights into the world, and they will benefit the young. The truth is different and far more alarming. There is nothing more important than writing well for the young, if literature is to have continuance. And they are the Lords of Time, in whose courts we beg for favors, hoping that the gifts we can bring them may secure their favor for our cause.

For though some of us may be struck by freak longevity and some of them by untimely disaster, they do stand differently in the flow of time, and nothing is more certain than that they will survive us. They will inherit the earth; and nothing that we value will endure in the world unless they can be freely persuaded to value it too.

☆   U.S. GOVERNMENT PRINTING OFFICE: 1980 O-299-724